# Prosperity in the Twenty-First Century

# GLOBAL PROSPERITY IN THOUGHT AND PRACTICE

*Series editors*
Christopher Harker
Yuan He
Henrietta Moore

**Global Prosperity in Thought and Practice** draws together research that rethinks what prosperity means for people around the globe. Contributions challenge the prevailing understanding of prosperity by developing alternative models and ways of thinking; presenting robust empirical evidence, innovative policies and emerging technologies for securing prosperity; and starting compelling public discussions about how we can flourish in the future.

# Prosperity in the Twenty-First Century

*Concepts, models and metrics*

Edited by

Henrietta L. Moore,
Matthew Davies, Nikolay Mintchev
and Saffron Woodcraft

First published in 2023 by
UCL Press
University College London
Gower Street
London WC1E 6BT

Available to download free: www.uclpress.co.uk

Collection © Editors, 2023
Text © Contributors, 2023
Images © Contributors and copyright holders named in captions, 2023

The authors have asserted their rights under the Copyright, Designs and Patents Act 1988 to be identified as the authors of this work.

A CIP catalogue record for this book is available from The British Library.

Any third-party material in this book is not covered by the book's Creative Commons licence. Details of the copyright ownership and permitted use of third-party material is given in the image (or extract) credit lines. If you would like to reuse any third-party material not covered by the book's Creative Commons licence, you will need to obtain permission directly from the copyright owner.

This book is published under a Creative Commons Attribution-Non-Commercial 4.0 International licence (CC BY-NC 4.0), https://creativecommons.org/licenses/by-nc/4.0/. This licence allows you to share and adapt the work for non-commercial use providing attribution is made to the author and publisher (but not in any way that suggests that they endorse you or your use of the work) and any changes are indicated. Attribution should include the following information:

Moore, H., Davies, M., Mintchev, N. and Woodcraft, S. (eds). 2023. *Prosperity in the Twenty-First Century: Concepts, models and metrics*. London: UCL Press. https://doi.org/10.14324/111. 9781800084452

Further details about Creative Commons licences are available at https://creativecommons.org/licenses/

ISBN: 978-1-80008-447-6 (Hbk.)
ISBN: 978-1-80008-446-9 (Pbk.)
ISBN: 978-1-80008-445-2 (PDF)
ISBN: 978-1-80008-448-3 (epub)
DOI: https://doi.org/10.14324/111.9781800084452

Printed and bound by CPI Group (UK) Ltd, Croydon, CR0 4YY

# Contents

| | |
|---|---|
| *List of figures* | vii |
| *List of tables* | ix |
| *Notes on contributors* | xi |
| *List of abbreviations* | xv |
| *Acknowledgements* | xvii |

    Introduction: prosperity in the twenty-first century    1
    *Henrietta L. Moore*

1  What is prosperity?    25
    *Henrietta L. Moore and Nikolay Mintchev*

2  The discourses of prosperity: metaphors, transformations and pathways    49
    *Nikolay Mintchev and Henrietta L. Moore*

3  Local meanings and 'sticky' measures of the good life: redefining prosperity with and for communities in east London    75
    *Henrietta L. Moore and Saffron Woodcraft*

4  Rethinking livelihood security: why addressing the democratic deficit in economic policy making opens up new pathways to prosperity    105
    *Saffron Woodcraft, Hannah Collins and Iona McArdle*

5  Building co-designed infrastructures in Lebanon's spaces of displacement    127
    *Hanna Baumann, Joana Dabaj, Nikolay Mintchev, Henrietta L. Moore and Andrea Rigon*

6  Decentralised renewable energy: a pathway to prosperity
   for Lebanon?                                                    149
   *Henrietta L. Moore, Hannah Collins and Diala Makki*

7  Prosperity in crisis and the longue durée in Africa             179
   *Henrietta L. Moore*

8  Emergent prosperity, time and design: farming in
   Marakwet, Kenya                                                 201
   *Matthew Davies, Samuel Lunn-Rockliffe, Timothy Kipkeu Kiprutto
   and Wilson Kipkore*

   Epilogue                                                        221
   *Henrietta L. Moore*

*Index*                                                            225

# List of figures

| | | |
|---|---|---|
| 1.1 | Co-designed prosperity model for east London. Source: IGP, 2022 | 33 |
| 1.2 | Co-designed prosperity model for Hamra, Beirut. Source: IGP, 2022 | 34 |
| 1.3 | Co-designed prosperity model for informal settlements in Dar es Salaam. Source: IGP, 2022 | 35 |
| 3.1 | Differences in prosperity across London. Source: Legatum Institute, 2022 | 78 |
| 3.2 | Prosperity over time: Hackney. Source: Legatum Institute, 2022 | 80 |
| 3.3 | Prosperity over time: Newham. Source: Legatum Institute, 2022 | 80 |
| 3.4 | Data points by research method for prosperity in east London. Source: IGP, 2015 | 82 |
| 3.5 | Map of research sites for the prosperity in east London study. Source: IGP, 2015 | 83 |
| 4.1 | Infrastructure for secure livelihoods. Source: IGP, 2022 | 109 |
| 4.2 | Local government policy levers for inclusive growth. Source: IGP, 2021 | 119 |
| 4.3 | Expanded range of levers linked to broader definition of inclusion. Source: IGP, 2021 | 120 |
| 5.1 | Bar Elias residents at the Participatory Planning Workshop, October 2018. Source: Hanna Baumann | 134 |
| 5.2 | A child playing on the circular bench. Source: CatalyticAction | 135 |
| 5.3 | The green space behind the MSF hospital after clean-up and planting. Source: CatalyticAction | 136 |
| 5.4 | Access ramp onto high pavement. Source: CatalyticAction | 136 |
| 5.5 | Shade incorporating laser-cut phrases and recycled materials above newly installed seating. A sign in the background points passers-by to the revitalised garden. Source: CatalyticAction | 137 |
| 5.6 | Overview of Participatory Spatial Intervention. Source: Catalytic Action | 138 |

| | | |
|---|---|---|
| 5.7 | Gathering around the seating area during the Lebanese revolution, October 2019. Source: Moayad Hamdallah, citizen scientist | 140 |
| 5.8 | Gathering to celebrate the Prophet's Birthday, 2019. Source: Moayad Hamdallah, citizen scientist | 140 |
| 5.9 | One of the trees planted as part of the PSI providing shade to a street seller 2021. Source: CatalyticAction | 142 |
| 6.1 | The Hamra Prosperity Model highlighting affordable and reliable utilities and public services, such as electricity, as a foundation of prosperity. Source: IGP, 2022 | 160 |
| 6.2 | Household survey results from Hamra showing 59.2 per cent of households are connected to private generators. Source: RELIEF Centre & UN-Habitat, 2020 | 161 |
| 6.3 | Household survey results from El Mina showing 84.6 per cent of households are connected to private generators. Source: Pietrostefani et al., 2022 | 162 |
| 6.4 | Building survey results from El Mina and Hamra showing buildings' connection to electricity versus building age. Source: Pietrostefani et al., 2022 | 163 |
| 6.5 | Building survey results from El Mina and Hamra showing buildings' connection to electricity versus structural condition of buildings. Source: Pietrostefani et al., 2022 | 163 |
| 6.6 | Household survey results from Hamra showing residents' connection to electricity versus education and income of head of household. Source: Pietrostefani et al., 2022 | 164 |
| 6.7 | Household survey results from El Mina showing residents' connection to electricity versus education and income of head of household. Source: Pietrostefani et al., 2022 | 165 |
| 6.8 | Household survey results from El Mina showing the rate of residents' connection to electricity based on nationality. Source: Pietrostefani et al., 2022 | 166 |
| 6.9 | Household survey results from El Mina showing Lebanese and Syrian expenditure on 5 amperes of private electricity. Source: Pietrostefani et al., 2022 | 167 |
| 8.1 | Location and geography of Elgeyo-Marakwet. | 205 |
| 8.2 | Noah Kiplagat, PROCOL Kenya citizen scientist, helps to dig a trench for the piping of the irrigation scheme. Source: Davies, 2014 | 206 |
| 8.3 | Digital elevation model of the Elgeyo Escarpment displaying the distribution of irrigation furrows. For more detailed diagrams see Davies, Kiprutto & Moore, 2014. | 209 |

# List of tables

| | | |
|---|---|---|
| 3.1 | What does prosperity mean to you? Most common responses from research participants. Source: IGP, 2015 | 86 |
| 3.2 | Categorisation of factors that are essential or important for a prosperous life in east London. Source: IGP, 2016 | 94 |
| 3.3 | Prosperity Index Dashboard – Foundations of Prosperity Domain. Source: Woodcraft & Anderson, 2019 | 96 |

# Notes on contributors

Dr **Hanna Baumann** is a Senior Research Fellow at the Institute for Global Prosperity. Her work is concerned with questions of urban inclusion and participation expressed at the intersection of global and local scales. This includes refuge and displacement in the city as well as urban contestations over infrastructural and memory projects. Her ongoing research project examines the role of public services in the urban participation of non-citizens in Beirut, Berlin and London.

**Hannah Collins** is a Research Associate working with the Institute for Global Prosperity at University College London (UCL) and Prosperity Co-Laboratory UK. Her recent work explores livelihood security as a framework for effective and locally driven policy intervention to support prosperous futures for all.

**Joana Dabaj** is the Co-founder of and Director of Programmes at CatalyticAction. She holds an MSc from University College London (UCL) and a Bachelor of Architecture from the American University of Beirut. She is an architect and researcher whose recent work focuses on co-designing research and built interventions with displaced and host communities.

Dr **Matthew Davies** is Deputy Director of the McDonald Institute for Archaeological Research at the University of Cambridge. Before this he was Associate Professor and Director of Education at the Institute for Global Prosperity, University College London (UCL). He has held appointments in African Studies and Archaeology and at the British Institute in Eastern Africa, Nairobi. He has worked with the Marakwet Research Citizen Science team on a range of issues since 2009. This work has been funded by the Global Challenges Research Fund, the Arts and Humanities Research Council, the Economic and Social Research Council and the Leverhulme Trust.

Dr **Wilson Kipkore** is a Senior Lecturer and manager in natural resource management at the University of Eldoret, Kenya. He has a range of experience working with leading East African environmental NGOs and as the Chief Executive of the Permanent Presidential Commission on Soil Conservation and Afforestation, Kenyan government.

**Timothy Kipkeu Kiprutto** is Director of the Marakwet Research Station and Chief Citizen Scientist of the Marakwet Research team. He is a trained forester with over a decade of experience of anthropological research in the region including project design, interview and focus group work, and landscape mapping.

Dr **Samuel Lunn-Rockliffe** is an Early Career Research Fellow at the McDonald Institute for Archaeological Research, University of Cambridge, and an Honorary Fellow at the Institute for Global Prosperity. He has worked closely with the Marakwet Research citizen science team in Kenya since 2014, focusing on histories of agricultural innovation.

**Diala Makki** is a Senior Research Officer at the London Borough of Newham. Her work with the Institute for Global Prosperity included investigating prosperity indexes in Lebanon and unpacking cultural and economic geographies of urban poverty, informal work, and everyday coping strategies in contexts of precarious urban environments.

**Iona McArdle** is an economic development professional with a background in regeneration and housing. Her work focuses on developing inclusive economy strategies and implementing delivery to tackle economic exclusion and achieve social value. In 2019/20, she was a visiting policy fellow at the Institute for Global Prosperity at University College London (UCL), working on livelihood security. She is a Fellow of the RSA, a member of the London Prosperity Board and an alumna of the Clore Social Leadership Programme.

Dr **Nikolay Mintchev** is Senior Research Associate at the Institute for Global Prosperity at University College London (UCL) and Prosperity Co-Laboratory (PROCOL) Lebanon. His most recent work explores how theory and methods in the social sciences can lead to social impact and contribute to more sustainable and prosperous futures.

Professor **Henrietta L. Moore** is the Founder and Director of the Institute for Global Prosperity and Chair in Culture Philosophy and Design at University College London (UCL). A leading global thinker on prosperity, Professor Moore challenges traditional economic models of growth, arguing that, in order to flourish, communities, businesses and governments need to engage with diversity and systemic injustice, and work within environmental limits. Her work crosses disciplines, from social science to the arts, business innovation and the natural sciences, and she applies these different perspectives to inform research and policy at all levels.

Dr **Andrea Rigon** is an Associate Professor at the Bartlett Development Planning Unit, UCL. He directs the MSc in Social Development Practice. He has 17 years of international experience in the international development and humanitarian sectors, working for NGOs and in academia, and consulting for the United Nations, donors and government in 14 countries.

Dr **Saffron Woodcraft** is Principal Research Fellow and Executive Lead of IGP's Prosperity Co-Laboratory UK. She leads Prosperity in east London 2021–2031, a 10-year study tracking the prosperity of over 4,000 households in east London using IGP's Citizen Prosperity Index to measure changes. Saffron works collaboratively with citizen scientists, community organisations, government policy makers and business decision makers to bring lived experiences of prosperity into place-based strategies and investments. She has led the development of UCL's Citizen Science Academy and Citizen Science Certificate, recognising community-based, practice-led research training.

# List of abbreviations

| | |
|---|---|
| ALDP | African Land Development Program |
| AUB | American University of Beirut |
| BDL | Banque du Liban (Lebanese central bank) |
| BRSS | Beirut River Solar Snake |
| BTR | build to rent |
| CA | citizen assembly |
| CEDRO | Community Energy Efficiency and Renewable Energy Demonstration Project for the Recovery of Lebanon |
| CoM | Council of Ministers (Lebanon) |
| EDL | Electricité du Liban |
| GDP | gross domestic product |
| GHG | greenhouse gas |
| GIS | geographic information system |
| GoL | Government of Lebanon |
| GVA | gross value added |
| IGP | Institute for Global Prosperity |
| IPCC | Intergovernmental Panel on Climate Change |
| IPP | independent power productions (Lebanon) |
| IRENA | International Renewable Energy Agency |
| KVDA | Kerio Valley Development Agency |
| LCEC | Lebanese Centre for Energy Conservation |
| LOOT | life outcomes, life opportunities and life together |
| LPB | London Prosperity Board |
| MENA | Middle East and North Africa |
| MoEW | Ministry of Energy and Water (Lebanon) |
| MSF | Médecins sans Frontières |
| MSM | men who have sex with men |
| MWh | megawatt hour |
| MWp | megawatt peak |
| NEEAP | National Energy Efficiency Plan (Lebanon) |

| | |
|---|---|
| NEEREA | National Energy Efficiency and Renewable Energy Action (Lebanon) |
| NGO | non-governmental organisation |
| NREAP | National Renewable Energy Action Plan (Lebanon) |
| OECD | Organisation for Economic Co-operation and Development |
| PPA | purchase power agreement |
| PPES | Policy Paper for the Electricity Sector (Lebanon) |
| PRS | private rented sector |
| PSI | Participatory Spatial Intervention |
| PV | photovoltaic |
| RE | renewable energy |
| RHDI | real household disposable income |
| RSA | Royal Society for the Encouragement of Arts, Manufactures and Commerce |
| SDGs | Sustainable Development Goals |
| SWH | solar water heater |
| TWh | terawatt hour |
| UNDP | United Nations Development Programme |
| UN ESCWA | United Nations Economic and Social Commission for Western Asia |
| UNICEF | United Nations Children's Fund |
| WEGo | Wellbeing Economy Governments |

# Acknowledgements

Professor Henrietta L. Moore thanks Fabio Battaglia, Hannah Collins, Yukiko Fujimoto, Katrina Mosely and Louise Roberts for their contribution to this volume and the wider workings of the IGP, Simon Nyokabi and Josh Olins for assistance with the cover image, as well as Chris Penfold and the team at UCL Press for their work putting this volume together.

## Chapter 1

Parts of this chapter are adaptations of arguments made in a previous publication: H. L. Moore and N. Mintchev (2021), 'What is prosperity?' Institute for Global Prosperity, London. https://doi.org/10.14324/000.wp.10126424.

## Chapter 3

The authors wish to thank the citizen scientists Sue Ansarie, Peter Bailey, Rhajesh Bhattacherjee, Miriam Chapman, Farhana Ibrahim, Montana Joseph, Akbar Khan, Leila Lawal, Nathalie Limon, Tony McKenzie, Jonathan Murray, Kyronne Parkes, Carrie Svinning, Ivy Tanzila, Ines Tercio, Fatima Uddin, Angela Williams, Nileema Yesmin, Nesrin Yurtoglu, and the London Prosperity Board Partners.

Parts of this chapter are adaptations of arguments made in previous publications: H. L. Moore and S. Woodcraft (2019), 'Placing sustainable prosperity in East London: Local meanings and "sticky" measures of the good life', *City & Society*, 31(2), 275–98, https://doi.org/10.1111/ciso.12208; and S. Woodcraft and B. Anderson (2019), 'Rethinking prosperity for London: When citizens lead transformation', Institute for Global Prosperity, London.

## Chapter 4

Iona McArdle wishes to thank Michelle May and Emma Frost from the London Legacy Development Corporation, Vanessa Pilla at Lendlease, and Rebecca Davey, Assistant Director of Employment, Business and Skills at the London Borough of Waltham Forest, who allowed her to go on secondment.

Parts of this chapter are adaptations of arguments made in a previous publication: S. Woodcraft, H. Collins and I. McArdle (2021), 'Re-thinking livelihood security: Why addressing the democratic deficit in economic policy-making opens up new pathways to prosperity', Institute for Global Prosperity, London.

## Chapter 5

The authors wish to thank the citizen scientists who were essential to the conception, implementation, monitoring and evaluation of the Participatory Spatial Intervention. They are Moayad Hamdallah, Asmaa Al-Hajj Khalil, Mehdi Al-Homsi, Ali Al-Rhayel, Amro Al-Mays, Nour Hamadi and Maysam Salah. We are also grateful to the residents of Bar Elias who provided input, the municipality of Bar Elias, and the team of CatalyticAction, the lead partner on the Participatory Spatial Intervention, especially Ramona Abdallah and Ghina Kanawati for their work on the PSI monitoring and impact assessment.

Parts of this chapter are adaptations of arguments made in previous publications: N. Mintchev, H. Baumann, H. L. Moore, A. Rigon and J. Dabaj (2019), 'Towards a shared prosperity: Co-designing solutions in Lebanon's spaces of displacement', *Journal of the British Academy* 7(S2), 109–35; and A. Rigon, J. Dabaj and H. Baumann (2021), 'Participatory design and diversity: Addressing vulnerabilities through social infrastructure in a Lebanese town hosting displaced people', in Andrea Rigon and Vanesa Castán Broto (eds), *Inclusive Urban Development in the Global South: Intersectionality, inequalities, and community* (pp. 198–212). London: Routledge.

## Chapter 6

The authors wish to thank the citizen scientists who produced the data on El Mina, Hamra and Ras Beirut presented in this chapter: Grace Abi Faraj,

Nazih Adra, Fatmeh Ahmad, Sara Ahmad, Zainab Alawieh, Dina Arakji, Aya Ashram, Razi Ayoub, Nour Bachacha, Sara Badawiyeh, Ghassan El Bakri, Elissar Bou Hussein, Fouad Bou Mjahed, Hiba Chaarani, Maya Chalabi, Jamal Chatila, Riwa Chatila, Sara Coptan, Mohamad Al Esrawi, Ghadir Ghamrawi, Osama Ghaya, Heba El Haji, Mohamad Hammoud, Assia Al Harrache, Ziad El Hayek, Adel Ali Ismail, Ahmad Itani, Aya Itani, Abdel Karim Janki, Sara Jilinkirian, Houda Kabbara, Mohammad Kanoun, Mohammad Said Khalaf, Mona Kolom, Mustafa Kolom, Mohammad Kaawash, Sara Abdel Latif, Amanie Majed, Alaa El Merehby, Taha Mersalli, Mohamad Mkayes, Sageda Moubarak, Salaheddine Naous, Alaa Nouri, Ralph Obeid, Amina Saad, Waseem Al Sakhleh, Manuella Shaweesh, Fawaz Shehab, Abed El Sattar Salameh, Mahmoud Sleiman, Lory Yaacoub, Yara Younes, Rahaf Zaher and Bassem Zawdeh, and the team that supported the projects: Ramona Abdallah, Sima El Cheikh, Joana Dabaj, Mariam Daher, Mayssa Jallad, Sara Maassarani, Nikolay Mintchev, Elisabetta Pietrostefani, Jonas Röllin, Rachel Saliba, Ala'a Shehab, Soheila Shourbaji, Yara Sleiman and Ana Tomičić.

Parts of this chapter are adaptations of arguments made in a previous publication: H. L. Moore and H. Collins (2019), 'Decentralised renewable energy and prosperity for Lebanon', *Energy Policy* 137. https://doi.org/10.1016/j.enpol.2019.111102.

## Chapter 7

Parts of this chapter are adaptations of arguments made in a previous publication: H. L. Moore (2018), 'Prosperity in crisis and the longue durée in Africa', *Journal of Peasant Studies*, 45(7), 1501–17. https://doi.org/10.1080/03066150.2018.1446001.

## Chapter 8

The authors wish to thank the Marakwet Citizen Science Research Team: Helena Cheptoo, Nelson Balilengo, William Chukor, Noah Kiplagat, Joseph Cheptorus, Andrew Yano and David Kay.

# Introduction: prosperity in the twenty-first century

Henrietta L. Moore

The impetus to redesign prosperity for the twenty-first century has been building momentum since the global financial crash of 2008, although the true origins of the contemporary movement more precisely date to the Club of Rome's famous report *The Limits to Growth* (Meadows et al., 1972); 2022 is the 50th anniversary of its publication. The report warned of the dangers of excess material consumption and global environmental degradation, and catalysed a series of conversations about rethinking economic growth, arguing that the underlying dynamics of modern industrialism are unsustainable.

The value of the report lay in its attempt to provide a conceptual framework, and the chapters gathered in this volume build on that momentum; they elaborate on the ideas, frameworks, concepts, narratives, models and metrics being co-developed and co-designed by the Institute for Global Prosperity (IGP) at University College London (UCL). The IGP is working in concert with many others, not just the citizen scientists and communities who shape and engage with our research, interventions and policy work, but the many other stakeholders in government, business, academia, local government and civil society whom the IGP works alongside in co-design, collaborating to improve quality of life for communities around the world. The ripples of inclusion grow wider to flow into the initiatives, ideas and frameworks of the many others across the world who are actively engaged in trying to reimagine an economic system fit for the twenty-first century (see Chapter 1). The work of the IGP is inspired and guided all the while by their struggles and insights.

## A new economy for people and planet

The search for new conceptual, theoretical and policy languages is an arduous one, involving as it does the relinquishing of many consoling narratives of purpose and intent (see Chapter 2). The prosperity many seek around the world is not synonymous with material wealth, although incomes and sustainable livelihoods are key parts of its constitution (see Chapter 3); its character and forms derive more directly from desires and practices linked to hope, aspiration, belonging, identity, culture and history. All such are aspects of human flourishing that draw on intrinsic values and connect to the physical, psychological and social dimensions of self-realisation and community fulfilment. These desires are powerfully felt and propel discussion in even the poorest parts of the globe and the most challenging of circumstances. I am often asked how prosperity can matter to people who are so poor. In truth, I remain perplexed by this question since self-realisation denied is one of the most pernicious features of poverty, and one of the first freedoms to be wrested from people and their communities through violence, oppression, systemic injustice and political repression.

One of the glimmers of hope in these grim and Covid-torn times comes from the call for fresh thinking on community wellbeing and quality of life rather than a focus on the growth of gross domestic product (GDP) as a metric of success (see Chapter 1). GDP measures the monetary value of the goods and services that are produced and consumed within the economy, but it takes no account of inequality, environmental degradation, unpaid domestic work, caring responsibilities, subsistence farming or voluntary activities. The merits and demerits of GDP have been extensively discussed (for example, Coyle, 2015; Fioramonti, 2013, 2017; Stiglitz, 2009; Stiglitz et al., 2010), but there is an emerging consensus across generations, nations and political divisions that GDP cannot and should not be the measure of any country's economic and social progress:

> It is finally becoming broadly recognized that maximizing GDP, which was never meant to measure societal wellbeing, is not an appropriate goal for national policy. Although no single measure will satisfy all purposes, the GDP has gained enormous power to influence national and international economic policies because of the broad consensus of its use over many years and countries.
> (Weizsäcker & Wijkman, 2018: 55)

However, it is worth noting that while many call for a move beyond GDP (for example, Van den Bergh, 2022), it is for the most part alive and well in national treasuries where policy makers shrug their shoulders and declare that, while they recognise its faults, it is the best on offer. Arguably, the debate about GDP is a slight red herring, because it is not the metric itself which is so problematic, but the commitment to economic growth as a policy goal, and the concomitant measurement of society and environment in market terms. What is needed is not a new metric, but a reconceptualisation of economic value and of the economic system itself. Here, much ground-breaking work has been done, including that of Bob Costanza (2022), Tim Jackson (2017, 2021) and Colin Mayer (2018). The main argument is that our societal goals need to shift from maximising the growth of the market economy to enhancing and delivering quality of life for people and planet.

The call, then, is not just for a new metric, but for a fundamental revision of the relationship between the economic and the social in the context of urgent and increasingly alarming sets of crises in life-supporting Earth systems (Steffen et al., 2015; Xu et al., 2020). On the positive side, there are many who claim that the historical period of the neoliberalism that has held sway since the 1970s is now in decline and about to be replaced by a new phase of economic history yet to be named. Janet Yellen, the US Treasury Secretary, recently espoused something called modern supply-side economics:

> What we are really comparing our new approach against is traditional 'supply side economics', which also seeks to expand the economy's potential output, but through aggressive deregulation paired with tax cuts designed to promote private capital investment. It is, unquestionably, important to properly implement regulation and maintain a pro-growth tax code, but they are not sufficient and can often be overdone. Modern supply side economics, in contrast, prioritizes labor supply, human capital, public infrastructure, R&D, and investments in a sustainable environment. These focus areas are all aimed at increasing economic growth and addressing longer-term structural problems, particularly inequality. ... Essentially, we aren't just focused on achieving a high topline growth number that is unsustainable – we are instead aiming for growth that is inclusive and green.
>
> (Yellen, 2022)

During its recent presidency of the G7, the German government committed to evolving its economy into an ecological social market economy:

> [W]e need to focus more on and do more to tackle the negative consequences of economic activity. We must stop funding economic activity which contributes to the consumption of fossil fuel, to the destruction of the environment, and to social inequity. Rather, the challenge is to break the link between growth, the consumption of resources and greenhouse gas emissions. ... [W]e want to engage in an open debate about what ultimately is really meant by prosperity and quality of life, about the ways sustainability and growth can complement each other, and about where we need to weigh up conflicting interests.
>
> (Federal Ministry for Economic Affairs and Climate Action (BMWK), 2022: 6)

Neither government is moving away from GDP or from economic growth, but they are questioning the premise of growth for growth's sake as it relates to both social inequality and planetary wellbeing. This is most definitely a step forward, and one of some significance. Arguably, they are latecomers to the party rather than prime movers. The governments of Ecuador and Bolivia enshrined *buen vivir* (living well) in their constitutions, national development plans and public policies in the early 2000s. Versions of the concept have found broad resonance in other Latin American countries, including Peru, Chile and Nicaragua. *Buen vivir*, often referred to by the indigenous terms *sumak kawsay* and *suma qamaña*, derives from the spiritual traditions and world views of indigenous communities and emphasises the rights of nature, and commitment to living in dignity and harmony with nature and all cultures. It explicitly recognises the structural inconsistencies of neoliberal globalisation, and the contradictions of market-led forms of development that depend on extracting natural resources, deepening socioeconomic inequalities and historic injustices (Artaraz et al., 2021; Carpio Benalcázar & Ullán de La Rosa, 2021). *Buen vivir* is a composite notion comprising many different traditions and political ideologies; it is by no means a settled concept (Gudynas, 2011, 2016; Hidalgo-Capitán & Cubillo-Guevara, 2017), and its interpretation and practice by indigenous communities have often been at variance with ongoing government policies on mining and economic development (Forero, 2021; Veltmeyer & Záyago Lau, 2021; Radcliffe, 2012).

New Zealand delivered its fourth wellbeing budget in 2022 (New Zealand Government, 2022) based on the principle of He Ara Waiora, an indigenous and uniquely New Zealand approach to raising living standards using 'a waiora framework built on te ao Māori knowledge and perspectives of wellbeing' (New Zealand Goverment, n.d.). Māori knowledge sees humans as embedded within nature, living in a unified socio-spiritual ecology; a life force (*mauri*) connects all creatures and allows them to flourish (Rout et al., 2021). Acknowledging these forms of connection sets limits on the human domination of the environment; the deep imbrication of *whānau* (people) and *whenua* (land) is expressed in and through personal and kinship relationships with all natural things, providing a sense of place and belonging (Rout & Reid, 2020). Bringing these principles to bear on community and environmental wellbeing through extensive consultation and co-creation with Māori elders does provide New Zealand with a very distinctive alternative approach to understanding values and outcomes (Ruwhiu et al., 2022).

Other examples could be provided; the Wellbeing Economy Governments (WEGo) group was launched at the OECD World Forum in 2018 and now includes Scotland, Iceland, New Zealand, Wales and Finland. Canada and Norway have both announced new national wellbeing indices that seek to go beyond GDP. In 2021, the European Council agreed the EU's 8th Environment Action Plan, enshrining commitments to bring the consumption of resources of the member states within planetary boundaries and to introduce an indicator set to measure progress in wellbeing that goes beyond GDP (Council of the European Union, 2021). Wales has led the way by bringing into law the Wellbeing of Future Generations Act. All these governments and bodies have important policies, strategies and indicators which guide government decision making, and this is key to bringing about change. However, beyond those countries demonstrating leadership are a series of less choate and formalised propositions, actions and directions. Dissatisfaction with economic outcomes and their increasing interdependence with striking political and social unrest has unleashed a series of terminologies, debates, strategic directions and potential responses to a series of interconnected challenges. The debates are often fierce and deeply felt; there are also profound ideological differences at play. What all share is the recognition that there are new challenges to be faced and a narrowing window of opportunity in which to tackle them. A series of possible futures and policy directions prevail in popular discussion: green deal, post-capitalism, post-growth, inclusive growth, great reset. This language of renewal is positive, but lacks specificity. Terms like 'build back better' and 'inclusive growth' are worryingly undertheorised, and have no procedural content (Moore & Collins, 2021): the implication is that we are building back better than before Covid, but if we could not do it before, how can we do it now? Everything that was difficult pre-crisis – raise productivity, turn economic growth into wellbeing, protect the planet's resources, transition to renewables – has not suddenly become easier.

In addition, phrases such as 'the great reset' and 'the left-behind' are purely descriptive terms, and they lack analytical and processual heft. Their solutions tend to be exceptionally broad: improve productivity, retrain for the fourth industrial revolution, build innovative potential, invest in infrastructure. Even where governments have laid down a clear road map between values, strategies and targets, as in the case of the United Kingdom's levelling-up White Paper, which designates six forms of capital and 12 missions, with associated metrics, looked at in the round they do not represent a change in direction or new forms of thinking about the economy. In addition, because they are a series of siloed actions with no specified intersections between them, they are most unlikely to bring about transformative change in the relationships between human flourishing and environmental regeneration; nor will they level anything up (HM Government, 2022a, 2022b; Moore & Collins, 2021)! How these debates and terms are useful is in adding to an emerging critique of how we think about economies, and the relationship of society and politics to the economy. What does seem to be shifting is the idea that our societies should be in service to our economies rather than the other way around; we have lived too long in the service of the market and it has not served us or the planet well.

Chapter 1 discusses why we need new theories about what prosperity means and entails in the twenty-first century. It explores the value of the economic in social life, and challenges the structural features of the dominant economic models on which we depend and the value premises on which they are built. The chapter moves beyond merely discussing new ideas to explore how such ideas open the door to innovative practices that will allow us to address inequalities in new ways. What makes the approach distinctive is that rather than focusing just on how to define and measure prosperity, it formulates what we need to do to make prosperity a realisable proposition for specific people living in specific locales, and delineates what are the pathways to prosperity. This pushes the debate on prosperity forward, emphasising that visions of the good life are diverse and require empirical work co-designed with local communities and stakeholders, in order to develop well-founded frameworks and pathways for sustainable prosperity that can be operationalised by communities, policy makers, business, civil society and government.

Diversity is at the core of successful prosperity interventions, recognising that the specifics of place, history, culture, identity, voice and purpose are key to its success. The various philosophical and methodological problems of scale and comparison this raises are discussed, and distinguished from both aggregate approaches to prosperity and those based on individual wellbeing. The chapter discusses the conceptualisation and methodological realisation of the IGP's prosperity index, the formulation of its indicators and metrics, and the whole-systems approach which underlies it. It is contextualised through examples from the IGP's three Prosperity Co-Laboratories in the UK, Africa and Lebanon. A key principle in the work is to explore the intersections and interdependencies of the different elements of prosperity in each context, with the aim of identifying and explaining what brings potential success, unlocking previous deadlocks. The conclusion is that prosperity is an emergent feature of a complex assemblage of elements, resources and embedded interactions over time (Moore & Woodcraft, 2022).

The issue raised in Chapter 1 is how we can shape innovation and change under conditions of such complexity, and still keep in focus quality of life for individuals, communities and the planet. The chapter proposes an alternative theory of change to that deployed in most macroeconomic policy initiatives, focusing on visualising how multiple forms of agency, materiality, organisational structures and types of knowledges can be brought together to create new relationships and new forms of value in specific locales, drawing on assets and resources that are distributed across many sectors, actors, networks, practices and institutions. The emphasis is on how to build complex ecologies and maximise system learning. This is an approach much more sophisticated and powerful than simply trying to raise GDP and hoping that it will trickle down. Even established texts on redefining prosperity and moving beyond GDP link rethinking the economy to devolved governance, community initiatives, distributed energy schemes and localised job creation schemes without any clear discussion of how this will be done, or how they will be built out of and through specific geographical and historical assets and place-based capacities and capabilities. Part of the difficulty here is that many prescriptions begin either with proposed macroeconomic levers and solutions – such as training more apprentices or inclusive growth – or with a list of community initiatives on the ground that offer potential solutions, but without a firm understanding of the specificities of place or a theory of effective place-based innovation.

The approach outlined in Chapter 1 is explicitly transdisciplinary and brings together concepts and tools in a novel framework drawn from anthropology, geography, economics, development studies, sociology, political theory and organisation science, and inspired by work in the global South, to explore how we can repurpose the ideas and methods we have to hand to drive further innovation. Chapter 2 returns to the question 'What is prosperity?', but does so from the perspective of the philosophy of language, discourse analysis and semiotics; it addresses the all-important question of what a new discourse on economics and prosperity can and should do, and what role it will play in creating pathways to transformation. In other words, does it matter that people from government treasuries to civil society, organisations, social activists and local communities are talking about prosperity in new ways, having different kinds of conversations?

The short answer, of course, is that it does, but, equally, both the public and policy discourses on growth, and its centrality to conceptual frameworks in economics, have proved remarkably resistant. The chapter discusses the mechanisms through which new metaphors evolve into concepts, frameworks, models and metrics in academic, policy and public discourse, bringing certain issues into the foreground and displacing and masking others. However, such processes are far from uniform, and cultural and historical contexts play an important role. The emerging space of prosperity in contemporary debates is one of plurality, and many narratives of prosperity exist and operate at different levels of experience and analysis, from the personal to the communal, to the organisational and the national, and all interact to shape emerging discursive spaces. The consequence is that concepts, notions and narratives can circulate within different sectors, communities and action spaces, and can be interpreted differently, in part because of the way they are linked to radically different phenomenological experiences: a term like inclusive capitalism resonates somewhat differently in discussions in Davos and Singapore as compared to those in Lagos or the London Borough of Barking and Dagenham.

The purpose of redefining prosperity is not therefore about producing a fixed, final, unified, invariant definition of prosperity that corresponds to single sets of clearly identifiable material objects, resources and experiences. As a term its work is to assist in redefining the world in a fundamentally different way, one that focuses on an approach to problems in terms of quality of life, environmental sustainability, democratic participation, and hope for a better future for people and planet. Certainly, redefining prosperity for the twenty-first century is about reconceptualising it away from income-based indicators and aggregate GDP growth, but this process of reconceptualisation is ongoing and responds to the diversity of voices, stakeholders, locales and visions brought to bear. Bringing communities into the process entails new perspectives and approaches, new answers to the questions of what is prosperity, and prosperity for whom. This is why collaborations and partnerships are of crucial importance, as is the implementation of mechanisms and methods, such as citizen science (see Chapters 3, 4 and 6), that encourage active inclusion and participation. Plurality of voices, approaches, ideas and values offers new ways of conceptualising prosperity that can lead to the realisation of alternative pathways to prosperity. There is no one-size-fits-all. Locale is not just a backdrop, but a form of entanglement in place, where the multiple elements that make up prosperity are assembled in specific ways that allow the identification of additional levers for policy intervention, driving forward the possibilities for social innovation to address situated challenges.

Chapter 3 lays out how this approach was applied in east London, emphasising how prosperity as a lived experience is shaped by situated social and cultural values, and dynamic place-specific factors. The analysis underlines how, despite emerging critiques of prosperity defined by material wealth and growth, lived prosperity itself remains understudied and undertheorised. What emerges from working with local communities and citizen scientists on understanding prosperity in terms of the quality and challenges of lives lived is a clear picture of how individual lives and household necessities intersect with larger institutional, structural and historical challenges, and how these intersections are lost in macroeconomic analysis using aggregate data sets. Analysis of the data demonstrates that individuals, households and social networks draw on a range of diverse, multidimensional and multiscalar elements to discern, manage and try to bring into being their vision of a good life. This point is underscored in Chapters 7 and 8, which describe how research in the very different context of rural Kenya emphasises once again that individuals, households and social networks work actively to assemble, manage and enhance realisable visions of the good life. Chapter 4 describes how, in the case of east London, good-quality work, functioning public services, choice, opportunity, political freedoms and intergenerational justice all came to the fore in discussions with residents. Respondents described how they employed a combination of institutions, social networks, community and care facilities, transport, and education providers, to build a secure livelihood. People often described failures in such systems as holding them back and impeding their ability to make a living

(Woodcraft & Anderson, 2019). Focusing on the misalignments between policy and lived experience revealed new forms of knowledge and spaces for action that are mostly overlooked by local authorities, public agencies and business, but are crucial if pathways to prosperity are to be equitable and achievable.

## What is to be done about growth?

The world is close to irretrievable climate breakdown (Wunderling et al., 2021). The United Nations environment agency (UNEP) has declared that there is no credible pathway to 1.5°C in place, and that progress on cutting carbon emissions is woefully inadequate, while Shell and TotalEnergies and other oil and gas companies continue to enjoy obscenely high profits, benefiting from the war in Ukraine (United Nations Environment Programme, 2022). The health of people and planet is at the mercy of fossil fuels, exacerbating the fragilities of the most vulnerable populations (*Lancet*, 2022). What is evident is that the economic losses associated with climate change, and the concomitant pressure from the biodiversity crisis, are massively increasing the pressure on households, communities and economies, and all this on top of the costs of Covid-19, conflict and the international cost-of-living and energy crises. Proactive adaptation is extremely poor. For example, urban green spaces provide local cooling and overall health benefits, but only 277 out of 1,038 global urban centres in 2021 were moderately green, and the number of households with air conditioning increased by 66 per cent from 2000 to 2020, worsening the energy crisis and increasing urban heat, air pollution and greenhouse gas emissions. Global electricity generation is still dominated by fossil fuels, with renewable energy contributing to 8.2 per cent of the total. Fossil fuel dependency is undermining global health through increases in climate change impacts, but also through unpredictable and poorly regulated markets, frail supply chains, and geopolitical and sectarian conflict. Millions of people do not have access to the energy they need to manage healthy temperatures at home, preserve food and medicine, and support learning outcomes (*Lancet*, 2022).

Chapter 5 describes the situation in Lebanon, where a detailed assessment by the IGP's Prosperity Co-Laboratory (PROCOL) Lebanon research team, as part of the development of localised prosperity indexes for two urban areas, demonstrates how dependency on imported fossils fuels has indebted the country, exacerbated sectarian tensions, undermined investment in infrastructures and led to an erosion of quality of life, food and education security, housing provision and trust in government. Data on the largest oil and gas companies shows that they will exceed their share of emissions consistent with 1.5°C by 37 per cent in 2030 and 103 per cent in 2040, and yet governments continue to incentivise their production and consumption through subsidies and tax breaks. The subsidies to the energy sector in Lebanon amount to 4.5 per cent of GDP annually, and account for around 40 per cent of government debt, undermining its ability to invest in other critical physical and social infrastructure.

There is widespread recognition of the strong relationship between GDP growth and energy, material and fossil fuel use. This has led to a heated debate about growth and what is known as relative and absolute decoupling. These apparently uncontentious terms mask significant ideological differences. Relative decoupling implies a decline in material and emission intensity of economic output, through technological advancement and improved efficiency. This is what is implied by the terms green growth, sustainable growth, smart growth. Absolute decoupling means a decline in resource use and emissions in absolute terms even as economic output rises: degrowth (Hickel, 2019; Kallis et al., 2018; Büchs & Koch, 2018). Chapter 2 describes how deeply sedimented the language of growth is in the very definition of the notion of economy and why the first step in transformative change is to develop a new language, an alternative set of metaphors for understanding alternative methods of value creation. What is clear is that profound emission and resources cuts cannot be achieved without confronting the structure of market economies (Jackson, 2021). We need not just to live within planetary boundaries (Steffen et al., 2015), but to regenerate the planet, the natural ecosystems on which we all depend.

The latest evidence suggests that a rapid and global absolute decoupling of environmental impact from economic growth at the scale required is highly unlikely and that there are no realistic scenarios currently on offer (Muhirwa et al., 2021; Hickel & Kallis, 2020; Parrique et al., 2019; Haberl et al., 2020; Wiedenhofer et al., 2020; Vadén et al, 2021). Green growth protagonists continue to argue that technological progress and structural changes in the economy will enable a decoupling of natural resource consumption and environmental impacts from economic growth. Green growth narratives dominate in most political circles; the Organisation for Economic Co-operation and Development (OECD), the European Union (EU) and the United Nations Environment Programme (UNEP) have strategies based on green growth, and decoupling is a specific target in the United Nations Sustainable Development Goals (SDGs).

There is no doubt that future technology will bring new opportunities, and that relative decoupling is needed. It is also the case that social transformations will take time, and action needs to start now with what can pragmatically be done with the technology and knowledge we already have. Those who are critical of green growth and support a planned and democratic reduction in production and consumption as a solution to the current crisis castigate both the association of economic growth with social progress, and the assumption that continued economic growth can be compatible with living within planetary boundaries (Hickel, 2019, 2021). These include proponents of no-growth, degrowth, a-growth and post-growth perspectives, and even though recent usage favours post-growth as an overarching term, it is a multilayered concept with strong ties to feminist critiques, decolonisation theories, social justice, ecology, wellbeing and critiques of capitalism and consumerism. The divisions between the eco-modernists (green growth) and the post-growth advocates are rebarbative, complex and often ideological, and many positions, affiliations and disagreements exist within the post-growth alternatives (Van den Bergh & Kallis, 2011; Spash, 2021). However, there are various issues that need to be considered in relation to the post-growth agenda.

All economic challenges are political, and part of the challenge arises from questions of public trust and the social appetite for the kinds of transformations envisaged by a degrowth scenario, with its significant changes in habits and consumption levels (Brand et al., 2021). More challenging and morally complex is the question of how to develop, design and maintain a just transition, especially for those countries in the global South, and communities everywhere, who are afflicted by poverty, disadvantage and systemic injustice and conflict: why should they be moderating their consumption levels (Gough, 2017; Hickel, 2019, 2021; Muradian, 2019)? Changing consumption patterns in the global North would require an ethical commitment to reduced levels, and many proponents have attempted to set out the value systems and benefits of a new economic lifestyle with social relationships at its core, allowing more free time, and more fulfilling ways of working and living (Jackson, 2021), an economy of radical abundance (Hickel, 2019), and an alternative hedonism (Soper, 2020). Public debate has barely started on defining and refining these issues, in part because there are many who just believe that degrowth is politically unfeasible (Keyßer & Lenzen, 2021), while others highlight the considerable work that needs to be done to envisage what an economy without growth would look like, and the potential consequences for employment, social protection plans and financial security (Jackson, 2018: 221).

A recent review of the degrowth literature concluded that policy proposals put forward under degrowth narratives lacked precision, and that many were merely referred to, with little effort expended to link them concretely to outcomes or to understand how they would work together to drive systemic change. The most commonly mentioned were universal basic incomes, work-time reductions, job guarantees with a living wage, maximum income caps, reduced caps on resource use and emissions, not-for-profit co-operatives, deliberative forums, reclaiming the commons, eco-villages, and housing co-operatives (Fitzpatrick et al., 2022). All of these suggestions have merit and there are examples of best practice to be found across the globe, but much more critical and experimental work needs to be done to lay out plausible pathways for transformation in specific locales. This needs to be much more than a mere list of the kinds of projects, initiatives, institutions and innovations that might work or prove useful. The purpose of this volume is to lay the ground for an approach that focuses on improving quality of life for people and planet in the specific locations where the communities concerned live, using a whole-systems approach to the intersections that need to drive transformative change. This is a significant step forward, based on new concepts, frameworks, models and metrics as set out in Chapters 1 and 2, and grounded in working actively with local communities, authorities and stakeholders to chart specific pathways to prosperity.

In addition, the intellectual debate on green growth (efficiency) versus post-growth (sufficiency) has two major flaws. First, it is not a question of either/or, but of both. We cannot afford to wait until the post-growth coalition has won the argument, not least because there will be no winners from a continued stand-off. What is most important is to proceed with both efficiency and sufficiency at speed, but with a changed economic goal in mind. It is most definitely the case that if we continue to hold GDP growth as an end in itself, we will fail to design, deliver and manage the social, material, economic and political transformations that are necessary to drive sustainable prosperity for people and planet. The barriers to low-carbon transitions are political, cultural and behavioural rather than simply technological or economic, and governments, change makers of all types, and communities, need to act quickly and in the interest of many and of social justice. Social cohesion, compensation and equity will be central to a just transition; many of the biggest risks involved in transformation are social and political, and markets and financial systems cannot manage those risks (Agarwala et al., 2021).

The second failing of the green-versus-post-growth debate is the confidence it presupposes in the notion of a designed future. Given the uncertainty of making changes in many critical systems at once, and the specifics of culture, identity, history and politics involved in confronting change, we cannot know all the outcomes and answers in advance. We are going to need to move together, experimenting and refining, bringing government and local authorities into innovative partnerships with local business, communities and civil society organisations to drive change directed at improving quality of life as it is. The longer we wait to make the transition, the higher will be the transaction costs and the greater the risks. There is a strong imperative to work with local communities to map out plausible pathways based on the social innovations needed to drive transformation and build new institutions that deliver new ways of managing specific challenges. This will also require macroeconomic policy based on whole-system approaches to socio-ecological risk, and system-analysis models that take account of the functioning of biophysical systems, but also integrate real-world dynamics involving social and behavioural heterogeneity. A fundamental challenge to managing systemic risks is the need to understand the intersections of social and biophysical systems in the context of complex networks of individual, community, sectoral and institutional actors with different views and goals (Hynes et al., 2020). This requires not only new theoretical frameworks and languages, but also new models and metrics based on an understanding of those intersections in complex sets of relationalities. This is the purpose of developing local prosperity indexes that can lay out for all involved the goals and pathways towards sustainable prosperity in context.

Chapter 5 of the volume picks up the question of what it takes to bring people together, across socially fragmented urban settings in which communities are affected by displacement, conflict and compounding crises, to develop shared plans for pathways to prosperity. Lebanon has a long history of receiving refugees and migrants, but the Syrian crisis now means that the country has the highest number of refugees per capita in the world. Migration is one of the most contentious issues in contemporary political debate, and movement of people is fuelled by economic collapse, political turmoil and climate change. National policies, humanitarian interventions, educational and health systems, decent public services and infrastructures are all crucial for dealing with mass displacement, and all are in short supply in Lebanon. How, then, can actions at the local level translate into shared ideas and spaces for prosperity with concrete outcomes for improvements in quality of life, when populist and nationalist responses focus on protecting prosperity for local communities by keeping refugees out?

IGP research begins with community co-creation of ideas about prosperity, but is always followed by the implementation of co-designed community solutions to identified challenges. In this case, urban interventions in the town of Bar Elias in the Beqaa Valley near the Syrian border were co-designed and created by refugees and Lebanese citizens, focusing on how the vulnerabilities created by a lack of public services are shared by the two communities. An evaluation two years later found that one of the newly created spaces had become known locally as the 'new town square', used by caregivers, children and visitors to the polyclinic in the day, and by young men in the evening. It had also become a local landmark, and the site of communal celebrations (Ramadan, Hijri New Year and the Prophet's Birthday), as well as of public demonstrations during the October 2019 revolution. More importantly, it had fostered a sense of shared space, and of how refugees and Lebanese citizens could work together for mutual benefit, resulting in additional initiatives on the part of residents to improve the quality of local urban spaces. Small-scale interventions of this kind are not a solution in themselves to large-scale problems associated with displacement, but they are a mechanism through which divided communities can begin to take ownership of potential pathways to improvement in quality of life for all.

## Whose ideas count?

One of the major challenges for any kind of designed solution or transformative pathway is to establish whose voices are heard and whose knowledge counts. There has been a long debate, with many critical perspectives, on the relationship between development and Western capitalism and Western science. Other epistemologies, other ways of knowing and doing, other ways of imagining development, simply do not get heard or recognised; colonialism continues in the production and valuing of knowledge (Andreasson, 2007; Demaria & Kothari, 2017; Escobar, 2011; Mathews, 2022; Matunhu, 2011; Mazzone et al., 2022; Moore, 2015; Patel, 2020; Ruwhiu et al., 2022; Santos, 2007, 2014; and Suleiman, 2016). There are no permitted alternatives to development, since all include and equate economic growth with material and social progress, and ignore the links between human wellbeing and the natural environment, drawing on anthropocentric views that separate humanity from the planet's ecosystems. Communities in the global South work with sustainability and stewardship values that try to counteract the histories of colonialism, capitalism and globalisation, and their consequences in the present. What characterises these very diverse discussions is a recognition of the embeddedness of humans in the natural and non-human worlds, and the disproportionate impact of ecological crises on indigenous people and communities in the global South. One of the key issues in defining and charting transformative change is the question of power: who decides what prosperity is, and for whom? Prosperity without self-determination and aspiration, and the means to realise both, would not be prosperity.

The IGP's PROCOL Africa works in Kenya, Tanzania and Ethiopia. Chapters 7 and 8 describe research carried out in north-west Kenya with local Marakwet communities and citizen scientists on their complex, intensive agriculture system and pathways to prosperity. Many external commentators have remarked on the ingenuity of hundreds of kilometres of gravity-fed irrigation channels and a diverse range of landrace and introduced crops, as well as soil management techniques. The Marakwet system of cultivation is based on a detailed understanding of the soil/food/water nexus, and it has remained remarkably resilient in the face of colonialism, development initiatives, food shortages, climate change, conflict, population growth and outward migration. When I was working there in 2021, local communities were simultaneously managing Covid, plagues of locusts, floods and mudslides. The Marakwet are highly sophisticated farmers, but regular and repeated warnings of collapse from outside observers and experts reframe them as balanced on the precipice of agricultural failure and collapse. Chapter 7 discusses the long history of such tropes, and their connection to colonial and development narratives based on idealised notions of the improved farmer, the demand for more efficiency under the guise of poverty alleviation, and frameworks of teleological progress curated through Western economic and scientific norms. Such tropes and frameworks leave little room for alternative technologies, forms of agency and aspiration, knowledges and ideas, even when they are clearly effective.

Chapter 8 discusses how Marakwet communities seek to improve their own lifeways through experimentation, improvisation and innovation in ways that allow them to thrive. This does not mean that there are not instances of failure, water pollution, soil erosion, deforestation and food shortage. This is very far from an ideal or idealised situation. Work for the prosperity index has revealed that individuals and communities have their own visions of prosperous livelihoods conceptualised not simply as income, although that is crucial, but based on a more holistic understanding of the good life: *maisha bora* (Kiswahili) or *tasampo tai* (Kimarakwet). Quality education, human health, clean and healthy environments, inter-clan solidarity, secure housing and work, and a voice in decision-making processes were all identified by local communities as important for sustainable prosperity. But what was of particular importance was the idea that good lives in Marakwet have to exist through time and across generations; it is this vision that guides the maintenance of lifeways, including forms of farming and food production, the persistence of households, lineages and clans, the retention and evolution of local social institutions, and a wider maintenance of biodiversity. Through time, the Marakwet have maintained their own ways and means of solving and addressing ecological, economic and engineering challenges so as to generate forms of lived prosperity. Such activities have often proceeded and been enacted in antithesis to external actors and their development plans.

Generating prosperity is not about the enactment of a singular developmental design or blueprint; rather it resides in experiences, aspirations, actions and decisions that play out through time in specific socio-ecological contexts. As discussed in Chapter 2, the realisation of prosperity is a temporally contingent, emergent phenomenon of complex socio-natural systems, assembled and reassembled by knowledgeable agents on the ground.

Chapter 7 shows that networked knowledge, pooled resources and distributed decision making across diverse social and ecological landscapes are characteristic of forms of flourishing in rural communities in Kenya and Zambia, but were persistently reconfigured by colonial and post-colonial states as wasteful and non-productive, and in need of modernisation. Quality of life depended on the maintenance of social and ecological diversity, and this was very often expressed as embeddedness in a series of social networks laid out across ecological zones that provided families with direct access both to land and to a range of resources that could be called on as needed, or indeed shared with others.

What is of interest here is that these modes of flourishing were – and are – designed for flexibility and diversity; they were intentionally extensible so that, as the need arose, the system could be expanded or enhanced with new capabilities and features. At certain times, there were definitely shortages of labour, resources, skills and knowledge. The introduction of new crops, and new ideas and aspirations, shaped the emergent features of the system, sometimes for good and sometimes for bad. Experimentation and the management of risk were always a calculation, but built into the system were forms of redundancy, paths not taken, resources not used, social relationships whose operationalisation was saved for another day. These were not systems based on maximising efficiency and productivity, extracting everything from the soil and the land and the people who farmed it; flourishing meant being there next year, and your children and land and animals after you. Recent levels of deforestation in Marakwet, soil degradation and water pollution have all come from maximising maize and potato production using inorganic fertilisers, maximising the profit that can be made from the land, using diesel generators to pump water rather than gravity-fed systems. This is not to idealise the farming system; it has benefited and will benefit further from new crop varieties, new skills, new knowledge, better energy and water access, roads, health and education. But what it does draw attention to is a different way of managing the complexities of socio-ecological systems over time.

Diversity of response has come into focus in quite different contexts through the Covid-19 pandemic and through the experience of fragile and overextended intersecting systems tipping and causing catastrophic sets of cascading failures. Covid was an ecological failure that became a health failure and then an economic and now a socio-political failure. As the Ukraine war shows, if you block one set of connections in the global food system, other areas quickly begin to fail, causing further system failure. The pursuit of economic efficiency and maximisation on the trail of ever-increasing GDP growth has produced systems that have no redundancy, flexibility, diversity or extensibility by design (Trump et al., 2021; Hynes et al., 2020). Covid was a multisystem problem that reached a tipping point (Roggema, 2021). Many now recognise that biophysical systems have these features (Mestre et al., 2021) and that we humans have been trying to design these features out, with disastrous results. It is strange, really, because we routinely design redundancy into our IT and road systems, into engineering projects and buildings, making sure that if something fails, there is another element ready to come into play. We know how complex systems work and yet we are not apparently willing to share that knowledge with communities like the Marakwet or listen to what they have to say. Economic systems that are premised on maximising profitability and efficiency, with maximum value extracted by a very few, are unlikely to be resilient or to offer pathways to sustainable prosperity.

## Conclusion

In this volume, our key argument is that the ability to generate prosperous lives principally resides with the people who live that prosperity. We lay out a theory of prosperity as a dynamic emergent assemblage, and thus develop theories, models and metrics appropriately. What makes this volume distinctive is that it is a sustained attempt to discuss what prosperity means and entails for local communities on the ground, how they conceive of it and how they can be involved in its design, delivery, mobilisation and implementation. The examples of various challenges to defining and realising prosperity are discussed in both rural and urban locales, and in examples drawn from the Middle East, Europe and Africa.

The discussion on redefining prosperity develops a new theoretical language which makes it much more amenable to local and policy action. It also makes visible to governments what is required if their green growth plans are to take hold, and maps out why a convincing macroeconomic policy for a post-growth society has to begin with social innovation and with the voices, experiences and aspirations of the people who will build the prosperity of the future. There are transformations to come in the global economy and each country will need to build the capacities and capabilities of their communities to thrive as those transformations take hold. This is a question not just of fixing the problems of the present – although that has barely begun – but of hastening the advances of the future and repairing and remaking the relationships between place and the economy and between social, planetary and economic prosperity.

## Bibliography

Agarwala, M., Burke, M., Klusak, P., Mohaddes, K., Volz, U. & Zenghelis, D. (2021). Climate change and fiscal sustainability: Risks and opportunities. *National Institute Economic Review*, 258(1), 28–46. https://doi.org/10.1017/nie.2021.37.

Andreasson, S. (2007). Thinking beyond development: The future of post-development theory in Southern Africa. Draft paper. School of Politics, International Studies and Philosophy, Queen's University Belfast. Available at: https://www.researchgate.net/publication/237460730_Thinking_Beyond_Development_The_Future_of_Post-Development_Theory_in_Southern_Africa (accessed 13 December 2022).

Artaraz, K., Calestani, M. & Trueba, M. L. (2021). Introduction: *Vivir bien/Buen vivir* and post-neoliberal development paths in Latin America: Scope, strategies, and the realities of implementation. *Latin American Perspectives*, 48(3), 4–16. https://doi.org/10.1177/0094582X211009461.

Brand, U., Muraca, B., Pineault, E., Sahakian, M., Schaffartzik, A., Novy, A., Streissler, C. Haberl, H., Asara, V., Dietz, K., Lang, M. et al. (2021). From planetary to societal boundaries: An argument for collectively defined self-limitation. *Sustainability: Science, Practice and Policy*, 17(1), 264–91. https://doi.org/10.1080/15487733.2021.1940754.

Büchs, M. & Koch, M. (2018). Challenges for the degrowth transition: The debate about wellbeing. *Futures*, 105, 155–65. https://doi.org/10.1016/j.futures.2018.09.002.

Carpio Benalcázar, P. & Ullán de La Rosa, F. J. (2021). The institutionalized *Buen Vivir*: A new hegemonic political paradigm for Ecuador. *Revista Brasileira de Política Internacional*, 64(1). https://doi.org/10.1590/0034-7329202100101.

Chertkovskaya, E., Paulsson, A. & Barca, S. (eds). (2019). *Towards a Political Economy of Degrowth*. Lanham, MD: Rowman & Littlefield.

Costanza, R. (2022). *Addicted to Growth: Societal therapy for a sustainable wellbeing future*. Abingdon: Routledge.

Council of the European Union (2021). 8th EAP: Member states endorse provisional political agreement reached with Parliament. 10 December. Available at: https://www.consilium.europa.eu/en/press/press-releases/2021/12/10/8th-eap-member-states-endorse-provisional-political-agreement-reached-with-parliament/ (accessed 13 December 2022).

Coyle, D. (2015). *GDP: A brief but affectionate history*. Rev. edn. Princeton, NJ: Princeton University Press.

Dell, K., Spiller, C. & Staniland, N. (2021). Do Indigenous metaphors have universal applicability? Learnings from Māori in New Zealand. Available at: https://researchspace.auckland.ac.nz/bitstream/handle/2292/56393/Dell%20et%20al.%2014072021.pdf?sequence=2 (accessed 13 December 2022).

Demaria, F. & Kothari, A. (2017). The *Post-Development Dictionary* agenda: Paths to the pluriverse. *Third World Quarterly*, 38(12), 2588–99. https://doi.org/10.1080/01436597.2017.1350821.

Douglas, R. (2022). Bringing postgrowth research into policy. CUSP Working Paper no. 33. Centre for the Understanding of Sustainable Prosperity, Guildford. Available at: https://cusp.ac.uk/themes/aetw/wp33/ (accessed 13 December 2022).

Escobar, A. (2011). *Encountering Development: The making and unmaking of the Third World*. Princeton, NJ: Princeton University Press.

Federal Ministry for Economic Affairs and Climate Action (BMWK). (2022). *Annual Economic Report*. Available at: https://www.bmwk.de/Redaktion/EN/Publikationen/Wirtschaft/annual-economic-report-2022.pdf?__blob=publicationFile&v=2 (accessed 13 December 2022).

Fioramonti, L. (2013). *Gross Domestic Problem: The Politics Behind the World's Most Powerful Number*. London: Zed Books.

Fioramonti, L. (2017). *The World after GDP: Politics, business and society in the post-growth era*. New York: Wiley.

Fitzpatrick, N., Parrique, T. & Cosme, I. (2022). Exploring degrowth policy proposals: A systematic mapping with thematic synthesis. *Journal of Cleaner Production*, 365, 132764. https://doi.org/10.1016/j.jclepro.2022.132764.

Forero, J. E. (2021). *Buen vivir* as an alternative development model: Ecuador's bumpy road toward a postextractivist society. *Latin American Perspectives*, 48(3), 227–44. https://doi.org/10.1177/0094582X211008147.

Foroohar, R. (2022). *Homecoming: The path to prosperity in a post-global world*. New York: Crown.

Galvez, R., Zrinyi, N., Péloffy, K. & Laviolette, S. (2020). Building forward better: A clean and just recovery from the COVID-19 pandemic. White Paper. The Senate of Canada. Available at: https://rosagalvez.ca/en/initiatives/clean-and-just-recovery/ (accessed 13 December 2022).

Gough, I. (2017). *Heat, Greed and Human Need: Climate change, capitalism and sustainable wellbeing*. Cheltenham: Edward Elgar.

Gudynas, E. (2011). Buen Vivir: Today's tomorrow. *Development*, 54, 441–7. https://doi.org/10.1057/dev.2011.86.

Gudynas, E. (2016). Beyond varieties of development: Disputes and alternatives. *Third World Quarterly*, 37(4), 721–32. http://dx.doi.org/10.1080/01436597.2015.1126504.

Haberl, H., Wiedenhofer, D., Virág, D., Kalt, G., Plank, B., Brockway, P., Fishman, T., Hausknost, D., Krausmann, F., Leon-Gruchalski, B., Mayer, A. et al. (2020). A systematic review of the evidence on decoupling of GDP, resource use and GHG emissions, part II: Synthesizing the insights. *Environmental Research Letters*, 15(6), 065003. https://doi.org/10.1088/1748-9326/ab842a.

Hickel, J. (2019). Degrowth: A theory of radical abundance. *Real-World Economics Review*, 87, 54–68.

Hickel, J. (2021). What does degrowth mean? A few points of clarification. *Globalizations*, 18(7), 1105–11. https://doi.org/10.1080/14747731.2020.1812222.

Hickel, J. & Kallis, G. (2020). Is green growth possible? *New Political Economy*, 25(4), 469–86. https://doi.org/10.1080/13563467.2019.1598964.

Hidalgo-Capitán, A. L. & Cubillo-Guevara, A. P. (2017). Deconstruction and genealogy of Latin American good living (*buen vivir*): The (triune) good living and its diverse intellectual wellsprings. In *Alternative Pathways to Sustainable Development: Lessons from Latin America*, edited by Gilles Carbonnier, Humberto Campodónico and Sergio Tezanos Vázquez, pp. 23–50. Leiden: Brill Nijhoff. https://doi.org/10.4000/poldev.2351.

Hough-Stewart, L., Trebeck, K., Sommer, C. & Wallis, S. (2019). What is a wellbeing economy? Different ways to understand the vision of an economy that serves people and planet. Wellbeing Economy Alliance. Available at: https://weall.org/wp-content/uploads/2019/12/A-WE-Is-WEAll-Ideas-Little-Summaries-of-Big-Issues-4-Dec-2019.pdf (accessed 13 December 2022).

Hynes, W., Trump, B., Love, P. & Linkov, I. (2020). Bouncing forward: A resilience approach to dealing with COVID-19 and future systemic shocks. *Environment Systems and Decisions*, 40(2), 174–84. https://doi.org/10.1007/s10669-020-09776-x.

Institute for Public Prosperity Research (2018). *Prosperity and Justice: A plan for the new economy.* Cambridge: Polity.

Jackson, T. (2017). *Prosperity without Growth: Foundations for the economy of tomorrow.* 2nd edn. Abingdon: Routledge.

Jackson, T. (2021). *Post Growth: Life after capitalism.* Cambridge: Polity.

Kallis, G., Kostakis, V., Lange, S., Muraca, B., Paulson, S. & Schmelzer, M. (2018). Research on degrowth. *Annual Review of Environment and Resources*, 43, 291–316. https://doi.org/10.1146/annurev-environ-102017-025941.

Keyßer, L. T. & Lenzen, M. (2021). 1.5 °C degrowth scenarios suggest the need for new mitigation pathways. *Nature Communications*, 12, 2676, 1–16. https://doi.org/10.1038/s41467-021-22884-9.

HM Government (2022a). *Levelling Up the United Kingdom.* London: HM Government. Available at: https://assets.publishing.service.gov.uk/government/uploads/system/uploads/attachment_data/file/1052706/Levelling_Up_WP_HRES.pdf (accessed 13 December 2022).

HM Government (2022b). *Levelling Up the United Kingdom: Measures and metrics: Technical Annex.* London: HM Government. Available at: https://assets.publishing.service.gov.uk/government/uploads/system/uploads/attachment_data/file/1054766/Technical_annex_-_missions_and_metrics.pdf (accessed 13 December 2022).

*Lancet* (2022). The 2022 global report of the *Lancet* Countdown. Available at: https://www.lancetcountdown.org/2022-report/ (accessed 13 December 2022). https://doi.org/10.1016/S0140-6736(22)01540-9.

Mathews, S. (2022). Moving from postcolonial critiques of development towards alternatives to development in Africa. In F. López-Castellano, C. Lizárraga & R. Manzanera-Ruiz (eds), *Neoliberalism and Unequal Development: Alternatives and transitions in Europe, Latin America and sub-Saharan Africa*, 175–91. Abingdon: Routledge.

Matunhu, J. (2011). A critique of modernization and dependency theories in Africa: Critical assessment. *African Journal of History and Culture*, 3(5), 65–72.

Mayer, C. (2018). *Prosperity: Better business makes the greater good.* Oxford: Oxford University Press.

Mazzone, A., Fulkaxò Cruz, D. K., Tumwebaze, S., Ushigua, M., Trotter, P. A., Carvajal, A. E., Schaeffer, R. & Khosla, R. (2022). Indigenous cosmologies of energy for a sustainable energy future. *Nature Energy*, 1–11. https://doi.org/10.1038/s41560-022-01121-7.

Meadows, D. H., Meadows, D. L., Randers, J. & Behrens, W. W., III. (1972). *The Limits to Growth: A report for the Club of Rome's Project on the Predicament of Mankind.* New York: Universe Books.

Mestre, N., Roig, E. & Almestar, M. (2021). Beyond nature-based rhetorics: A prospect on the potentials of redundancy in ecology-oriented design. *Sustainability*, 13(23), 13293. https://doi.org/10.3390/su132313293.

Moore, H. L. (2015). Global prosperity and sustainable development goals. *Journal of International Development*, 27(6), 801–15. https://doi.org/10.1002/jid.3114.

Moore, H. L. & Collins, H. (2021). *Assembling Prosperity in a Post-Covid United Kingdom: New approaches to levelling up.* London: Institute for Global Prosperity. Available at: https://discovery.ucl.ac.uk/id/eprint/10131207/ (accessed 13 December 2022).

Moore, H. L. & Woodcraft, S. (2022). Conceptualising and measuring prosperity. GOLD VI Working Paper Series #11. Available at: https://gold.uclg.org/sites/default/files/11_conceptualising_and_measuring_prosperity_by_henrietta_l._moore_and_saffron_woodcraft.pdf (accessed 13 December 2022).

Muhirwa, F., Shen, L., Elshkaki, A., Velempini, K., Hirwa, H., Zhong, S. & Mbandi, A. M. (2021). Decoupling energy, water, and food resources production from GHG emissions: A footprint perspective review of Africa from 1990 to 2017. *Energies*, 14(19), 6326. https://doi.org/10.3390/en14196326.

Muradian, R. (2019). Frugality as a choice vs. frugality as a social condition: Is de-growth doomed to be a Eurocentric project? *Ecological Economics*, 161, 257–60. https://doi.org/10.1016/j.ecolecon.2019.03.027.

New Zealand Government (2022). *Wellbeing Budget 2022: A secure future*. Available at: https://www.treasury.govt.nz/sites/default/files/2022-05/b22-wellbeing-budget.pdf (accessed 13 December 2022).

New Zealand Government (n.d.). He Ara Waiora – brief overview. Available at: https://www.treasury.govt.nz/sites/default/files/2021-05/He%20Ara%20Waiora%20-%20brief%20overview%20A3.pdf (accessed 13 December 2022).

Obeng-Odoom, F. (2018). Critique of development economics. *Japanese Political Economy*, 44(1–4), 59–81.

Parrique, T., Barth, J., Briens, F., Kerschner, C., Kraus-Polk, A., Kuokkanen, A. & Spangenberg, J. H. (2019). Decoupling debunked: Evidence and arguments against green growth as a sole strategy for sustainability. European Environmental Bureau. Available at: https://eeb.org/wp-content/uploads/2019/07/Decoupling-Debunked-FULL-for-ONLINE.pdf (accessed 13 December 2022).

Patel, K. (2020). Race and a decolonial turn in development studies. *Third World Quarterly*, 41(9), 1463–75. https://doi.org/10.1080/01436597.2020.1784001.

Radcliffe, S. A. (2012). Development for a postneoliberal era? *Sumak kawsay*, living well and the limits to decolonisation in Ecuador. *Geoforum*, 43(2), 240–9. https://doi.org/10.1016/j.geoforum.2011.09.003.

Roggema, R. (2021). From nature-based to nature-driven: Landscape first for the design of Moeder Zernike in Groningen. *Sustainability*, 13(4), 2368. https://doi.org/10.3390/su13042368.

Rout, M., Awatere, S., Mika, J. P., Reid, J. & Roskruge, M. (2021). A Māori approach to environmental economics: Te ao tūroa, te ao hurihuri, te ao mārama – The old world, a changing world, a world of light. In *Oxford Research Encyclopedia of Environmental Science*, edited by Herman H. Shugart. https://doi.org/10.1093/acrefore/9780199389414.013.715.

Rout, M. & Reid, J. (2020). Embracing indigenous metaphors: A new/old way of thinking about sustainability. *Sustainability Science*, 15(3), 945–54. https://doi.org/10.1007/s11625-020-00783-0.

Ruwhiu, D., Amoamo, M., Carter, L., Bargh, M., Ruckstuhl, K., Carr, A. & Awatere, S. (2022). Ngā whai take: Reframing indigenous development. In K. Ruckstuhl, I. A. Velásquez Nimatuj, J.-A. McNeish and N. Postero (eds), *The Routledge Handbook of Indigenous Development*, 297–308. Abingdon: Routledge.

Santos, B. de S. (2007). *Another Knowledge is Possible: Beyond northern epistemologies*. London: Verso.

Santos, B. de S. (2014). *Epistemologies of the South: Justice against epistemicide*. Abingdon: Routledge.

Schmid, B. (2022). What about the city? Towards an urban post-growth research agenda. *Sustainability*, 14(19), 11926, 1–16. https://doi.org/10.3390/su141911926.

Soper, K. (2020). *Post-Growth Living: For an alternative hedonism*. London: Verso.

Spash, C. L. (2021). Apologists for growth: Passive revolutionaries in a passive revolution. *Globalizations*, 18(7), 1123–48.

Steffen, W., Richardson, K., Rockström, J., Cornell, S. E., Fetzer, I., Bennett, E. M., Biggs, R., Carpenter, S. R., De Vries, W., De Wit, C. A., Folke, C., Gerten, D., Heinke, J., Mace, G. M., Persson, L. M., Ramanathan, V., Reyers, B. & Sörlin, S. (2015). Planetary boundaries: Guiding human development on a changing planet. *Science*, 347(6223), 1259855. https://doi.org/10.1126/science.1259855.

Stiglitz, J. E. (2009). GDP fetishism. *The Economists' Voice*, 6(8). https://doi.org/10.2202/1553-3832.1651.

Stiglitz, J. E., Sen, A. & Fitoussi, J.-P. (2010). *Mismeasuring our Lives: Why GDP doesn't add up*. New York: New Press.

Suleiman, M. R. (2016). African development: A critical review. *International Journal of Humanities & Social Science Studies* 2(6), 320–30.

Trump, B. D., Keenan, J. M. & Linkov, I. (2021). Multi-disciplinary perspectives on systemic risk and resilience in the time of COVID-19. In I. Linkov, J. M. Keenan & B. D. Trump (eds), *COVID-19: Systemic risk and resilience*, 1–9. Cham: Springer. https://doi.org/10.1007/978-3-030-71587-8_1.

United Nations Development Programme and University of Oxford (2021). *The Peoples' Climate Vote*. UNDP and University of Oxford. Available at: https://www.undp.org/publications/peoples-climate-vote (accessed 13 December 2022).

United Nations Environment Programme (2022). *The Closing Window: Climate crisis calls for rapid transformation of societies*. Emissions Gap Report 2022. UNEP. Available at: https://www.unep.org/resources/emissions-gap-report-2022 (accessed 13 December 2022).

Vadén, T., Lähde, V., Majava, A., Järvensivu, P., Toivanen, T. & Eronen, J. T. (2021). Raising the bar: On the type, size and timeline of a 'successful' decoupling. *Environmental Politics*, 30(3), 462–76. https://doi.org/10.1080/09644016.2020.1783951.

Van den Bergh, J. C. J. M. (2011). Environment versus growth: A criticism of 'degrowth' and a plea for 'a-growth'. *Ecological Economics*, 70(5), 881–90. https://doi.org/10.1016/j.ecolecon.2010.09.035.

Van den Bergh, J. C. J. M. (2022). A procedure for globally institutionalizing a 'beyond-GDP' metric. *Ecological Economics*, 192, 107257, 1–5. https://doi.org/10.1016/j.ecolecon.2021.107257.

Van den Bergh, J. C. J. M. & Kallis, G. (2011). Growth, a-growth or degrowth to stay within planetary boundaries? *Journal of Economic Issues*, 46(4), 909–20. https://doi.org/10.2753/JEI0021-3624460404.

Veltmeyer, H. & Záyago Lau, E. (eds). (2021). *Buen Vivir and the Challenges to Capitalism in Latin America*. Abingdon: Routledge.

Weizsäcker, E. U. von & Wijkman, A. (2018). *Come On! Capitalism, short-termism, population and the destruction of the planet*. New York: Springer.

Wellbeing Economy Alliance (2017). Wellbeing Economy Policy Design Guide: How to design economic policies that put the wellbeing of people and the planet first. Available at: https://wellbeingeconomy.org/wp-content/uploads/Wellbeing-Economy-Policy-Design-Guide_Mar17_FINAL.pdf (accessed 13 December 2022).

Wiedenhofer, D., Virág, D., Kalt, G., Plank, B., Streeck, J., Pichler, M., Mayer, A., Krausmann, F., Brockway, P., Schaffartzik, A., Fishman, T., Hausknost, D., Leon-Gruchalski, B., Sousa, T., Creutzig, F. & Haberl, H. (2020). A systematic review of the evidence on decoupling of GDP, resource use and GHG emissions, part I: Bibliometric and conceptual mapping. *Environmental Research Letters*, 15(6), 063002. https://doi.org/10.1088/1748-9326/ab8429.

Woodcraft, S. & Anderson, B. (2019). *Rethinking Prosperity for London: When citizens lead transformation*. London: Institute for Global Prosperity. Available at: https://static1.squarespace.com/static/5a0c05169f07f51c64a336a2/t/5d03c62b56b1ce0001bf6266/1560528440423/LPI_Report_single_140619_update.pdf (accessed 23 February 2023).

Wunderling, N., Donges, J. F., Kurths, J. & Winkelmann, R. (2021). Interacting tipping elements increase risk of climate domino effects under global warming. *Earth System Dynamics*, 12(2), 601–19. https://doi.org/10.5194/esd-12-601-2021.

Xu, C., Kohler, T. A., Lenton, T. M., Svenning, J.-C. & Scheffer, M. (2020). Future of the human climate niche. *Proceedings of the National Academy of Sciences of the United States of America*, 117(21), 11350–5. https://doi.org/10.1073/pnas.1910114117.

Yellen, J. K. (2022). Remarks by Secretary of the Treasury Janet L. Yellen at the 2022 'Virtual Davos Agenda' hosted by the World Economic Forum. Available at: https://home.treasury.gov/news/press-releases/jy0565 (accessed 13 December 2022).

# 1
# What is prosperity?

Henrietta L. Moore and Nikolay Mintchev

## 1.1 Rethinking prosperity

This chapter is about why we need new theories about what prosperity means and entails in the twenty-first century. To redefine prosperity is to challenge both the structural features of our economies and the value premises on which they are built. We are concerned here with how a redesigned prosperity opens the door not just to innovative ideas, but to new practices, allowing us to address inequalities in novel ways. Searching for the means and mechanisms through which these new frameworks and activities may be operationalised quickly reveals that we need fresh approaches to how systems change and knowledge is shared. We begin then with three points of reference: the value of the economic in our lives, the purpose of sharing knowledge, and the means of operationalising change.

The broad brush of prosperity must be about the relationship between individual lives – their quality, aspiration and purpose – and the larger systems and constraints in which they are embedded. In analytic terms, this is a question of scale, but it is simultaneously one of scope: what does prosperity comprise and embrace, for whom, when and where? In contemporary societies, questions of scale and scope are simultaneously matters of politics. 'Build back better', 'great reset', 'green new deal', 'inclusive growth' are just some of the terms animating public debate as we struggle to reframe and manage the fractured relationship between politics and economics. These terms have variable purpose and localised inflections, but they crop up in indigenised forms across the globe, provoking a range of responses from anxiety to outrage and passion. Such phrases have more import for citizens in some places than in others, and some find variable salience for governments and place-based organisations hoping to appease anger and perhaps deliver genuinely new solutions to long-running difficulties. It is easy to overlook the significance of what appear to be definitional skirmishes, but questions of range, reach, scope and content can have huge consequences in terms of policy and investment.

We see this most prominently in macroeconomic policy and its directed compass towards increased growth and productivity. The Covid-19 pandemic has revealed the structural frailties and systemic injustices of social systems built on economies thus mandated, with their targets focused on increased GDP. The widening gaps in quality of life and opportunity between those who benefit from the value created and extracted in our economies and societies and those who do not has resulted in a well-established case for looking for measures of progress beyond economic growth and GDP (Fioramonti, 2017; Helliwell et al., 2020; Institute for Public Policy Research, 2018; Ngamaba, 2017; OECD, 2020; Stiglitz et al., 2010; Stiglitz, 2011, 2019; World Bank, 2010). It is widely recognised that the pursuit of constantly augmented growth is not sustainable in the context of limited planetary resources, nor does it provide us with appropriate pathways for addressing today's pressing challenges of inequality, environmental degradation, and climate change, among others (for example, Cassiers, 2015; Dalziel et al., 2018; Hickel, 2020a; Jackson 2017; Maxton and Randers, 2016; Moore, 2015). Yet even in this time of crisis such realisations have had very little impact on policy formulation and how we might address the prosperity deficit of individuals and communities within regions and nations (Moore, 2015; Moore & Woodcraft, 2019), with conventional policy frameworks continuing to rely on national and regional aggregates and statistics with very little relevance to the quality of people's lives. What is needed is a redefinition of prosperity that is less concerned with aggregate economic wealth and growth, and more attentive to the things that people care about and need: secure and good-quality livelihoods, good public services, a clean and healthy environment, planetary and ecosystem health, a political system that allows everyone to be heard, and the ability to have rich social and cultural lives.

The work of redefining prosperity is part of an emerging critique of the 'economics first' approach to progress. The critique includes: theories of happiness (Layard, 2011; Dolan, 2014) and wellbeing (Huppert et al., 2009; Diener and Seligman 2004) that have enriched our understandings of the physical and psychological factors that allow us to 'feel good' and 'do well' in terms of pleasure and purpose in life; work on social progress (Social Progress Imperative, 2022; Stiglitz et al., 2010) that has developed a series of measures to assess social, non-economic development beyond GDP; the Foundational Economy Collective, which has emphasised the social as well as the material infrastructures on which we all depend (Calafati et al., 2019; Foundational Economy Collective, 2018; Froud et al., 2018); the Legatum Institute, whose annual prosperity index ranks countries according to their pathways from poverty to prosperity (Legatum Institute, 2020, 2019); the OECD's Better Life Initiative, which charts whether life is getting better across the OECD and partner countries (OECD, 2020); the Sustainable Development Index, which uses aggregate data to assess the ecological efficiency of countries in delivering human development (Hickel, 2020b); and the United Nations Sustainable Development Goals (United Nations Development Programme, 2016), which have established a global agenda for action centred on the five principles of people, prosperity, planet, peace and partnership. Our work on redefining and building pathways to prosperity in the Institute for Global Prosperity (IGP) at UCL is part of this broader ecology of initiatives, but its specific value lies in four innovative approaches: the first involves working with local communities to understand what prosperity means for them in the context of lives lived; the second entails situating these local understandings within the structural features of the economy, infrastructure, public services provision, and systemic social and political inequalities; the third consists in developing pathways to sustainable prosperity based on novel understandings of how complex systems change; the fourth situates the mechanisms for change within new forms of collaboration and governance.

## 1.2 The question of context

Macroeconomics is an unusual social science in that it believes that aggregate outcomes can be read from the preferences and utilities of individuals. It is virtually isolated in this orthodoxy, while other disciplines continue to struggle with the central problem of the relationship between structure and agency in human societies. The dilemma of how the individual meshes with the social is a philosophical conundrum, but it has two kinds of consequences for redesigning prosperity. The first is that it is not a matter just of defining and measuring prosperity, but of formulating what we actually need to do to make sustainable prosperity a realisable proposition for specific people living in specific locales. This shift in priority is significant, because prosperity then commutes from an abstract national or regional goal to a locally situated requirement, with all the complexity and cultural and historical impedimenta this implies and entails. The specifics of location also necessitate a recognition of the meanings, values, practices and systems that shape the meanings and experiences of the good life in particular contexts. There is no singular vision of prosperity (according to its redefined meaning), no 'one size fits all', and in consequence the goal is not focused only on improving a set of metrics, but on developing attainable versions of the good life for communities and mapping out plausible pathways for achieving those visions. This is a problem both of scale and of scope, and what it demonstrates is that despite the post-growth/post-GDP conversations in vogue and the various metrics and methodologies for wellbeing and social progress in play, we do not have well-founded frameworks and pathways for sustainable prosperity that can be operationalised by communities, policy makers, business, civil society and government.

The second challenge is related to issues of place and diversity. In order to operationalise the concept of prosperity (redefined), we need a conceptual definition with specific content, but one that is also sensitive to time and place, to the context-specific visions of prosperity derived from engagement with community members. In short, we need to confront another familiar problem in philosophy and the social sciences: what is the relationship between the universal and the particular? Visions of the good life are diverse and attached to history, culture and circumstance, so what, if anything, do they share, these pluralistic versions of prosperity? One response is to assert that such questions are best approached through critical reflection and practical engagement in specific locales, involving, in essence, a sophisticated sorting and sifting exercise; while this is undoubtedly true it does not on its own provide a sufficiently robust riposte. There are quite a number of key words in the social sciences and humanities whose conceptual meanings differ across time and space: justice, culture, rights, for example. These terms always carry local inflections but are held to refer to identifiable sets of concerns or terrains of action and thought. While such concepts are wide-ranging, philosophical discussion and critical reflection most often proceed through a dual process of identifying those elements that are present whenever the term is invoked, and examining the different forms they take in specific contexts of application and practice. However, while it is recognised that intellectual discussion often follows this dualistic route, divisions remain as to whether we need to identify core aspects of the concept that run through all the known instances like a golden thread, or whether we should treat these concepts as possessing a family resemblance which is such that different combinations of features appear with each instantiation.

This query has both methodological and operational consequences, raising, as it does, the important issue of how a conceptual definition can be developed, operationalised and validated in a way that allows prosperity to become a useful conceptual framework for delivering positive social and economic change through policy initiatives as well as through community-based interventions. Broadly speaking, there are two types of intellectual procedure, and both are well evidenced in the literature on human needs and human development. The first is necessarily reductive and tries to establish the baseline minimum for individual and community wellbeing by providing a specification of needs (usually a list), accompanied by an undergirding assumption that if all these minimal needs are met then individuals and communities will flourish. This is in no small measure because well-specified theories of social justice require theories of human needs. There is no dispute that humans require shelter, food, security and other basic necessities, but universal specifications (lists, most often) have a tendency to be very abstract and generalised; the moment they become more specific their universal character is in doubt and charges of ethnocentrism begin to sprout. Needs can shade into values, and we see this struggle in Martha Nussbaum's famous list of the capabilities individuals need to lead a life of valuable functioning, where its very generality derives from the requirement to permit the possibility of multiple specificities of each of the components (Nussbaum, 2000). The more empirical content is provided, the more policy relevance builds, but so does the likelihood of claiming as objective or universal needs that are in reality historically, socially and culturally conditioned. This presents formidable challenges for forms of authority of all kinds that have responsibility for matters of access and distribution (see, for example, Scott, 2012; Atkinson et al., 2020).

A second avenue offers a plural way of proceeding. Doyal and Gough's (1991) well-regarded solution makes a distinction between universal needs (participation, health and autonomy) and a set of intermediate needs through which the former would be satisfied. These intermediate needs are common to societies and cultures at all times, but their means of satisfaction will necessarily be divergent and specific. Thus, it is the intermediate needs that provide the yardstick by which levels of deprivation and failures of satisfaction can be specified so that interventions and welfare strategies might be justified and judged objectively. This approach has enormous value, but it is wise to recall that from a philosophical point of view it is unlikely to solve the problem of universalism versus contextualism definitively. Consider, for example, whether issues of participation and health can be said to be equally universal, or universal in the same way; it seems logical that possible claims about a universal need for health of body and mind are not of the same order as those that might be made about participation, which must necessarily be context-dependent.

However, a more practical consideration is to ask what our aim in redefining prosperity is. Broadly, we suggest two responses. The first is that, since we have embarked on a redefinition of prosperity, it must follow that variations at the level of conceptualisation and theorisation are consequential. Second, the aim is to redefine prosperity so as to improve people's quality of life, and this entails a recognition that any theory or framing of prosperity that is developed must be one that is specific: it must materialise for specific persons in specific locales. If this is the case, then we might agree that we cannot be interested in simply developing a general definition of the good life. What benefit would that provide?

Yet if prosperity is simply whatever it turns out to be in a specific locale, it is going to be difficult to deliver policy objectives. There are further considerations here of equity and distribution, and these connect to the manner in which locales are embedded in larger geographical entities with interconnected consequences and potentially intersecting moral frameworks. For example, a community convinced that prosperity must involve swimming pools in every house would likely be depriving nearby communities of water, as well as asserting a framework of need that exceeded reasonable policy objectives for attaining the good life. In short, a prosperity expanded to include everyone having whatever they desired would not only be unsustainable socially, economically and ecologically, but would likely no longer be a recognisable version of the good life. It is a feature of the world we live in that prosperity is relational and interconnected.

While many of today's most pressing challenges are global in scale and relevance, they translate into locally specific effects on people's lives. The responses that address these problems must therefore be (at least in part) locally driven, guided by context-specific visions of prosperity, led by actors with skills and knowledges that are sensitised to their contexts, and supported by community members committed to improving the places where they live. Research conducted at the IGP begins with the premise that communities must play a central role in both rethinking prosperity and developing pathways to better quality of life. The assumption here is not only that change must be effected at the local level, but that informed localised agency is a necessary condition for change to take place and for delineating pathways towards prosperity.

Prosperity redefined includes notions of voice, recognition and community self-realisation which preclude compromising the agency of others; it also insists that, in contexts of policy change where power is unevenly distributed, any notion of improving quality of life or meeting the specific needs of communities has to respect and be derived from the skills, knowledge and agency of those who are the designated beneficiaries. Solutions imposed from outside are not only ineffective and costly, but would undermine several principles of what constitutes prosperity or the good life. A prosperity that involved meeting needs while compromising agency and self-determination would not be a sustainable prosperity.

Research at the IGP has examined how we might redefine prosperity for the twenty-first century by working with local communities to understand what prosperity means for them and how those local understandings relate to structural features of the economy, infrastructure, public services provision, and systemic social and political inequalities. The operationalisation of the prosperity framework therefore provides a new and innovative approach to analysing the lived experience of local livelihoods and communities within the complex set of interlocking systems and structures that make up the social, economic and political life of a specific community: lived experience and structural constraints must come together. It follows that, in this formulation, prosperity must be more than individual wellbeing, for wellbeing is too often characterised as a set of attributes pertaining to the individual, rather than as a series of effects produced in specific times and places through the relationships established by living well together in functioning social, economic and political systems and ecosystems (see Chapter 2; Moore & Woodcraft, 2019; Moore & Collins, 2020). It is a weakness of much work on wellbeing that it takes little account of long-run considerations of planetary sustainability and ecosystem health, even if it incorporates provision of green spaces and environmental assets in terms of their impact on individuals' health. Prosperity redefined incorporates individual wellbeing, but lays emphasis on living well with others and with the planet (Atkinson, 2013; Atkinson et al., 2017; White, 2015). The focus is thus on relationality in context.

## 1.3 Practices of context

The starting point for constructing a context-sensitive understanding of prosperity is talking to people about their hopes, challenges and opportunities for a good-quality of life in different sites of inquiry. These conversations take place through semi-structured interviews with residents, workshops with multiple stakeholders (including academics, businesses, local authorities and NGOs, among others), and brainstorming sessions with citizen scientist researchers from the relevant local communities who work as members of the research team. The findings that these evidence-collection exercises produce become the conceptual material for a prosperity model for each site of inquiry, and subsequently inform the co-design of household surveys for quantitative data collection for the development of a prosperity index. Simultaneously, detailed statistical information from extant data sources, such as national statistical services and government departments, is used to build up a detailed picture of the local landscape. These latter data sources provide information which is not routinely accessible to local communities and stakeholders, such as information on spending on public services and infrastructure, levels of biodiversity loss or soil toxicity, or the number of children going to school hungry, but which is shared in processes of co-design to inform discussions around the visualisation of the prosperity model at the local level.

The IGP's prosperity model is divided into five domains: (1) belonging, identities and culture, (2) health and healthy environments, (3) foundations of prosperity (referring to key aspects of material security that support the possibility of a good life and strengthen other elements of prosperity), (4) opportunities and aspirations, and (5) power, voice and influence (see Chapter 3, and Moore & Woodcraft 2019). These five domains were identified through a process that involved the critical evaluation of existing wellbeing and human development indices at national and international levels, and a process of qualitative co-design with local communities. The five domains represent a range of concerns that include, but go well beyond, issues of income, jobs, skills and productivity. The qualitative data collected through research and co-design with local communities in the different research locales plays the all-important role of operationalising and giving concrete content to each domain, as well as the manner in which it is experienced in each specific context. What is most significant is not just the investigation of the content and character of each domain but the exploration of the specific manner in which domains intersect in each locale. This careful exploration of domains, and of their content and intersectionality, is part of the process of operationalising and subsequently visualising each prosperity model, and it is accomplished through a collaborative effort with local citizen scientists who play a key role in steering the curation and visualisation of the domains. The significance of this process of visualisation is that it elucidates the specific intersections and interlocking constraints and opportunities in each locale, thereby indicating potential pathways for motivation, opportunity and change. Processes of change and pathways for achieving potential prosperity thus begin with

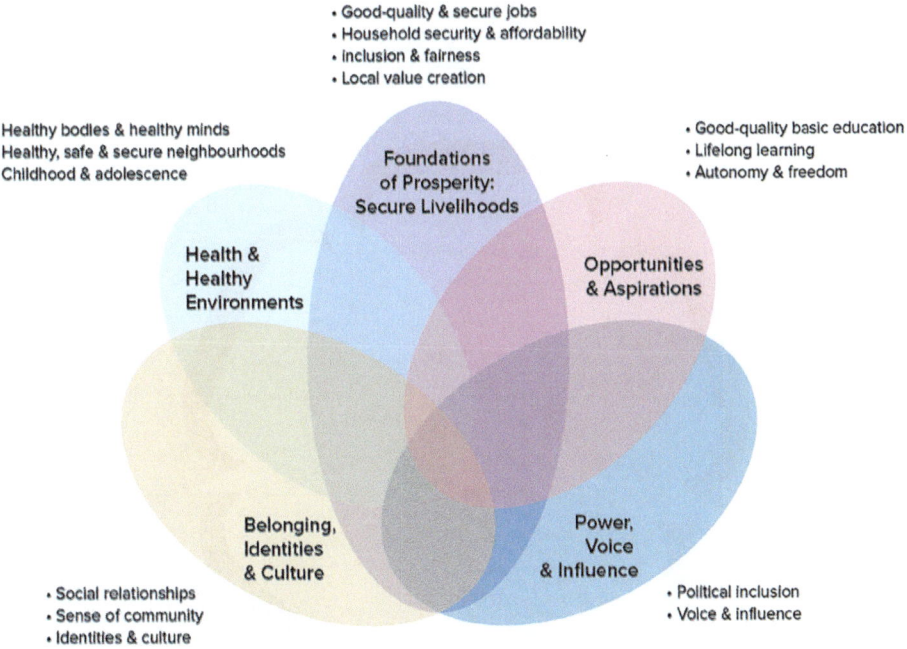

**Figure 1.1** Co-designed prosperity model for east London.
Source: IGP, 2022

a detailed understanding of situation that brings local understandings together with existing data sets and statistical analysis, thus providing a deep three-dimensional understanding of context.

Figures 1.1 to 1.3 are diagrams of the prosperity models for three different sites: east London (United Kingdom), Hamra, Beirut (Lebanon), and an informal settlement in Dar es Salaam (Tanzania).

## 1.4 Categorising and characterising change

The final stage in the process of developing a prosperity index for each locale involves the choice of indicators and indicator development for each domain. Indicators are derived from local and national data sets, and combined with specific localised indicators developed through quantitative and qualitative work with local communities (IGP, 2017). The aim is to develop a new multidimensional measurement tool that accurately represents the things that matter to people, yet sets them within a detailed understanding of larger determinants and constraints. While other efforts to develop new measures of prosperity have been successful in bringing together a range

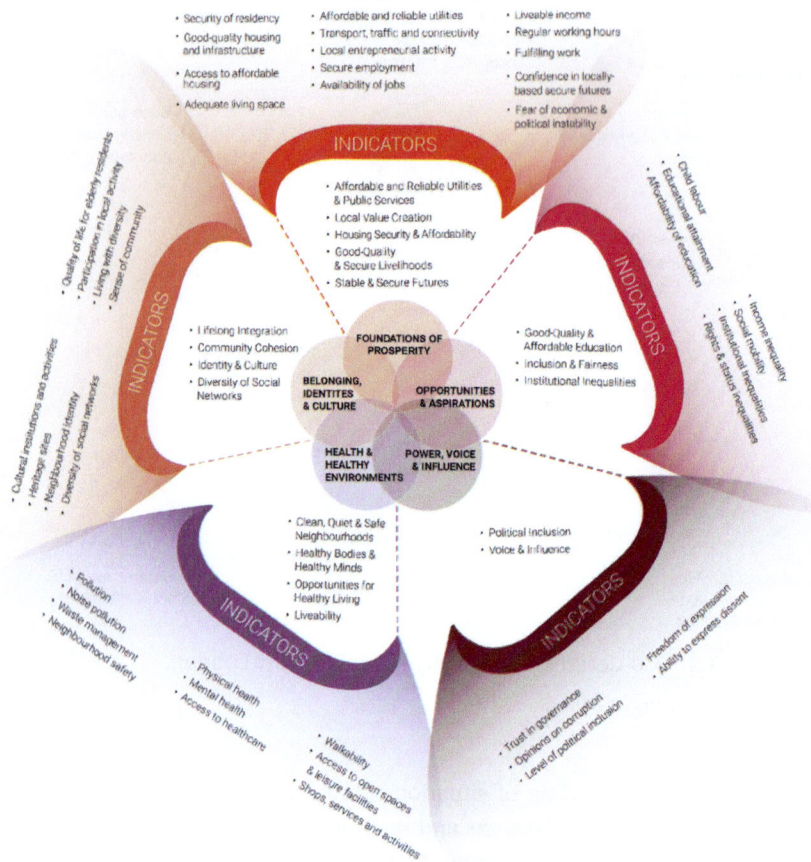

**Figure 1.2** Co-designed prosperity model for Hamra, Beirut.
Source: IGP, 2022

of economic and non-economic indicators (for example, United Nations Habitat City Prosperity Initiative, 2019; Legatum Institute, 2020), their focus on the city, regional and national levels has made it difficult to capture differences in quality of life within smaller geographical locales, and their expert-led approaches to defining prosperity have meant that the public's concerns are only partially reflected in the indicators that comprise the measuring tool (see Mintchev et al., 2019: 112). In comparison, the IGP's prosperity index is citizen-led, but it also aims to lay down a groundwork for pathways to prosperity in three distinct ways. First, it brings the significance of quality of life into public conversation and debate, seeking definitions and understandings validated by data on what matters to people. It thereby challenges social and political narratives that focus on economic

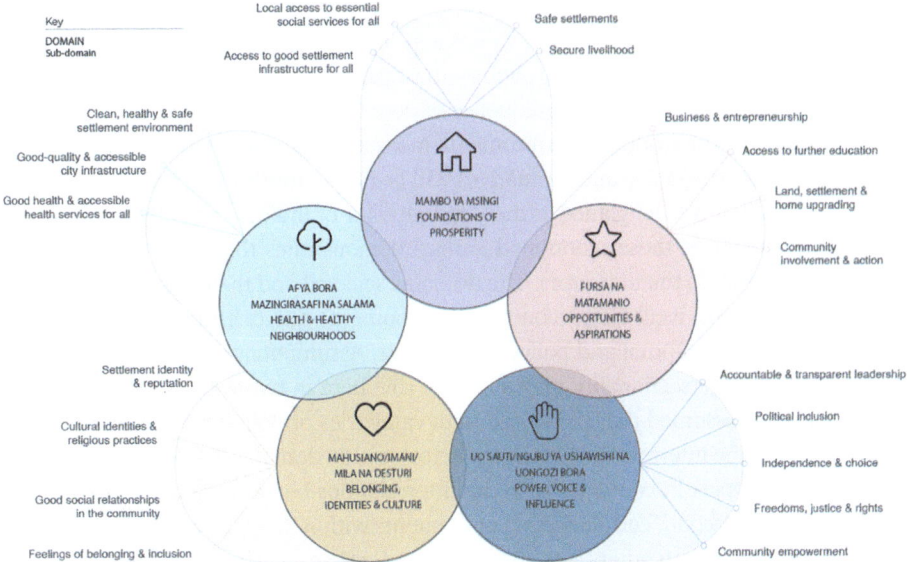

**Figure 1.3** Co-designed prosperity model for informal settlements in Dar es Salaam.

Source: IGP, 2022

initiatives that often fail to bring better opportunities and improved living conditions for the greater public. Second, it enables new forms of evidence-based governance. Measurement and governance are always closely linked, because the things that get measured define the problems that need to be addressed, and vice versa. Measuring prosperity via the mechanism of lived experience enables stakeholders such as NGOs and local governments to use their resources more effectively to respond to people's needs. Third, the prosperity index allows communities to monitor their progress towards better quality of life. Data on local prosperity indicators is an important tool that pinpoints the strengths and weaknesses in different domains of quality of life. This tool in turn enables people to hold governments to account and to make a stronger case for the change they want to see, and to work together to implement that change.

Issues of change and how change is envisaged are a critical feature both of the conceptual frameworks underlying policy initiatives and of the means through which evidence is gathered to support such frameworks. This connects to the earlier point about scope. All indices and forms of measurement are underpinned by categories; in our work they are termed domains, and in the Legatum Prosperity Index, for example, they are labelled pillars (Legatum Institute, 2019). The determination of the boundaries and content of these categories is a political decision, and, while informed by critical review of data, expert opinion and community co-design, it is always a matter of values and therefore politics (Scott, 2012), because categories/domains/pillars – the designated building blocks of the various indices – are the consequence of decisions about preferred ways of dividing up the world. When it comes to measurement, a series of indicators (objective, subjective and evaluative) will be nested inside these categories or domains. A brief glance at the large number of indices currently available, including those mentioned earlier, demonstrates that the domains vary and so do the indicators. The domains selected and their labels (such as health and wellbeing, economy, environment) reflect established and emerging conceptual and policy frameworks. Assumptions about relationality and intersectionality play a crucial role here in two ways. First, it is generally assumed that the selection of categories or domains reflects the fact that the interrelations between factors within domains are denser and more complex in comparison to the interrelations between factors across domains. Second, certain factors or elements within domains will be more determinant than others, possibly playing a larger role in how the intersections between other related elements will take shape, and, because not all factors or elements within domains are equal, indices frequently weight certain factors to give them more significance to reflect their determinant role (e.g. Legatum Institute, 2019). The consequence of this is that theories of change or directions of travel for policy priorities are already partly built into the scope of specific frameworks through the manner in which they give weight and priority to certain factors and elements.

Thus, questions of change, unsurprisingly, turn out to be a matter of relationality, of how relations are perceived. This is one of the strongest reasons for developing a prosperity framework that reflects the concerns and life experiences of residents and communities. Understandings and experiences of prosperity may vary, but they always matter for all, and the manner in which they have import matters also. The determination of domains within the IGP's prosperity framework allows for the possibilities that the content of domains will vary across space and time, and that the significance of the relations between factors and elements within and across the domains may vary too. However, the key purpose of the prosperity framework is to determine what is needed to bring about effective change and put communities on pathways to sustainable prosperity by improving the quality of people's lives. In order to foreground this policy focus and to develop a clearer analytical framework for identifying key areas where change is necessary, the IGP has developed a specific framework drawn from its comparative work between and within national and regional contexts. This framework starts from the premise of relationality and provides the means to explore and explain how change occurs.

From the work IGP has conducted in the UK, Kenya, Tanzania and Lebanon (see also Woodcraft & Anderson, 2019; Woodcraft et al., 2020; Sender et al., 2020), it is clear that relationalities between the key elements driving quality of life are unsurprisingly denser at what we might term the meso level, the level at which people live their lives, interact, communicate and become interdependent, and experience dislocation, constraint and immiseration. The question of what exactly constitutes the meso level is a matter of investigation and specification. The boundaries of human social, economic and political systems are at once porous and sharply defined. At times the meso level will be a small town, and at others a specific area within a city; it might be a series of villages or a specific region bounded by natural resources or other factors; it is rarely congruent with named social, class, ethnic or religious groupings. The meso should not be collapsed into identitarian social groupings, because, while religious, ethnic, class and other important social distinctions will always be present and consequential within the meso level, they do not define its boundaries. The meso is perhaps best understood as the manifestation of the significance of place and location in human life, and it varies depending on context. One noteworthy feature is that structures of governance very often provide important contours for the meso level because of the way in which they inevitably influence financial flows and investments, schooling and health provision, infrastructural decisions and policy responsibilities; places are often held together by a shared history of development and underdevelopment.

When we examine what drives changes in quality of life, or prosperity more broadly, at the meso level, it is apparent that a constellation of factors have to be taken into account, and that the internal dynamics of this constellation cannot be unravelled simply by looking at the influence of one domain or set of indicators on another: how health influences productivity, for example. This does not mean that broad trends and co-variance cannot be observed – they very often are – but the issue is how we might better provide insight into how the various domains interrelate in specific contexts, and how their constituent elements may or may not have import, and co-vary with others, in those particular locales. This is key to any well-targeted policy initiative designed to provide sustainable pathways to prosperity, because, as is evidenced from such initiatives around the world, we have much more success in providing evidence for what does not work than in explaining what brings about success. In exploring the configurations of intersections between and across domains, it is essential to retain the significance of what matters for individuals and communities as they seek to manage the constraints and challenges they face and to bring about change. The IGP's LOOT framework examines the key drivers of change by interrogating the data according to three main contributory constellations to prosperity as it is experienced by individuals and communities: life outcomes, life opportunities and life together (Moore et al., 2020). It uses the data across domains in each context and their constituent indicators (subjective, objective and evaluative) to explore the intersections between these three elements of prosperity, and to connect them to larger social, economic and political structures and constraints.

*Life outcomes* are the assets and capacities individuals and communities have in context: levels of education, employment, mental health, environmental quality and so on. *Life opportunities* are the capabilities and resources, including aspects of agency, effectiveness and local resources, that can be deployed to manage change and transformation now and in the future. *Life together* comprises the networks, social institutions, and forms of solidarity and connection that allow the management of co-operation and conflict, as well as knowledge sharing and innovation (Moore et al., 2020). What the LOOT framework does is provide the means to explore systematically the intersections between domains from the point of view of how the density and complexity of interrelations across and between domains connects to the mechanisms and means for driving change. This is a profoundly innovative step, because most indices of wellbeing, happiness and human development assume a theory of change – such as that GDP drives quality of life – and have no mechanisms for interrogating the best course of action when it does not. The LOOT framework is experimental and is currently being rolled out for further testing and refinement in the UK, Lebanon and Tanzania; for the theory behind it see Chapter 2.

## 1.5 Complex systems and assemblages

The value of the LOOT framework follows from the observation that prosperity is an emergent feature of a complex set of embedded interactions over time. Approaching the definition of prosperity from this perspective requires a different form of theorising from that current in economic policy formulations, in which considerable emphasis is placed on a small number of unidimensional levers which are thought, when activated, to result in improvements in quality of life, for example increases in GDP or productivity. The failure of such policy frameworks is evidenced by the long-running structural and systemic disadvantage experienced by regions, sectors and communities through time as others have benefited from globalisation, automation, investment and human capital accumulation. Rising tides do not raise all boats. So the question is: where do we turn for a suggestion of how complex systems might be better organised for innovation? what do we need to do to understand change better and make things happen?

As things stand at the moment, there are no good economic models for understanding pathways to prosperity as it has been redefined in this chapter. This is partly because economic models assume that community- or place-based prosperity is an aggregate of individual prosperity, as opposed to an outcome of complex and embedded interactions across multiple systems and actors, including local government, business, education systems, health services, social capital and trust, inward investment, ecological and natural capital services, individuals, civil society and community engagements. This statement hardly seems controversial, but when pursued more rigorously it has some surprising consequences. If prosperity is the outcome of the intersection of multiple systems with a large number of moving parts, it is best conceived of as an assemblage, a particular configuration that emerges in time through unpredictable interactions (Barry, 2013; Collier & Ong, 2007; DeLanda, 2006; Li, 2007; Marcus & Saka, 2006; Müller, 2015). These interactions are subject to the workings of power, and to various other forms of mobilisation through time, including pressures that can be brought to bear on the specific relational configurations between elements in context. In other words, the history of each place matters. However, the assemblages that make up prosperity are part of, and embedded in, wider human and natural systems which are themselves characterised by non-linear dynamics and sets of open-ended capacities that exceed the properties of their component parts (Goldstein, 2018; Dougherty & Dunne, 2011).

Understanding how collective prosperous lives and livelihoods might emerge within these complex ecologies of systems is crucial, but the first insight is to recognise that prosperity is not an entity in itself or something that simply describes the state of individuals or firms or regions, but an effect of the whole ecology, of the specific assemblage constituted by the specifics of time and place. This raises the question of if and how the emergent properties of assemblages can be shaped, and if so by whom and through what means. Imagine, if you will, interventions designed to reduce flooding and manage water pollution; these include and involve water and climate systems, regulations, markets, consumer organisations, farmer livelihoods, public health and infrastructure provision, and a wide variety of other actors and assets from engineers to plastic pipes, to mention only the most obvious. Different groups or stakeholders have diverse and divergent interests; goals and values compete and coalesce; power relations and new forms of knowledge intersect to provide practical and contingent solutions. The complexity of envisaging and managing complex systems to drive innovation for change requires a completely different theory of change from those we recognise from most macroeconomic policy initiatives, such as high-end technological innovation or infrastructural investment or co-ordinated regional financing through public–private partnerships. Here we are dealing with multiple forms of agency, materiality, organisational forms and knowledges with dynamic and uncertain outcomes. The emphasis has to be on visualising and testing how these heterogeneous elements can be brought together to create new relationships, new knowledges and new forms of value. This will require considerable realignment of actors, technologies, practices, organisations and knowledge, drawing on assets and resources that are distributed across many different spaces, places, actors, networks, practices and institutions. Understanding that change is a matter of bringing these disparate elements together requires the acceptance that it is not something that can be generated by single actors or entities alone, because it has to be an emergent feature of the entire ecology (Dougherty & Dunne, 2011; Dougherty, 2017a, 2017b).

So how can we shape innovation and change under conditions of such complexity? The first step is to recall that prosperity is about solving actual problems and improving people's quality of life where they are situated. Complex systems are characterised by extensive distributions of agency and purpose, and bringing knowledge and assets together in new ways to provide solutions to concrete problems creates new forms of value. The innovation that results is a consequence of new sets of actors coming together to bring diverse perspectives and skills to bear on known problems. In terms of improvements in prosperity, this has two consequences. The first is that change cannot be achieved through the imposition of top-down solutions or through unidirectional mechanistic levers, as already discussed. Change in complex systems has to be shaped through connecting knowledges, livelihoods, assets, identities, regulation and institutions, first into purposeful problem definition – what needs to be done here and now (Ansell, 2011) – and then into a set of potential solutions (Dougherty, 2017a). In such systems change cannot be driven by agents or firms or local governments or institutions working alone, or through established mechanisms that are not focused on improving the capabilities and capacities of communities to deliver improvements in quality of life. Working with communities to understand the problems and then envisage solutions is the starting point, but in making this claim there is more to be understood.

Once again, we need to begin by acknowledging that the individualising assumptions of macroeconomics take us off in the wrong direction, imagining that the capacities and capabilities of communities are simply the aggregate of the capacities and capabilities of individual agents. This underlying premise guides a conventional approach to the labour market through deep-seated ideas about education and skill acquisition. Economics – and thus most policy frameworks – expect individual capacities to vary and potentially to change over time differentially through education, skills acquisition and environmental interaction. As in Sen's theorisation of capabilities, differential freedoms or structural conditions determine how individuals are able to develop their capabilities and turn their capacities into functionings within social and economic systems (Sen, 1999). These ideas are persuasive and powerful, but they are of limited value for explaining how social systems embedded in complex ecologies develop over time.

Here we have to have more regard for the fact that social systems develop their complexity through the co-ordination of individuals' capacities and capabilities in a wide variety of action spaces (Reyes, 2018). Two points are of relevance: the first is that complexity builds through co-ordination and this is a process that can be shaped, the second that individuals have to be considered not as single entities with fixed educational and skill assets, but as a bundle of assets that can be differentially deployed in different domains of action. It is perhaps helpful to pause, and reflect on the point that human co-ordination requires many skills, including motivation, judgement and empathy. The water engineer we would have had need of in the example given above might equally be an imam whose pertinent skill sets for initiating change in their home town through motivation, empathy and discernment might not be well captured across all relevant action domains by an assessment of their labour market skills. This is of no surprise to anyone who has been involved in supporting change in their local community, where it is common to find individuals pooling and sharing skills, and redeploying the composite result in innovative contexts. But there is a wider point beyond the simple recognition that the capacities and capabilities of communities are more than just the sum of the education and skill sets of their individual members.

While social systems are self-organising and subject to self-regulation, they also respond to organisational learning which proceeds through various mechanisms that amplify system learning. But these organisational forms cannot be reduced to the aggregate outcome of individual learning processes or mechanisms. Most of the major challenges we face in the world today are whole-system problems with significant uncertainties as to how system processes will evolve and unfold. The co-ordination and development of social capacities and capabilities comprise one of these uncertainties, but new forms of value can only happen if there are enough connections between agents, organisations, resources and knowledges for new ideas, patterns of interaction and diversity of solutions to emerge. This means that the widest array of community institutions and actors across the whole ecology have to be brought to bear on the question of what prosperity is in this time and place, and how it might be achieved. The challenge is to create new forms of collaboration, and organisational forms and social institutions, that do not currently exist in most communities. Enhancing ideas, interactions and solutions drives system learning and increases system complexity through community capacities and capabilities which draw on the deep structures of cultures, values, regulation and frameworks for action that exist in specific places. Putting co-design with local communities at the core of prosperity builds new forms of collaboration and expands ideas, goals and outputs. Community and place-based capacities and capabilities can then be used to direct and focus local assets and resources towards shared purposes over time, adapting as those purposes shift and develop. Prosperity requires innovation through new forms of collaboration, and this is why redefining prosperity requires not only new theories of change, but a reorientation of policy goals and outcomes towards quality of life and reform of economic value. Place-based capacities and capabilities need to be developed to support a variety of innovations reoriented towards quality-of-life goals over time, and these will need to be based on new forms of collaboration and interaction that draw on the widest range of citizen and other expertise, including local government, business, universities, civil society organisations, finance institutions and many others (Moore et al., 2020).

Knowledge innovations that can build capacities and capabilities have to be about solving actual problems and realising that prosperity can only be achieved through concrete steps to intervene in existing systems and build new social institutions to deliver innovative solutions and experimental propositions. Designing new forms of governance, that is, social institutions that bring all interested parties together in new configurations, is essential for long-term change towards quality of life. For example, in the UK households account for around 40 per cent of all carbon emissions (Committee on Climate Change, n.d.), 8,500 people die each year because they are living in homes that are too cold (National Energy Action, 2020), and in England approximately 8.4 million people live in unaffordable, insecure and unsuitable housing (National Housing Federation, 2019). The ongoing housing crisis in the UK means that currently around 1.3 million new homes are required just to house those in greatest need (Shelter, 2019). The combination of these factors explains why tackling housing is high on local community lists for prosperity. Yet we have the solutions to integrate into working systems at the local level if we could hammer out how to bring engineers, architects, planners, suppliers, communities and businesses together to recycle building materials, use passive ventilation and heating, optimise windows, install heat pumps and solar systems, and deploy digital distribution systems and new technologies and regulations to collaboratively integrate alternative ideas into existing systems (Dougherty & Dunne, 2011). Co-ordinating, collaborating and sharing in this way would mean that most buildings could become net-positive over their lifetimes, producing more energy than they consume (Cheshire, 2016). If they did, this would cut heating and healthcare costs, improve quality of life, reduce carbon emissions and create local employment. Collaboratively solving such problems within communities derives from shared purpose, problem definition, defined strategies, clear pathways to deliver and social solidarity, all the while building the capacities and capabilities to meet the next challenge. When tackling prosperity, it is not just the what, it is also the how.

## 1.6 Conclusion

In this chapter, we have argued that redefining prosperity entails rethinking our approach to economic value and system change. It means moving away from mechanistic levers for change that are based on assuming that economic growth will necessarily benefit all, to explore innovative ways of tackling social inequality and improving quality of life. Prosperity as we redefine it here is more than income or wealth; it is, in essence, the value created with the wealth we have; much of that value resides in communities and places, but it needs to be repurposed to meet new challenges and to create new opportunities for those places. Driving a concerted set of place-based efforts to tackle problems in context – carbon net-zero, improved water quality, affordable and green housing – has the potential to create local employment and to provide local institutions with incentives to support the development of community capacities and capabilities.

Here we see the value of the prosperity index not just as a new measuring tool for evaluating and shaping the new configurations and collaborations that can bring about prosperity, but as a mechanism for defining purpose, strategy and outcome within overall processes of system change towards prosperity. Definitions of prosperity and pathways towards prosperity have to be citizen-led and deeply embedded in place, culture and context, but, definitional challenges aside, the approach to prosperity has to be a pragmatic, operational and embedded one that brings about improvements in people's quality of life wherever they are situated. The IGP's LOOT framework provides an innovative approach which, rather than dividing aspects of lives lived into familiar categories like economics, health, social capital and so on, provides a mechanism for exploring how all these areas intersect across the three main dimensions of prosperity as it is experienced in place: life outcomes, life opportunities and life together.

We conclude by suggesting that prosperity is an emergent feature of a whole ecology, and that recognising this has consequences for theories of change, for operationalising prosperity and for policy formation. The most immediate deficit lies in forms of knowledge sharing and collaboration that can build system complexity, and in community capacities and capabilities to deliver problem solving, shared strategies and solutions, and pathways for implementation. The new social institutions and organisational forms required will need to build community capacities and capabilities, not only for addressing the challenges of the day, but for addressing, too, those that will emerge. Prosperity is a grand challenge and, as such, is not a problem that can be solved, but a process of innovation that will always require adaptation.

## Bibliography

Ansell, C. K. (2011). *Pragmatist Democracy: Evolutionary learning as public philosophy*. New York: Oxford University Press.

Atkinson, S. (2013). Beyond components of wellbeing: The effects of relational and situated assemblage. *Topoi*, 32, 137–44. https://doi.org/10.1007/s11245-013-9164-0.

Atkinson, S., Bagnall, A.-M., Corcoran, R. & South, J. (2017). What is community wellbeing? Conceptual review. What Works Centre for Wellbeing, September. Available at: https://whatworkswellbeing.org/resources/what-is-community-wellbeing-conceptual-review/ (accessed 14 December 2022).

Atkinson, S., Bagnall, A.-M., Corcoran, R., South, J. & Curtis, S. (2020). Being well together: Individual subjective and community wellbeing. *Journal of Happiness Studies*, 21, 1903–21. Available at: https://link.springer.com/article/10.1007/s10902-019-00146-2 (accessed 14 December 2022).

Barry, A. (2013). *Material Politics: Disputes along the pipeline*. Chichester: Wiley Blackwell.

Calafati, L., Ebrey, J., Froud, J., Haslam, C., Johal, S. & Williams, K. (2019). How an ordinary place works: Understanding Morriston. Research report. Available at: https://foundational economycom.files.wordpress.com/2019/05/morriston-report-v6-13-may-2019.pdf (accessed 14 December 2022).

Cassiers, I. (2015). Introduction. In I. Cassiers (ed.), *Redefining Prosperity*, pp. 1–5. Abingdon: Routledge.

Cheshire, D. (2016). *Building Revolutions: Applying the circular economy to the built environment.* Newcastle upon Tyne: RIBA Publishing.

Collier, S. J. & Ong, A. (2007). Global assemblages, anthropological problems. In S. J. Collier & A. Ong (eds), pp. 3–21. *Global Assemblages: Technology, politics, and ethics as anthropological problems.* Malden, MA: Blackwell Publishing.

Commission on Growth and Development (2008). *The Growth Report: Strategies for sustained growth and inclusive development.* Washington, DC: World Bank. Available at: https://open knowledge.worldbank.org/handle/10986/6507 (accessed 23 February 2023).

Commission on Growth and Development (2010). *Globalization and Growth: Implications for a post-crisis world*, ed. M. Spence and D. Leipziger. Washington, DC: World Bank. Available at: https://openknowledge.worldbank.org/bitstream/handle/10986/ 2440/542530PUB0glob101Official0Use0Only1.pdf?sequence=1&isAllowed=y (accessed 15 December 2022).

Committee on Climate Change (n.d.). The fifth carbon budget. https://www.theccc.org.uk/ wp-content/uploads/2016/07/5CB-Infographic-FINAL-.pdf (accessed 15 December 2022).

Dalziel, P., Saunders, C. & Saunders, J. (2018). *Wellbeing Economics: The capabilities approach to prosperity.* Basingstoke: Palgrave Macmillan.

DeLanda, M. (2006). *A New Philosophy of Society: Assemblage theory and social complexity.* London: Continuum.

Diener, E. & Seligman, M. E. P. (2004). Beyond money: Toward an economy of wellbeing. *Psychological Science in the Public Interest*, 5(1), 1–31. https://doi.org/10.1111/j.0963-7214.2004. 00501001.x.

Dolan, P. (2014). *Happiness by Design: Finding pleasure and purpose in everyday life.* London: Penguin Books.

Dougherty, D. (2017a). Taking advantage of emergence for complex innovation systems. *Journal of Open Innovation: Technology, Market and Complexity*, 3, 14. https://doi.org/10.1186/ s40852-017-0067-y.

Dougherty, D. (2017b). Organizing for innovation in complex innovation systems. *Innovation: Organization and Management*, 19(1), 11–15. https://doi.org/10.1080/14479338.2016. 1245109.

Dougherty, D. & Dunne, D. D. (2011). Organizing ecologies of complex innovation. *Organization Science*, 22(5), 1214–23. https://doi.org/10.1287/orsc.1100.0605.

Doyal, L. & Gough, I. (1991). *A Theory of Human Need.* New York: Guilford.

Fioramonti, L. (2017). *Wellbeing Economy: Success in a world without growth.* Johannesburg: Pan Macmillan.

Foundational Economy Collective (2018). *Foundational Economy.* Manchester: Manchester University Press.

Froud, J., Haslam, C., Johal, S., Tsitsianis, N. & Williams, K. (2018). Foundational liveability: Rethinking territorial inequalities. Foundational Economy Collective Working Paper no. 5. Available at: https://foundationaleconomycom.files.wordpress.com/2018/12/ foundational-livability-wp-no-5-fe-collective.pdf (accessed 15 December 2022).

Goldstein, J. A. (2018). Emergence and radical novelty: From theory to methods. In E. Mitleton-Kelly, A. Paraskevas & C. Day (eds), *Handbook of Research Methods in Complexity Science: Theory and applications*, 507–24. Cheltenham: Edward Elgar Publishing.

Helliwell, J., Layard, R., Sachs, J. D. & De Neve, J.-E. (2020). *World Happiness Report 2020.* New York: Sustainable Development Solutions Network.

Hickel, J. (2020a). *Less is More: How degrowth will save the world.* London: William Heinemann.

Hickel, J. (2020b). The sustainable development index: Measuring the ecological efficiency of human development in the anthropocene. *Ecological Economics*, 167, 106331. https://doi. org/10.1016/j.ecolecon.2019.05.011.

Huppert, F. A., Marks, N., Clark, A., Siegrist, J., Stutzer, Alois, Vitterso, J. & Warhendorf, M. (2009) Measuring wellbeing across Europe: Description of the ESS Well-being Module and preliminary findings. *Social Indicators Research*, 91, 301–15. https://doi.org/10.1007/s11205-008-9346-0.

IGP (2017). Prosperity Index pilot wave 2017: Summary of methodology and description of indicators. https://doi.org/10.14324/000.wp.10080171.

Institute for Public Policy Research (2018). *Prosperity and Justice: A plan for the new economy*. Cambridge: Polity.

Jackson, T. (2017). *Prosperity without Growth: Foundations for the economy of tomorrow*. 2nd edn. Abingdon: Routledge.

Layard, R. (2011). *Happiness: Lessons from a new science*. Rev. edn. London: Penguin Books.

Legatum Institute (2019). The Legatum Prosperity Index™ 2019 methodology report. London: Legatum Institute. Available at: https://docs.prosperity.com/7515/8634/9002/Methodology_for_Legatum_Prosperity_Index_2019.pdf (accessed 15 December 2022).

Legatum Institute (2020). *The Legatum Prosperity Index 2020*. London: Legatum Institute. https://docs.prosperity.com/2916/0568/0539/The_Legatum_Prosperity_Index_2020.pdf (accessed 15 December 2022).

Li, T. M. (2007). *The Will to Improve: Governmentality, development, and the practice of politics*. Durham, NC: Duke University Press.

Marcus, G. E. & Saka, E. (2006). Assemblage. *Theory, Culture & Society*, 23(2–3), 101–6. https://doi.org/10.1177/0263276406062573.

Maxton, G. & Randers, J. (2016). *Reinventing Prosperity: Managing economic growth to reduce unemployment, inequality and climate change*. Vancouver: Greystone Books.

Mintchev, N., Baumann, H., Moore, H. L., Rigon, A. & Dabaj, J. (2019). Towards a shared prosperity: Co-designing solutions in Lebanon's spaces of displacement. *Journal of the British Academy*, 7(S2), 109–35. https://doi.org/10.5871/jba/007s2.109.

Moore, H. L. (2015). Global prosperity and sustainable development goals. *Journal of International Development*, 27(6), 801–15.

Moore, H. L. & Collins, H. (2020). Towards prosperity: Reinvigorating local economies through Universal Basic Services. IGP Working Paper 01-2020/04. London: Institute for Global Prosperity. Available at: https://discovery.ucl.ac.uk/id/eprint/10096789/ (accessed 15 December 2022). https://doi.org/10.14324/000.wp.10096789.

Moore, H. L., Moreno, J. M. & Melios, G. (2020). Identifying and understanding local priorities for developing an 'economy of belonging': A case study of eight areas in the UK. Working/discussion paper. London: Institute for Global Prosperity. Available at: https://discovery.ucl.ac.uk/id/eprint/10120021/ (accessed 15 December 2022).

Moore, H. L. & Woodcraft, S. (2019). Understanding prosperity in East London: Local meanings and 'sticky' measures of the good life. *City & Society*, 31(2), 275–98. https://doi.org/10.1111/ciso.12208.

Müller, M. (2015). Assemblages and actor-networks: Rethinking socio-material power, politics and space. *Geography Compass*, 9(1), 27–41. https://doi.org/10.1111/gec3.12192.

National Energy Action (NEA) (2020). New ONS figures reveal cold homes death toll. Available at: https://www.nea.org.uk/news/271120-01/ (accessed 23 February 2023).

National Housing Federation (NHF) (2019). 1 in 7 people in England directly hit by the housing crisis. Available at: https://www.housing.org.uk/news-and-blogs/news/1-in-7-people-in-england-directly-hit-by-the-housing-crisis/ (accessed 23 February 2023).

Ngamaba, K. H. (2017). Determinants of subjective well-being in representative samples of nations. *European Journal of Public Health*, 27(2), 377–82. https://doi.org/10.1093/eurpub/ckw103.

Nussbaum, M. C. (2000). *Women and Human Development: The capabilities approach*. Cambridge: Cambridge University Press.

OECD (2020). *How's Life? 2020: Measuring well-being*. Paris: OECD Publishing. Available at: https://read.oecd-ilibrary.org/economics/how-s-life/volume-/issue-/_9870c393-en#page1 (accessed 15 December 2022).

Reyes, A. (2018). Connecting higher education and innovation to local development. *Futures*, 103, 73–83. https://doi.org/10.1016/j.futures.2018.04.004.

Scott, K. (2012) *Measuring Wellbeing: Towards sustainability*? Abingdon and New York: Routledge.

Sen, A. (1999). *Development as Freedom*. Oxford: Oxford University Press.

Sender, H., Hannan, M. A., Billingham, L., Isaacs, J. & Ocitti, D. (2020). Rethinking prosperity: Perspectives of young people living in East London. IGP Working Paper 02-2020/05. London: Institute for Global Prosperity.

Shelter (2019). Three million new social homes key to solving housing crisis. Press release, 14 January. Available at: https://england.shelter.org.uk/media/press_release/three_million_new_social_homes_key_to_solving_housing_crisis2 (accessed 15 December 2022).

Social Progress Imperative. (2022). *2022 Social Progress Index*. Available at: https://www.socialprogress.org/global-index-2022overview (accessed 23 February 2023).

Stiglitz, J. E. (2011). Rethinking macroeconomics: What failed, and how to repair it. *Journal of the European Economic Association*, 9(4), 591–645. https://doi.org/10.1111/j.1542-4774.2011.01030.x.

Stiglitz, J. E. (2019). *People, Power, and Profits: Progressive capitalism for an age of discontent*. London: Allen Lane.

Stiglitz, J., Sen, A. & Fitoussi, J.-P. (2010). *Mismeasuring Our Lives: Why GDP doesn't add up*. New York: New Press.

United Nations Development Programme (2016). Sustainable Development Goals are a 'roadmap for peace, dignity and prosperity'. Available at: https://www.undp.org/content/undp/en/home/presscenter/pressreleases/2016/09/23/sustainable-development-goals-are-a-roadmap-for-peace-dignity-and-prosperity-.html (accessed 31 July 2019).

United Nations Habitat City Prosperity Initiative (2019). *City Prosperity Initiative*. Available at: https://unhabitat.org/knowledge/city-prosperity-initiative (accessed 15 September 2022).

White, S. C. (2015). Relational wellbeing: A theoretical and operational approach. Bath Papers in International Development and Wellbeing, Working Paper no. 43. Centre for Development Studies, University of Bath. Available at: https://www.econstor.eu/bitstream/10419/128138/1/bpd43.pdf (accessed 15 December 2022).

Woodcraft, S. & Anderson, B. (2019). *Rethinking Prosperity for London: When citizens lead transformation*. London: Institute for Global Prosperity. Available at: https://static1.squarespace.com/static/5a0c05169f07f51c64a336a2/t/5d03c62b56b1ce0001bf6266/1560528440423/LPI_Report_single_140619_update.pdf (accessed 23 February 2023).

Woodcraft, S. Osuteye, E., Ndezi, T. & Makoba, F. (2020). Pathways to the 'good life': Co-producing prosperity research in informal settlements in Tanzania. *Urban Planning*, 5(3), 288–302. https://doi.org/10.17645/up.v5i3.3177.

World Bank (2010). *Post-Crisis Growth in Developing Countries: A special report of the commission on growth and development on the implications of the 2008 financial crisis*. Washington, DC: World Bank. Available at: http://documents.worldbank.org/en/publication/documents-reports/documentdetail/658041468151762824/Post-crisis-growth-in-developing-countries-a-special-report-of-the-commission-on-growth-and-development-on-the-implications-of-the-2008-financial-crisis (accessed 23 February 2023).

# 2
# The discourses of prosperity: metaphors, transformations and pathways

Nikolay Mintchev and Henrietta L. Moore

## 2.1 Introduction

The present chapter addresses the same headline question as Chapter 1: 'What is prosperity?' But it does so from the intellectual perspective of discourse analysis, semiotics and the philosophy of language. It proposes an understanding of prosperity as a discursive concept that can be effectively used as an organising principle for research, policy change and interventions for improved quality of life for people and planet. It addresses the question of what a discourse on prosperity does, and what role it plays in creating pathways to social transformation.

Any attempt to redefine prosperity has to begin with a reflection on the relationship between language and the world, a consideration of how change comes about in that relation, and how the consequences of any changes may be realised. Metaphor was once the domain of literary critics, philosophers and linguists, but in recent years a substantial literature has emerged on metaphor as a driver of policy formation and change, as a factor in organisational change and leadership, and as a key element in responses to climate change and environmental degradation. What ties these diverse fields together is a concern about how changes come about, and how framing devices might be used to persuade people to see the world anew and respond differently.

As Ricoeur argues, metaphor has the power to redescribe reality and is set in motion by a tension between identity and difference, through the perception or the assertion of a similarity in things that are otherwise dissimilar, allowing us to grasp unknown relations between things (Ricoeur, 1977: 4, 92). For example, the attorney general is a jellyfish. However, here, we need to pay attention to how semantic innovation works. While the word remains the carrier of the effects of metaphorical meaning, it is the statement or the sentence that carries intention, that attaches metaphorical meaning to the world. This point is an important one, because it distinguishes the character of metaphor from what we might broadly call the history of word usage, the way the meaning of a particular word changes over time. These two processes are connected, evidently, but they should not be conflated. One way to characterise the connection, as Ricoeur suggests, is to see the word as the focus of meaning, but to recognise that it requires a frame, a discursive space in which its relevance to the world finds purchase. 'Words draw delegated efficacy from contexts' (Ricoeur, 1977: 89). Consequently, when we speak of redefining prosperity, it is not just a matter of naming prosperity differently, assigning new signifieds or meanings, or providing a typology of all possible meanings of prosperity. It is a matter of creating new discursive spaces or frames within which a redefined prosperity actively redescribes the world, bringing different affordances, visualising connections and processes anew, driving the delineation of possible pathways towards a redefined prosperity. It is language as used in action, 'which can take circumstances into account and have particular applications' (Ricoeur, 1977: 82).

## 2.2 Setting the frame

In the current moment, there are a series of new discourses emerging around prosperity, critiquing its narrow association with wealth and income (see Chapter 1), but despite these new developments the predominant frame for public policy and debate remains that of economic wealth shaped by, and firmly set within, a series of notions such as GDP, productivity, efficiency, progress and markets. These latter ideas are so well established that they do not need to be fully understood to serve as framing devices and levers in public and policy debates. New metaphors have entered the broad discursive space of the economy in the last 30 to 40 years. For example, discourses and policies relating to climate change draw on 'greenhouse', 'footprint', 'race', 'war' and 'emergency' (Nerlich & Hellsten, 2014; Flusberg et al., 2017), while continuing to inhabit a discursive space dominated by the 'market' metaphor (Cojanu, 2008). This applies also to recent economic metaphors that have emerged in response to growing scientific and policy engagement with, as well as public disquiet about, environmental degradation, biodiversity loss and climate risk (Coffey, 2016). The use of such metaphors, and how they are inserted into broader discursive frames, are not politically neutral, and it is a feature of their deployment that they can often serve divergent ideological positions simultaneously: capitalists and environmentalists can both espouse notions of green growth. This provides a picture of complexity, contestation and change.

Set around individual metaphors and framing devices are a series of conceptual metaphors that underpin broader theoretical frameworks. These conceptual devices are more abstract, less experientially near, for policy makers, citizens and analysts alike, and include such notions as control, sustainability, complexity, non-linearity, uncertainty and whole-systems change (Hughes et al., 2021). Broadly speaking, discursive parameters related to policy and innovation have shifted in the last 30 years, away from control towards uncertainty and whole-systems change and related concepts, combined with a new focus on the role of social actors, particularly citizens, in shaping policy direction and future envisioning (Dobuzinskis, 1992; Thibodeau et al., 2017). However, what has remained a constant in policy terms within these broader theoretical frameworks is the metaphor of growth. Despite criticism of growth models (for example, Raworth, 2017; Jackson, 2017; Moore, 2015; Moore & Woodcraft, 2019; Stiglitz et al., 2010), governments worldwide continue to see economic growth as a synonym for prosperity.

The result is that while elements of economic discourse are shifting and new models – including critiques of growth – are emerging, the overall framing devices underpinning economic models and policy making are relatively intact. A measure of how resistant this conceptualisation of the economy remains is evident in the ongoing debate as to whether economic productivity can be decoupled absolutely from resource use and environmental impact (Hubacek et al., 2021; Parrique et al., 2019; Ward et al., 2016), through what has been termed green growth, the green economy, sustainable capitalism for example. As these terms imply, the operating assumption is that technological changes and substitutions will enable economic expansion and continuing GDP growth alongside the protection of natural resources and ecosystems (Hickel & Kallis, 2020; Jackson & Victor, 2019; Söderholm, 2020). A substantial part of what makes green growth and other notions so appealing is that the existing model can be repurposed, and consequently business as usual will continue to offer the optimal solution.

This picture of continuity and change is further complicated by the fact that traffic in metaphors, concepts and framing devices can move in both directions. A consequence of economics being embedded in society is the provision of a rich stream of metaphors that connect the economy to social relations and institutions, as well as to the bodies of individuals. Common examples draw parallels between the economy and a healthy body, referring to a functioning economy as a 'healthy economy', in which key elements act as 'the life blood' of the economy; when things go wrong, the economy may suffer from market ills, paralysis and even depression. Features of the economy often reflect aspects of everyday life: the economy is envisaged as a pie or a garden. Such metaphors are subject to change, and while some are long-running, others gain purchase in particular historical moments, such as the notion of 'being as poor as a church mouse'. It is often argued that such metaphors are illustrative or explanatory, and not consequential in terms of our understandings of how an economy functions. However, a distinction needs to be drawn here between pedagogic/explanatory/interior metaphors and constitutive/framing/modelling metaphors inherent in scientific theorising and public discourse (Musacchio, 2011; Klamer & Leonard, 1994). This distinction is important, but by no means absolute, as the following discussion illustrates.

The relation between metaphors and models can be complex and deeply imbricated. As commentators have emphasised, metaphor is not just a piece of language, but 'a process of thought' (Schön, 1967: 37), and cognition itself 'is fundamentally metaphorical in nature" (Lakoff & Johnson, 1980: 2). Metaphor is a perspective or frame, a way of looking at things, but it is also the 'process by which new perspectives on the world come into existence' (Schön, 1979: 254), the mechanism through which we come to know the external world. Metaphors and discursive frames shape our views of the world in particular ways and allow us to act on it through specific practices, influencing thoughts and feelings, and creating expectations and desires. As Ernesto Laclau put it, 'Discourse is the primary terrain of the constitution of objectivity as such' (2005: 68). In other words, discourse is not something that reflects a pre-existing reality, but something that shapes and organises this reality and the relations between its different elements. Discourses form the identities of subjects and objects (Howarth & Stavrakakis, 2000: 3), the relations between them, and thus how we experience and organise our reality. All attempts to capture the world through language, to bridge the divide between subject and object, are irreducibly metaphorical. Knowing the world turns out to be very troublesome: 'The question of referring, in all its ramifications, is one that would put the fear of God into even the strongest among us' (Eco, 2000: 280).

Economics as a science is about making truth claims vis-à-vis the world, and Deirdre McCloskey pointed out four decades ago that metaphor is fundamental to economic thinking: 'to say that markets can be represented by supply and demand "curves" is no less a metaphor than to say that the west wind is the "breath of autumn's being"' (McCloskey, 1985: 74). Markets do not have supply and demand curves. Economic modelling is metaphorical because the lines, curves and points on diagrams and graphs are used metaphorically to represent the economy or economic variables. This is perhaps of minor significance if the modeller merely wishes to use metaphors as an aid to understanding, a means to grasp a complex and abstract domain in terms of a more concrete and familiar one, or provide a mechanism for representing complex relationships. But there are some further points of significance to be considered.

The first is the acknowledged challenge of literal or dead metaphors, that is, the point at which a metaphor as new meaning passes into ordinary usage so that its original innovation is lost and it becomes understood literally (lexicalised). For example, take the word 'skyscraper'. It has been argued that economics is full of dead metaphors, such as liquid money or liquid assets, which originally had a metaphorical meaning, but are now so moribund that they must not be taken literally. No economist thinks that money is literally a liquid, and the term 'liquid' has been given a new technical economic meaning which is unambiguously defined (Lagueux, 1999: 10–12). One interpretation of this position implies that metaphors are outside economic theory itself and suggests that the use of live metaphors by economists is just for the purpose of illustrative depictions and has no bearing on economic models or theories. But the situation is more complex than this, because metaphor affects the way we think about not only the two terms of the metaphor itself (the principal and the subsidiary), but the broader conceptual framework within which it sits and the world beyond it.

Science – including economics – proceeds through a process whereby metaphors evolve into concepts (Gibbs, 1996). While it is true that some metaphors decline into literalism, the more powerful of them tend to evolve into concepts that are powerful precisely because they move from predication to propagation (Graham, 2002); in other words, their ubiquity influences the discursive space within which models sit. This applies to such terms as growth and sustainability. Both are metaphors, and are important for comprehending abstract processes, but at the same time they are involved in creating material realities that provide further evidence of their importance and relevance. These kinds of constitutive metaphors are not disproved by scientific models, since they shape the discursive space within which models are applied and find purchase; they set the challenges and the questions. Such metaphors work through chains of metaphorical association, bringing certain issues to the foreground and displacing and masking others. Thus metaphor structures our understanding of concepts, and working together metaphorical chains create a coherent image of what we call the economy.

These kinds of metaphors play a major role in cognition and conceptualisation, structuring the character of scientific thought in profound ways, shaping scientific discourse and forms of knowledge (Lakoff & Johnson, 1980; Deignan, 2005). They also enter broader domains of social life, refiguring other relations and processes in economic terms via changes in associations and affordances, and we see the emergence of metaphors governed by economic theories. Take, for example, the phrase 'time is money'. The deployment of this phrase changes our views of time, but it also affects our notion of money. Human capital is another such example: education and skills are refigured as forms of investment that have productive outputs. Our social processes are understood as economic ones, and seamlessly apprehended as governed by the rules of the latter such as markets, outputs, efficiency, value added (Harvey, 2005; McKinnon, 2013). These processes of economisation change over time and are not the product of a single economic logic, but of several intersecting ones (Çalışkan & Callon, 2009; Griffen & Panofsky, 2021; Laruffa, 2022). As a process economisation is never complete, because alternative principles and norms for governing economic life survive alongside it. While capitalism may be dominant, many alternatives exist, even if they do not find general purchase (Balaguer Rasillo & Wirth, 2022; Taylor Aiken, 2019; Monticelli, 2018). Constitutive metaphors depict a terrain, and as such they contain many contradictions and antagonisms, which allows for different elements of emphasis in varying contexts. Paradoxically, it is the existence of such antagonisms and contradictions which means that constitutive metaphors can rarely be denied or disproved; most often they simply flex.

Natural language metaphors within such terrains covertly influence reasoning for citizens, scientists and policy makers alike. For example, the notions of jump-starting or levelling up the economy imply that the actions needed are both straightforward and technically feasible, as they would be in relation to cars or wall building. Analysis and policy making soon shift to what changes are needed in the dominant economic model to achieve these outcomes, without any prior questioning of the model itself or its grander animating metaphors such as growth and productivity, which structure wider values and support ideological positions. The result is that both the formation and the application of metaphors are influenced by economic ideologies in society; consequently the logic and character of the original source domains are often preserved and carried forward into the metaphorical understanding of the target. This has consequences not only for the development of economic models and how they relate to the world, but for the way in which metaphorical networks assemble constitutive metaphors (Holmgreen, 2003: 95; Resche, 2012). It is important here to remember that economic models are metaphors, in that they are representations of their objects of focus (Morgan, 2012).

Economics thinking has colonised thinking on the social, presenting itself as a series of self-evident propositions or truth claims for understanding how social life is and should be, and as such it shapes aspirations, desires and future trajectories of self and social realisation (Bourdieu, 1998; Foucault, 1982). Constitutive metaphors do not function in the same way as simple word or sentence metaphors. They proceed through chains of systematic associations, inflecting a series of intersecting discourses, producing and shaping values. The growth metaphor provides an excellent example. Growth is an ontological metaphor which draws on the experience of being human, as well as on bodily processes in other living things. It is conceptualised as natural and good, while the absence of growth is a lack or something bad, potentially life-threatening (Lakoff & Johnson, 1980: 14). As a metaphor it is pervasive, productive, and systematic, and in association with other associated metaphor chains it constitutes a rich and coherent lexical field (White, 2003: 148). Its very visibility in our language means that we can have difficulties envisaging a society not built on growth. Evidence for this comes from policy documents and decoupling debates, where concern about action on climate change is often expressed in terms of its effect on GDP growth, rather than the more pressing problem of the consequences for human lives and the planet of not taking action.

This is sometimes referred to as the economics-first approach, and is a feature of the current dominant economic model, as well as being a clear example of economisation. What is quite remarkable is that GDP growth is considered a measure of economic success across the world, and through the adherence to the underpinning dominant economic model by government treasuries, international institutions, professional economists and business, this model and the metaphors, values and policies that sustain it form a genuinely global model with widespread acceptance at all levels. This does not mean that criticisms and alternatives do not exist, but it does mean that the ideology of economic growth is pervasive and shapes possible futures and aspirations. However, the internal relations of this discourse are complex and allow for great flexibility, at national levels and also in different sectors and communities across the world and within individual countries (Schmidt, 2011). It is widely recognised that metaphors such as growth and sustainability can exhibit different metaphorical realisations, activating different idioms, associations and framing devices depending on specific cultural beliefs and values (White & Soler, 2007). Various social, historical, cultural and economic circumstances can cause modifications in economic metaphors, demonstrating the 'situatedness of metaphor usage' (Herrera-Soler & White, 2012: 5). Cultural specificity is one barometer of change, but it also emphasises the importance of contextual interpretation and localised narratives (Andryukhina 2021; Pamies & Ramos Ruiz, 2017). The pragmatics of metaphor usage and deployment determine its meaning as distinct from its syntax or intrinsic semantic sense (Klamer & Leonard, 1994: 30).

So within the broader framework of constitutive metaphors, interior or sub-metaphors evolve over time, and find specific purchase in particular contexts and circumstances, and, as noted earlier, this accounts in large part for the longevity of constitutive metaphors whose resilience arises from their capaciousness and the innovative potential of their constitutive metaphorical chains. However, where discourses with different world views and different definitions of central concepts collide, there is potential for contestation, even antagonism, as the meanings of concepts come under scrutiny. For example, what is sustainability or resilience or levelling up or inclusive growth? These debates do not unsettle constitutive metaphors, but they can be heated, and emphasise once again that there is no single economic logic or narrative that drives the dominant economic discourse, but rather a series of intersecting discourses that can compete, foregrounding certain elements and hiding others. This allows agents to pick and choose, to locate themselves in particular visions, aspirations and alternatives. However, the situation can shift when constitutive metaphors clash or are brought into a strongly contrastive relation; then the consequences can be not just disagreement, but schism (Klamer & Leonard, 1994: 43): communism versus socialism, degrowth versus growth. Here ideological assumptions and precedents come into play and what is at stake are world visions, value infrastructures and deeply held sentiments.

## 2.3 Prosperity: lexical fields and discourses

Let us turn now to the question of redefining prosperity, and to how a redefined prosperity might be characterised, actioned and implemented. The redefinition of prosperity within academic and policy discussions has led to a multiplication of the term's senses (see Chapter 1), but it has also led to a certain degree of paradigm crisis involving both contestation among the different groups, trends and agents involved in its redefinition, and ideological confrontation between the supporters of the dominant economic growth model and those who wish to critique it. Prosperity as a term designates a diverse field that defies a totalising logic, and several different discursive strands co-exist. The purpose in redefining prosperity for the twenty-first century is not to purify it, to stake a definitional claim. Language cannot be purged of ambiguity, because it always aims to refer to a reality outside itself. While a composite list of all the lexical meanings the term animates would be of interest, what is of more value is what the term does in the world and how that might change. The aim is not to definitively define a pre-existing entity, but to give an account of dynamic states of emergence, consolidation and transformation.

The first point to note here is that prosperity is not a new term; it is a term with a history, and the history of its metaphorical elaborations is one in which different elements have, at different times, and in different contexts, been foregrounded and occluded. While the narrow definition of prosperity as economic wealth has been accentuated in the last 100 years or so, and especially since the adoption of GDP as a measure of national accounts in 1953, the term still has a widely recognised connotation of hope and flourishing. As Isabelle Cassiers explains, the Latin *prosperus*, which forms the etymological root of 'prosperity', means 'to cause (a thing) to succeed, to render fortunate' (2015: 1). But, while older and newer meanings co-exist, it is evident that since the middle of the last century, ideas about prosperity and self-realisation have become increasingly associated with material consumption, as the goal of national prosperity has settled on continuous growth in GDP as its defining feature.

The emerging space of prosperity debates in the contemporary moment is one characterised by plurality, and part of that is the consequence of jostling between the various proponents of a redefined prosperity in universities, think tanks and policy contexts, as they seek to advance their particular understandings of the term, with their associated theories and metrics. But, as discussed in Chapter 1, many other narratives of prosperity exist and operate at different levels of experience and analysis, from the personal to the communal and the organisational, and all interact to shape the emerging discursive space. The consequence is that concepts, notions and narratives can circulate within different sectors, communities and action spaces and can be interpreted differently, in part because of the way they are linked to radically different phenomenological experiences (Taylor Aiken, 2019). For example, it is evident that what communities in Birmingham might associate with the term levelling up differs somewhat from what the UK government intends by the term, and the reasons for this link to their very different experiences of inequality. Concepts and narratives are always coloured by life as it is lived and experienced, and consequently a metaphor such as inclusive capitalism resonates somewhat differently in discussions in Davos as compared to those in the London Borough of Barking and Dagenham.

Given that this is the case, we might reasonably ask, 'What does the term prosperity mean?' The idea that words are arbitrary and conventional designations of things that exist in the world seems common sense. Linguistics makes a distinction between the sense of a word, its place within the internal system of language, and its reference, or ability to refer to a reality outside language. However, a word can never refer unambiguously to its referent, because their relations are never completely fixed (Eco, 1984). Ask yourself, 'What does the word "economy" mean?', and then try to list everything that you believe constitutes the economy. Would this description ever be complete? Have you remembered to include all the facets of what we now call the knowledge economy or what we mean when we speak of markets in health systems? If the market is everywhere, then what are its boundaries? Yet this does not stop any of us intuitively understanding what is meant by the economy or by the phrase 'there is a downturn in the economy' or 'a cost of living crisis'. Prosperity, like economy, is not just a word, but a concept, and as such is made up of a series of dynamically interrelating metaphorical chains and associations. A concept develops in consequence of the challenge of bringing a particular phenomenon into focus: what is prosperity? This begins with a tension between identity and difference set in motion by a process of semantic innovation: 'prosperity is quality of life'. The consequence is then a series of metaphorical associations which through the workings of context, power and governance highlight some aspects while occluding others. One way to comprehend what is at stake here is to say that prosperity is captured by a series of conceptual metaphors – wellbeing, quality of life, sustainable livelihoods – that emphasise and organise certain features and consequently assign value to them. This process of bringing the phenomenon into focus is about grasping unknown relations between things and identifying new sets of relations with innovative affordances.

The word 'prosperity' does not designate something precisely and uniquely symbolised. The work of redesigning prosperity is not about producing a fixed, unified and invariant definition of prosperity that corresponds to clearly identifiable objects, provisions and experiences in the material world. Such a definition would be of little value: 'some necessary overtones of meaning are lost when a word is precisely and uniquely symbolized. The vagueness of living languages as compared with mathematics is the price they pay for their applicability to the world and their capacity for growth' (Hesse, 1955: 88). The same dynamic capacity applies to a redefined prosperity whenever it is treated as a central signification or constitutive metaphor: it is a way of imagining the material world in a fundamentally different way that focuses the approach to problems in terms of quality of life, environmental sustainability, democratic participation, and hope for a better future for people and planet. So when prosperity as a term becomes integrated into the logics of signification in this manner, it becomes thought of and imagined in a fundamentally different way, and through this process of signification something new is added to it, a surplus that exceeds the materiality of what is signified; it is this surplus that is impossible to identify as the referent (see also Žižek, 2008 [1989]). The work of redefining prosperity is not about lexicalisation or about building a laborious typology, for once all the known meanings had been captured this would not mean that one had definitely captured all there is to prosperity.

The problem of defining concepts with precision was identified and elaborated by Wittgenstein in his *Philosophical Investigations* (2009 [1953]: 35–9). Wittgenstein's account of why exact conceptual definition is so problematic was specifically concerned with 'language games' – and with the notion of games more generally – but it does have clear implications for the understanding of other concepts. According to Wittgenstein, the things that we call games – card games, board games, athletic sports, for example – do not share a common essential quality. There is no single attribute by virtue of which they are all considered to be games. Instead, they have 'affinities' and 'resemblances'; they relate to one another through 'a complicated network of similarities overlapping and criss-crossing: similarities in the large and in the small'

(2009 [1953]: 36). Some games may share one type of resemblance, while others may share another type. Some games may have little, if anything, in common with one another. Nevertheless, the reason that we call them 'games' is that they are all part of the same loosely related group of activities that we have come to associate with the term. The concept of a game, as Wittgenstein understood it – like the concept of prosperity, as we understand it – is not 'a rigidly bounded concept', but rather 'a concept with blurred edges' (Wittgenstein 2009 [1953]: 37, 38).

A second, complementary, explanation for why it is difficult to define prosperity draws on the psychoanalytic argument that language and signification are always incomplete. Any attempt to describe something with words ends up in a cycle of perpetual deferral. A concept or an object can be described through predication, but this assertion can only point to a set of attributes or markers, without fully capturing the essence of the concept or thing beyond the cluster of attributes. Language can never present us with a full account of meaning or reality; it can only describe them in partial and incomplete ways. Peter Dews makes this point clearly in his analysis of Lacan's theory of language: 'No definition of a linguistic term can be self-explanatory, so that the explication of meaning involves the potentially indefinite series of interpretive substitutions made possible by the language as a whole' (2007 [1987]: 74). Dews points out that within this theoretical framework, ostension (pointing out examples or instances) cannot be a sufficient way of defining words. The aim of ostension is to connect words to things in the world through a process of differentiation, but even at this elementary level this connection is bound to fail if one kind of a thing cannot be clearly differentiated from another, and 'the attempt to establish a privileged point at which language would hook directly on to the world is condemned to failure' (2007 [1987]: 73; see also Boothby, 2019: 170–2). Language is effective, but it is only ever an attempt at representation.

Yet, at the same time, language permits us to experience things as having a stable and coherent identity in the face of partiality and change (Laclau 2005: Ch. 4; Žižek 2008 [1989]: Ch. 3, 2014: Ch. 4). Naming and labelling allow us to consolidate things into unities, albeit fragile ones, and to impose a certain amount of order on the world through the use of language. Once a name or label bestows an identity upon an object, that object's existence can appear stable even if all of its objective properties change over time. When a name or label bestows an identity upon a set of different objects, establishing relations between them, the objects in question appear to have an objective common ground by virtue of this articulation (as with the example of games). Language, then, produces two contradictory effects: on the one hand, it alienates us from the world, making it feel beyond reach because of the impossibility of fully describing and symbolising it; on the other hand, it grounds us as subjects in the world by helping us consolidate and unify our experience of people, things and processes.

However, we must recognise that the linguistic terms at play here are also ones in which subjects are politically, socially and psychologically invested (Žižek, 2014: 214–15). These include identity categories related to gender, ethnicity/race and class, as well as concepts such as 'community', which can carry historical significance in defining the identity and aspirations of people in relation to the culture and history of their area, and their conceptions of the good life (for example, Mintchev & Moore, 2017). In the context of such heavily invested terms, language is a vehicle of both power and agency, and it can have both constraining and empowering effects. On one level, the linguistic categories and the concomitant social norms that are imposed on the subject in any given context circumscribe the range of identities that the subject can develop. On another level, these same categories and norms are the condition of possibility of agency, because they can be subverted, reinterpreted, rejected or actively accepted and taken up (McNay, 2000: 3). This is why analyses of language and representation can be used to critique power – especially with regard to essentialist stereotypes that reproduce and justify social inequalities (for example Butler, 1990; Hall, 2017) – as well as to call for new types of agency by articulating novel configurations of identity as the basis for emancipatory social movements (for example Laclau & Mouffe, 2001 [1985]).

This theoretical view of language as both constraining and enabling has important implications for how we understand prosperity as a concept that is at the centre of a project for social change. Prosperity is a term whose referent is evasive; not only is it impossible to fully describe prosperity as a cluster of attributes (because of the slippage and deferral that characterise the process of describing a referent), but even if we could define it as a cluster of attributes, the complex and context-specific nature of the concept makes it impossible to agree on a fixed set of attributes that could then be used to determine if a referent satisfies the description. So while the singularity of the signifier creates the anticipation of a single, consolidated definition, as well as a clearly delineated set of instances that fit this definition, the complexity of social realities and the multiple experiences that make up prosperity as the good life cannot be summarised by a single term (for a similar argument about the categories of gender, see Butler, 2011 [1993]: 165). At the same time, the discourse of prosperity (defined as the good life) has the potential to connect and consolidate a diverse range of actors, capabilities, projects and resources into a network that can mobilise effectively in order to respond to emergent challenges. This network is what in Chapter 1 we call 'prosperity as an assemblage'. The point we add here is that the word 'prosperity' and the discursive practices that reiterate it not only name the assemblage but also support its unity; they help to keep it together and to connect its different elements, albeit with the necessary support of active and deliberate co-ordinating activities.

Such consolidation is brought about by articulating the multiple elements as parts of a broader project with a shared name, as well as by articulating the different elements as working towards shared aspirations, shared visions of the world that we want to achieve, and the processes through which we would like to achieve it. Consider as an example a community in which there is a business concerned with locally sourced and sustainable food production, a café where elderly people meet to socialise, a housing association that supports residents facing pressures to relocate, a group of academics researching young people's mental health, a charity campaigning for the preservation of green spaces, a start-up developing new technologies for affordable electricity, and a church that offers food support to low-income households. All of these actors make a specific contribution to securing a better quality of life or a more sustainable way of living for themselves and their community. The notion of prosperity as an assemblage, however, suggests that prosperity cannot be sufficiently understood or achieved as an aggregate of individual actors, capabilities and resources without co-ordination and collaboration that lead to innovative solutions to problems (see Chapter 1). Of course, interactions and collaborations may already be taking place, and some or all of the community's project-leading actors may see themselves – and be seen by others – as working towards a bigger collective vision of a good life. This vision, furthermore, may be associated with the term prosperity, but the function of a discourse of prosperity is to support and strengthen these collaborations, while encouraging investment in the capabilities and resources that will contribute to the realisation of the shared visions in question. This is achieved by building on local usage, narratives and experiences in order to co-design a discursive framing of social transformation for a multitude of diverse projects.

Central to the IGP's approach is the idea that prosperity is not only an academic and policy construct, associated with a corresponding set of debates, concerns, and forms of discourse and knowledge, but also a construct of communities and sectors outside academia/policy who might understand the concept through a different set of experiences and knowledges (see Moore & Woodcraft, 2019; Woodcraft et al., 2020; Jallad et al., 2022). The practice of co-design aims to create partnerships across a broad range of stakeholders, in order to create a prosperity model that is representative of a wide range of knowledges coming from different social and institutional positions. If accomplished, this process of co-design should lead to an epistemological decentring, as well as a transformation of the power dynamics of contestation over whose discourses are rendered legitimate.

Different types of discourse vary in the degree of authorisation and legitimacy they are ascribed in public life, and this is linked to the positions of the speakers and institutions from which the discourse originates, as well as to the content of what is said and how it is presented. Heterogeneous fields of discourse, with multiple enunciations, different positionalities and multiple narratives, are characterised by contestations, conflicts and power inequalities that are reproduced – and sometimes challenged and undermined – by the actions of actors with different agendas and interests (Bourdieu, 1991; Thompson, 1990: 154–62). The IGP practice of co-design between various institutions and stakeholders, including members of the public, is an attempt to reconfigure the horizon of collaboration and competition by focusing on co-production and sharing of resources (rather than on competing for them) as the basis for driving social transformation.

The notion of meaning deployed when we refer to the meaning of prosperity in the context of our theory is a very specific one. It entails a description of multiple elements, whose relationship to one another is dynamic, flexible and open to different configurations across space and time. Experiences of prosperity as the good life – insofar as they entail multiple dimensions of social, economic and political life – are never fixed, and neither are the referents of the term that represents those experiences. The process of building prosperity is thus always unfinished; it can address various challenges, improve quality of life, and contribute to more sustainable futures and regenerate the planet, but it can never reach a terminal point at which prosperity has been fully achieved or realised in all its complexity. In other words, the pathway has no ending; it only has gains and losses. Prosperity, in this sense, is a goal that can never be fully completed, and this has very specific implications for how we understand it, and what the possibilities and limitations are in defining and describing it. As we argued in Chapter 1, analytically speaking prosperity is not an entity or a steady state, but rather a dynamic assemblage set in the context of intersecting systems (social, economic, ecological, infrastructural). Reconceptualising and redefining prosperity involves repositioning the contextualised elements of the assemblage in new sets of relations, transforming values and metaphors to provide for new configurations and emergent affordances: a constant becoming of prosperity.

## 2.4 Prosperity: concepts, theories and methods

In consequence, when redefining prosperity for the twenty-first century, there can be no over-reliance on any one factor. As argued in the previous section, prosperity defies any easy or unambiguous definition. But if this is the case then how should we understand its nature and structure, how can we create it and build it, how can individuals and communities identify it and identify with it? Concepts, of course, take work; they do not arrive fully formed out of the head of Medusa. What is more, they change over time and find renewed purpose and relevance. Precisely because of the public and policy demands for relevance, we need to have some means of understanding what elements signify prosperity, and some understanding of how prosperity as a concept can be operationalised and tested. Current debates around the redefinition of prosperity actually deploy a number of different conceptualisations, definitions and operationalisations. These provide for productive debate about what are the specific sets of objects, provisions, infrastructures and experiences in the material world that can be identified as signalling prosperity for individuals, communities, neighbourhoods, cities and regions.

Philosophically, one of the difficulties in pointing to the prosperity that these questions raise is closely related to the challenge of determining whether the relationship between prosperity and the various elements that the term represents is one of equivalence or one of inference (see Eco, 1984: 35–6). Take for example the notion of 'good-quality and secure livelihoods', which is a key component of prosperity. Is its relationship to prosperity one of equivalence, whereby having a good-quality and secure livelihood is equivalent to being prosperous or having prosperity? Or is the relationship one of inference, where, if one has a good-quality and secure livelihood, we infer that one is also prosperous or has prosperity? To ask the same question from a slightly different angle: is 'having a good-quality and secure livelihood' the answer to the question 'what does prosperity mean to you?', or is it the answer to 'what do you need in order to be prosperous or have prosperity?' Regardless of whether the relationship is of equivalence or inference, we are faced with a significant philosophical challenge. If the relationship is one of equivalence, then we have the question of how many elements or components of prosperity we need in order to say that a person or community is prosperous or has prosperity. Is it one element? All elements? Or a number somewhere in between? Alternatively, if the relationship is one of inference, then the challenge becomes one of describing or identifying the prosperity, or the state of being prosperous, that emerges beyond these elements once they are in place. If a good-quality and secure livelihood leads to (as opposed to equates to) prosperity, the question then becomes about what exactly prosperity is and how it differs from a life with a good and secure livelihood. When prosperity is equated with wealth, ostension and reference appear to be a straightforward matter of pointing to examples of wealth, such as money or assets. However, when prosperity is defined as the good life and operationalised into multidimensional prosperity models, the processes of ostension and reference become very challenging.

To address these issues, it helps to turn to a brief reflection on the relationship between concepts, theories, methods and metrics, since they are at the heart of the question of what is prosperity and how it should be empirically, as well as philosophically, determined. Redefining prosperity is about reconceptualising it – away from income-based indicators and aggregate GDP growth – towards a more heterogeneous set of characteristics based on a different way of valuing quality of life. However, this process of reconceptualisation is ongoing, and new metaphors come into play as redefinition proceeds, because new data emerges, and we need new metaphors, mechanisms and means for representing emerging elements: a new language. Conceptualisation also responds to the diversity of voices, stakeholders, locales and visions. Bringing communities into the process entails new perspectives and approaches. New challenges also emerge. For example, we have to think very hard at this moment about what prosperity is and entails under conditions of climate and ecological uncertainty.

While a concept is an abstract notion or mental representation, a way of focusing on what is at issue, a theory is a set of explanatory propositions or credible explanations about the particular subject or set of processes that the concept brings into view. Concepts are useful because they bring things into focus and set the frame. Theories are only useful if they provide us with a deeper understanding of the problem in the world we are thinking about or focusing on. Rethinking prosperity thus entails new conceptualisations and new theories. The boundary between theories and concepts is a not a rigid one precisely because theories are about how elements or constructs within conceptualisations interrelate. Nomological networks are a key part of theory development

(Newman et al., 2015; Saad, 2020; Zhang & Venkatesh, 2017; Verma & Khatri, 2021), because they provide representations of the concepts under consideration (wellbeing, livelihoods, quality of life) and their interrelationships. For example, what is the relationship between sustainability and wellbeing? Nomological networks allow for the development of theoretical propositions that specify the interrelationships and linkages between different elements. For example, as democratic participation improves, life satisfaction rises. This process has the effect of operationalising concepts or constructs, allowing them to be studied and measured empirically. The work already conducted on prosperity, as well as related studies of wellbeing and quality of life, has demonstrated that while the interrelationships between different elements provide patterns, they also exhibit variance (Moore et al., 2020; Joshanloo et al., 2019; Ruggeri et al., 2020; Diener et al., 2010; Ng & Diener, 2019). In addition, the boundaries between theories, models and metrics are fuzzy and often porous. Prosperity models of the kind discussed in Chapter 1 and illustrated in Figure 2.1 are useful if they supply us with a deeper understanding of theories and of how different propositions, terms and processes within theories interrelate. A model is a more basic or scaled-down version of a theory; while a model is descriptive, a theory is both explanatory and descriptive. One of the purposes of a model is to explain or elucidate a theory (or set of theories) and allow the testing of propositions (are different elements related to each other or not, and if so how?), and this testing in turn allows the determination of methods, metrics and data collection.

As discussed in Chapter 1, there is a broad range of views regarding which dimensions or elements should be included in the measurement of prosperity. For example, the Legatum Prosperity Index has three domains, with four pillars within each domain: Inclusive Societies (safety and security, personal freedom, governance and social capital); Open Economies (investment environment, enterprise conditions, infrastructure and market access, and economic quality); Empowered People (living conditions, health, education and natural environment) (Legatum Institute, 2020, 2021a, 2021b). The OECD Better Life Index includes eleven topics: housing, income, jobs, community, education, environment, civic engagement, health, life satisfaction, safety and work–life balance (OECD, 2020). The criteria for selection, and especially for the delineation of boundaries between domains/pillars/topics and their associated indicators, are closely linked both to prior conceptualisations of prosperity and to implicit theories about the relationships between elements, as well as to ideas about assumed overlap between associated concepts, including wellbeing and quality of life (Otoiu et al., 2014; Durand, 2015; Phillips, 2006). In addition, as discussed in Chapter 1, individual indicators within pillars/topics/sections are often given differential weighting to signal varying degrees of importance, value or determination. These weightings, plus the various criteria for selection and decisions about boundary delineation, are often discussed in technical papers or descriptions of index construction, but they are rarely linked back to any sustained theoretical or conceptual discussion of what constitutes prosperity (Legatum Institute 2021a, 2021b; Durand, 2015). The dimensions and indicators chosen are driven by implicit values embedded in conceptualisations and theories. Given the large array of elements constituting and driving prosperity in different contexts, it is crucial to interrogate how researchers and policy makers identify the relevant underlying factors constituting and driving prosperity. Clearly not everything can be included, and since not everything can be included there have to be mechanisms (theories and models) for reducing the large array of variables to a smaller number of derived variables. This process is further complicated by the scale at which analysis proceeds; what is relevant for individual prosperity is not governed by the same criteria of selection, weighting and interrelation between elements as community-level or national prosperity (Moore et al., 2020; Joshanloo et al., 2019).

The redefinition of prosperity must work through an empirically oriented and pluralistic approach that allows new conceptualisations to emerge. The different elements that make up prosperity do coalesce and group into overlapping dimensions or domains, but these are not analytically or experientially distinct or discrete. The views of multiple stakeholders allow the determination of the character of prosperity (see Chapter 1) in each locale and comparison between locales. They also permit the integration of value elements, like culture, history and identity, alongside elements connected to larger-scale economic, ecological and social processes, such as infrastructure and investment. The aim is to provide an integrated, multidimensional and multiscalar framework for conceptualising and assessing quality of life and prosperity (and pathways towards future prosperity) that takes account of local concerns and actualities, as well as larger-scale processes and trends, but the focus of analysis and policy is the local level (see Chapter 1 for discussions of the meaning and definition of the local), and the particular assemblage of elements that characterises it.

## 2.5 Conclusion: not just words

In this chapter we have argued that redefining prosperity for the twenty-first century is intimately connected, as it must be, to the politics of signification, its aim being to question and reframe the status quo. We began by demonstrating the importance of understanding how language works in the world, drawing on linguistics and philosophy, and discussing what is at stake in attempts to drive change and re-present the world to ourselves and to others. Language is key to new ways of framing and knowing, and metaphor plays a central role in redescribing reality, setting up new epistemic affinities, forms of relationality, and affordances. It is its connective power that is most often evident, providing new openings, allowing us to use language (and subsequently concepts, theories and methods) to shape alternative ways of thinking and acting. Metaphor is extensive and allows for social innovation and experimentation. This is why the development of constructs in the social and natural sciences is so dependent on metaphorical thinking, where new possibilities drive new questions and new models. However, it is not only, or even primarily, in scientific discourse that this process unfurls, because public and policy discourses have this potential also.

As discussed earlier, the redefinition of prosperity is not a shared singular narrative, and investigating how narratives are negotiated and reproduced allows for the exploration of their role in social change processes and the delineation of alternative future pathways to prosperity (Wittmayer et al., 2019). Prosperity is the result of several intersecting logics, metaphorical chains of association deployed by different sets of actors in contexts of power and the determinations of place, history and culture. These differential deployments provide for the creation of new meanings, arising at the intersection of multiple perspectives and discourses, maintaining the relevance of debates on prosperity to people, places and changing circumstances. The very lively character of the current debate on redefining prosperity (and its related terms, such as wellbeing and sustainability) is evidence of the process of meaning transformation. However, this is not just a matter of words, but of interventions and practices in the world, many of which are connected to policy and investment decisions. The ongoing development of prosperity as a constitutive metaphor frees it from the restriction of current dominant economic models, and connects it through multi-stakeholder deliberation to situated understandings and relationships. In short, it allows for new forms of recognition, in part through the destabilising of existing boundaries and boundary assumptions, and allows assemblages of elements to be reassembled through shifting forms of value, power and governance (Blanco-Wells, 2021), elucidating new potential pathways to prosperity. This is one of the consequences of what Bourdieu has called a theory effect: 'by expressing in a coherent and empirically valid discourse what was previously ignored, ... science transforms the representation of the social world as well as simultaneously transforming the social world itself, at least to the extent that it renders possible practices that conform to this transformed representation' (Bourdieu, 1991: 133).

The discussion of metaphor, concepts, theories, models and metrics in this chapter (and in Chapter 1) lays the ground for a theory of change explaining how new concepts, ideas, values and methods can strengthen capabilities and support aspirations for a better social world. This is why collaborations and partnerships are of crucial importance, as is the implementation of mechanisms and methods (such as citizen science) that encourage inclusion and participation. The success of a given articulation, however, is never guaranteed. Collaboratively formulating a vision of prosperity and presenting it as a framework for change does not mean that it will be taken seriously by all. For a newly articulated transformative vision of prosperity to gain legitimacy and convince people that it is worthwhile, it has to demonstrate its value and its potential to benefit the community. This is the case even if the vision in question is operationalised by local partnerships, built on the basis of local terminologies, and designed to respond to local challenges. Our view is that the best way to demonstrate the value of a theory is by producing tangible outcomes that benefit stakeholders and lead to positive change. The delivery of outcomes is essential for legitimising both the concept and the aspirations it represents, including the aspiration to enhance and consolidate locally embedded assemblages (Moore & Woodcraft, 2019; Mintchev et al., 2019; Shehabi et al., 2021).

Examining prosperity as a constitutive metaphor draws attention to the central set of relationships that comprise it, providing a series of responses to questions concerning its nature and character. It also creates a series of means and mechanisms for focusing on and maximising attention to complex realities, through what Tsing has called the art of noticing (Tsing, 2015). Metaphors are not just simple semantic variations, because they work through processes of identity and difference to create new opportunities both epistemological and ontological. Key here, as we have argued throughout this chapter, is the focus on locale, the situated context of relationships and assemblages. Locale is not just a backdrop, but a form of entanglement, a space/place where emergent processes and interdependencies can be explored. The multidimensionality of interrelationships between elements in specific contexts allows for the identification of additional levers for policy intervention, driving forward the possibilities for social innovation to address situated challenges. Plurality of voices, approaches, ideas and values offers new ways of conceptualising prosperity and of identifying new ways of being and acting in the world that can lead to the realisation of alternative pathways to prosperity:

> every situation can be cracked open from the inside, reconfigured in a different regime of perception and signification. To reconfigure the landscape of what can be seen and what can be thought is to alter the field of the possible and the distribution of capacities and incapacities. ... This is what a process of political subjectivation consists in: in the action of uncounted capacities that crack open the unity of the given and the obviousness of the visible, in order to sketch a new topography of the possible.
> 
> (Rancière 2009: 49)

## Bibliography

Andryukhina, T. V. (2021). Metaphor variation in economic discourse. *Professional Discourse & Communication*, 3(4), 9–20. https://doi.org/10.24833/2687-0126-2021-3-4-9-20.

Balaguer Rasillo, X. & Wirth, M. (2022). Alternative economies and commoning practices in Catalonia: Unpacking *Ecoxarxes* from a social studies of economisation perspective. *Antipode*, 54(6), 1694–1714. https://doi.org/10.1111/anti.12867.

Baranzini, R. & Besomi, D. (eds) (2022). *Metaphors in the History of Economic Thought: Crises, business cycles and equilibrium*. Abingdon: Routledge.

Blanco-Wells, G. (2021). Ecologies of repair: A post-human approach to other-than-human natures. *Frontiers in Psychology*, 12, 633737, 1–10. https://doi.org/10.3389/fpsyg.2021.633737.

Boothby, R. (2019). Lacan's thing with Hegel. *Continental Thought & Theory*, 2(4), 164–79. Available at: https://ir.canterbury.ac.nz/bitstream/handle/10092/17117/11%20Boothby%20Hegel%20Final.pdf?sequence=5 (accessed 16 December 2022).

Bourdieu, P. (1991). *Language and Symbolic Power* (trans. G. Raymond & M. Adamson). Cambridge: Polity Press.

Bourdieu, P. (1998). *Acts of Resistance: Against the new myths of our time* (trans. R. Nice). Cambridge: Polity Press.

Bracker, N. & Herbrechter, S. (2005). *Metaphors of Economy*. Amsterdam: Rodopi.

Brown, N. (2003). Hope against hype: Accountability in biopasts, presents and futures. *Science & Technology Studies*, 16(2), 3–21. https://doi.org/10.23987/sts.55152.

Butler, J. (1990). *Gender Trouble: Feminism and the subversion of identity*. Abingdon: Routledge.

Butler, J. (2011 [1993]). *Bodies that Matter: On the discursive limits of 'sex'*. Abingdon: Routledge.

Buzila, E. (2018). The power of metaphor. Available at: https://papers.ssrn.com/sol3/papers.cfm?abstract_id=3292066 (accessed 16 December 2022).

Çalışkan, K. & Callon, M. (2009). Economization, part 1: Shifting attention from the economy towards processes of economization. *Economy and Society*, 38(3), 369–98. https://doi.org/10.1080/03085140903020580.

Cassiers, I. (2015) Introduction. In I. Cassiers (ed.), *Redefining Prosperity*, pp. 1–5. Abingdon: Routledge.

Coffey, B. (2016). Unpacking the politics of natural capital and economic metaphors in environmental policy discourse. *Environmental Politics*, 25(2), 203–22. https://doi.org/10.1080/09644016.2015.1090370.

Cojanu, V. (2008). The 'market' metaphor and climate change: An epistemological application in the study of green economics. *Internal Journal of Green Economics*, 2(3), 284–94. https://doi.org/10.1504/IJGE.2008.021423.

Deignan, A. (2005). A corpus linguistic perspective on the relationship between metonymy and metaphor. *Style*, 39(1), 72–91.

Dews, P. (2007 [1987]). *Logics of Disintegration: Post-structuralist thought and the claims of critical theory*. London: Verso.

Diener, E., Ng, W., Harter, J. & Arora (2010). Wealth and happiness across the world: Material prosperity predicts life evaluation, whereas psychosocial prosperity predicts positive feeling. *Journal of Personality and Social Psychology*, 99(1), 52–61. https://doi.org/10.1037/a0018066.

Dobuzinskis, L. (1992). Modernist and postmodernist metaphors of the policy process: Control and stability vs. chaos and reflexive understanding. *Policy Sciences*, 25, 355–80. https://doi.org/10.1007/BF00138019.

Durand, M. (2015). The OECD Better Life Initiative: *How's Life*? and the measurement of well-being. *Review of Income and Wealth*, 61(1), 4–17. https://doi.org/10.1111/roiw.12156.

Eco, U. (1984). *Semiotics and the Philosophy of Language*. Bloomington: Indiana University Press.

Eco, U. (2000). *Kant and the Platypus: Essays on language and cognition* (trans. Alastair McEwen). London: Vintage.

Flusberg, S. J., Matlock, T. & Thibodeau, P. H. (2017). Metaphors for the war (or race) against climate change. *Environmental Communication*, 11(6), 769–83. https://doi.org/10.1080/17524032.2017.1289111.

Foucault, M. (1982). The subject and power. *Critical Inquiry*, 8(4), 777–95. https://doi.org/10.1086/448181.

Gibbs, R. W. (1996). Why many concepts are metaphorical. *Cognition*, 61(3), 309–19. https://doi.org/10.1016/S0010-0277(96)00723-8.

Goodman, N. (1968). *Languages of Art: An approach to a theory of symbols*. Indianapolis: Bobbs-Merrill.

Graham, P. (2002). Predication and propagation: A method for analyzing evaluative meanings in technology policy. *Text and Talk*, 22(2), 227–68. https://doi.org/10.1515/text.2002.009.

Griffen Z. & Panofsky, A. (2021). Ambivalent economizations: The case of value added modeling in teacher evaluation. *Theory and Society*, 50(3), 515–39. https://doi.org/10.1007/s11186-020-09417-x.

Hall, S. (2017). *The Fateful Triangle: Race, ethnicity, nation*. Cambridge, MA: Harvard University Press.

Hardt, L. (2014). Metaphors as research tools in economics. *On the Horizon*, 22(4), 256–64. https://doi.org/10.1108/OTH-11-2013-0059.

Harvey, D. (2005). *A Brief History of Neoliberalism*. Oxford: Oxford University Press.

Herrera-Soler, H. & White, M. (2012). Metaphor and mills: Figurative language in business and economics. Introduction. In H. Herrera-Soler & M. White, (eds) *Metaphor and Mills: Figurative language in business and economics*, pp. 1–24. Berlin, Boston: De Gruyter.

Hesse, M. (1955). *Science and the Human Imagination: Aspects of the history and logic of physical science*. New York: Philosophical Library.

Hickel, J. & Kallis, G. (2020). Is green growth possible? *New Political Economy*, 25(4), 469–86. https://doi.org/10.1080/13563467.2019.1598964.

Holmgreen, L.-L. (2003). Setting the neo-liberal agenda: How metaphors help shape socio-economic 'realities'. *Metaphorik.de*, 5, 90–114. Available at: https://www.metaphorik.de/sites/www.metaphorik.de/files/journal-pdf/05_2003_holmgreen.pdf?origin=publication_detail (accessed 20 September 2022).

Howarth, D. & Stavrakakis, Y. (2000). Introducing discourse theory and political analysis. In D. R. Howarth, A. J. Norval & Y. Stavrakakis (eds), *Discourse Theory and Political Analysis: Identities, hegemonies and social change*, pp. 1–23. Manchester: Manchester University Press.

Hubacek, K., Chen, X., Feng, K., Wiedmann, T. & Shan, Y. (2021). Evidence of decoupling consumption-based $CO_2$ emissions from economic growth. *Advances in Applied Energy*, 4, 1–10. https://doi.org/10.1016/j.adapen.2021.100074.

Hughes, I., Byrne, E., Mullally, G. & Sage, C. (eds) (2021). *Metaphor, Sustainability, Transformation: Transdisciplinary perspectives*. Abingdon: Routledge.

Hutton, C. (1989). The arbitrary nature of the sign. *Semiotica*, 75(1–2), 63–78. https://doi.org/10.1515/semi.1989.75.1-2.63.

Jackson, T. (2015). Foreword. In I. Cassiers (ed.), *Redefining Prosperity*, xii–xiii. Abingdon: Routledge.

Jackson, T. (2017). *Prosperity without Growth: Foundations for the economy of tomorrow*. 2nd edn. Abingdon: Routledge.

Jackson, T. & Victor, P. A. (2019). Unravelling the claims for (and against) green growth. *Science*, 366(6468), 950–1. https://doi.org/10.1126/science.aay0749.

Jallad, M., Mintchev, N., Pietrostefani, E., Daher, M. & Moore, H. L. (2022). Citizen social science and pathways to prosperity: Co-designing research and impact in Beirut, Lebanon. *International Journal of Social Research Methodology*, 25(6), 769–82. https://doi.org/10.1080/13645579.2021.1942664.

Joshanloo, M., Jovanović, V. & Taylor, T. (2019). A multidimensional understanding of prosperity and well-being at country level: Data-driven explorations. *PLoS ONE*, 14(10), e0223221. https://doi.org/10.1371/journal.pone.0223221.

Klamer, A. & Leonard, T. C. (1994). So what's an economic metaphor? In P. Mirowski (ed.), *Natural Images in Economic Thought: 'Markets read in tooth and claw'*, pp. 20–51. Cambridge: Cambridge University Press.

Laclau, E. (2005). *On Populist Reason*. London: Verso.

Laclau, E. & Mouffe, C. (2001 [1985]). *Hegemony and Socialist Strategy: Towards a radical democratic politics*. 2nd edn. London: Verso.

Lagueux, M. (1999). Do metaphors affect economic theory? *Economics and Philosophy*, 15(1), 1–22. https://doi.org/10.1017/S0266267100003564.

Lakoff, G. (2010). Why it matters how we frame the environment. *Environmental Communication*, 4(1), 70–81. https://doi.org/10.1080/17524030903529749.

Lakoff, G. & Johnson, M. (1980). *Metaphors We Live By*. Chicago: University of Chicago Press.

Langer, T. (2015). Metaphors in economics: Conceptual mapping possibilities in the lectures of economics. *Procedia Economics and Finance*, 25, 308–17. https://doi.org/10.1016/S2212-5671(15)00741-8.

Laruffa, F. (2022). Neoliberalism, economization and the paradox of the new welfare state. *European Journal of Sociology*, 63(1), 131–63. https://doi.org/10.1017/S0003975622000169.

Legatum Institute (2020). Defining prosperity. Available at: https://docs.prosperity.com/6516/0586/8116/Defining_Prosperity.pdf (accessed 17 December 2022).

Legatum Institute (2021a). The United Kingdom Prosperity Index: Measuring prosperity. Available at: https://li.com/wp-content/uploads/2021/08/2021-UK-Prosperity-Methodology-report.pdf (accessed 17 December 2022).

Legatum Institute (2021b). *The Legatum Prosperity Index 2021: Methodology*. Available at: https://www.prosperity.com/about/methodology (accessed 20 September 2022).

McCloskey, D. N. (1985). *The Rhetoric of Economics*. 2nd edn. Madison: University of Wisconsin Press.

McGinn, C. (2015). *Philosophy of Language: The classics explained*. Cambridge, MA: MIT Press.

McKinnon, A. M. (2013). Ideology and the market metaphor in rational choice theory of religion: A rhetorical critique of 'religious economies'. *Critical Sociology*, 39(4), 529–43. https://doi.org/10.1177/0896920511415431.

McNay, L. (2000). *Gender and Agency: Reconfiguring the subject in feminist and social theory*. Cambridge: Polity Press.

Mintchev, N., Baumann, H. L., Moore, H. L., Rigon, A. & Dabaj, J. (2019). Towards a shared prosperity: Co-designing solutions in Lebanon's spaces of displacement. *Journal of the British Academy*, 7(2), 109–35. https://doi.org/10.5871/jba/007s2.109.

Mintchev, N., Daher, M., Jallad, M., Pietrostefani, E., Moore, H. L., Ghanrawi, G., Al Harrache, A., Majed, A. & Younes, Y. (2022). Sustained citizen science from research to solutions: A new impact model for the social sciences. *International Journal of Qualitative Methods*. https://doi.org/10.1177/16094069221133232.

Mintchev, N. & Moore, H. L. (2017) Community and prosperity beyond social capital: The case of Newham, East London. *Critical Social Policy*, 37(4), pp. 562–81. https://doi.org/10.1177/0261018316683461.

Monticelli, L. (2018). Embodying alternatives to capitalism in the 21st century. *Triple C*, 6(2), 501–17. https://doi.org/10.31269/triplec.v16i2.1032.

Moore, H. L. (2015). Global prosperity and sustainable development goals. *Journal of International Development*, 27(6), 801–15. https://doi.org/10.1002/jid.3114.

Moore, H. L., Moreno, J. M. & Melios, G. (2020). *Identifying and Understanding Local Priorities for Developing an 'Economy of Belonging': A case study of eight areas in the UK*. London: Institute for Global Prosperity. Available at: https://discovery.ucl.ac.uk/id/eprint/10120021/ (accessed 17 December 2022).

Moore, H. L. & Woodcraft, S. (2019). Understanding prosperity in East London: Local meanings and 'sticky' measures of the Good Life. *City & Society*, 31(2), 275–98. https://doi.org/10.1111/ciso.12208.

Morgan, M. S. (2012). *The World in the Model: How economists work and think*. Cambridge: Cambridge University Press.

Musacchio, M. T. (2011). Metaphors and metaphor-like processes across languages: Notes on English and Italian language of economics. In K. Ahmad (ed.), *Affective Computing and Sentiment Analysis: Emotion, metaphor and terminology*, pp. 89–98. Dordrecht: Springer.

Nerlich, B. & Hellsten, I. (2014). The greenhouse metaphor and the footprint metaphor: Climate change risk assessment and risk management seen through the lens of two prominent metaphors. *Technikfolgenabschätzung: Theorie und Praxis*, 23(2), 27–33. Available at: https://nottingham-repository.worktribe.com/output/999398 (accessed 17 December 2022).

Newman, I., Hitchcock, J. H. & Newman, D. (2015). The use of research syntheses and nomological networks to develop HRD theory. *Advances in Developing Human Resources*, 17(1), 117–34. https://doi.org/10.1177/1523422314559810.

Ng, W. & Diener, E. (2019). Affluence and subjective well-being: Does income inequality moderate their associations? *Applied Research in Quality of Life*, 14(1), 155–70. https://doi.org/10.1007/s11482-017-9585-9.

Nietzsche, F. (1979). On truth and lies in a nonmoral sense. In F. W. Nietzsche (ed.), *Philosophy and Truth: Selections from Nietzsche's notebooks of the early 1870's* (trans. D. Breazeale), pp. 79–100. Atlantic Highlands, NJ: Humanities Press International.

OECD (2011). *Towards Green Growth*. OECD Green Growth Studies. Paris: OECD Publishing. https://doi.org/10.1787/9789264111318-en.

OECD (2020). *How's Life? 2020: Measuring well-being*. Paris: OECD Publishing. https://doi.org/10.1787/9870c393-en.

Otoiu, A., Titan, E. & Dumitrescu, R. (2014). Are the variables used in building composite indicators of well-being relevant? Validating composite indexes of well-being. *Ecological Indicators*, 46, 575–85. https://doi.org/10.1016/j.ecolind.2014.07.019.

Pamies, A. & Ramos Ruiz, I. (2017). Metaphors of economy and economy of metaphors. *Europhras*, 60–9. https://doi.org/10.26615/978-2-9701095-2-5_008.

Parrique, T., Barth, J., Briens, F., Kerschner, C., Kraus-Polk, A., Kuokkanen, A. & Spangenberg, J. H. (2019). Decoupling debunked: Evidence and arguments against green growth as a sole strategy for sustainability. European Environmental Bureau. Available at: https://eeb.org/wp-content/uploads/2019/07/Decoupling-Debunked.pdf (accessed 17 December 2022).

Peichl, A. & Pestel, N. (2013). Multidimensional well-being at the top: Evidence for Germany. *Fiscal Studies*, 34(3), 355–71. https://doi.org/10.1111/j.1475-5890.2013.12010.x.

Phillips, D. (2006). *Quality of life: Concept, policy and practice*. Abingdon, New York: Routledge.

Rancière, J. (2009). *The Emancipated Spectator* (trans. G. Elliott). New York: Verso.

Raworth, K. (2017). *Doughnut Economics: Seven ways to think like a 21st century economist*. White River Junction, VT: Chelsea Green Publishing.

Resche, C. (2012). Towards a better understanding of metaphorical networks in the language of economics: The importance of theory-constitutive metaphors. In H. Herrera-Soler & M. White (eds), *Metaphor and Mills*, 77–102. Berlin, Boston: De Gruyter.

Ricoeur, P. (1977). *The Rule of the Metaphor: The creation of meaning in language* (trans. R. Czerny, K. McLaughlin & J. Costello, SJ). Toronto: University of Toronto Press.

Ruggeri, K., Garcia-Garzon, E., Maguire, Á., Matz, S. & Huppert, F. A. (2020). Well-being is more than happiness and life satisfaction: A multidimensional analysis of 21 countries. *Health and Quality of Life Outcomes*, 18(1), 192. https://doi.org/10.1186/s12955-020-01423-y.

Saad, G. (2020). Building a global database of nomological networks of cumulative evidence. *Evolutionary Behavioral Sciences*, 14(4), 368–72. https://doi.org/10.1037/ebs0000223.

Schmidt, V. A. (2011). Speaking of change: Why discourse is key to the dynamics of policy transformation. *Critical Policy Studies*, 5(2), 106–26. https://doi.org/10.1080/19460171.2011.576520.

Schön, D. (1967). *Invention and the Evolution of Ideas*. London: Tavistock Publications.

Schön, D. (1979). Generative metaphor: A perspective on problem-setting in social policy. In A. Ortony (ed.), *Metaphor and Thought*, 254–83. Cambridge: Cambridge University Press.

Shehabi, A., Al-Masri, M., Obeid, J., Ayoub, M., Jallad, M. & Daher, M. (2021). *A Pilot Citizens' Assembly on Electricity and Energy Justice in Hamra, Lebanon*. London: Institute for Global Prosperity. https://doi.org/10.14324/000.wp.10129878.

Söderholm, P. (2020). The green economy transition: The challenges of technological change for sustainability. *Sustainable Earth*, 3, 6, 1–11. https://doi.org/10.1186/s42055-020-00029-y.

Stiglitz, J. E., Sen, A. & Fitoussi, J.-P. (2010). *Mismeasuring Our Lives: Why GDP doesn't add up*. New York: New Press.

Strauss, C. (2006). The imaginary. *Anthropological Theory*, 6(3), 322–44. https://doi.org/10.1177/1463499606066891.

Talib, N. & Fitzgerald, R. (2016). Micro-meso-macro movements: A multi-level critical discourse analysis framework to examine metaphors and the value of truth in policy texts. *Critical Discourse Studies*, 13(5), 531–47. https://doi.org/10.1080/17405904.2016.1182932.

Taylor Aiken, G. (2019). Community as tool for low carbon transitions: Involvement and containment, policy and action. *Environment and Planning C: Politics and Space*, 37(4), 732–49. https://doi.org/10.1177/2399654418791579.

Thibodeau, P. H., Frantz, C. M. & Berretta, M. (2017). The earth is our home: Systemic metaphors to redefine our relationship with nature. *Climatic Change*, 142, 287–300. https://doi.org/10.1007/s10584-017-1926-z.

Thompson, J. B. (1990). *Ideology and Modern Culture: Critical social theory in the era of mass communication*. Cambridge: Polity Press.

Tsing, A. L. (2015). *The Mushroom at the End of the World: On the possibility of life in capitalist ruins*. Princeton, NJ: Princeton University Press.

Verma, N. & Khatri, P. (2021). The nomological network of organizational attachment: A systematic review approach. *Journal of Decision Systems*, 1–22. https://doi.org/10.1080/12460125.2021.2002507.

Ward, J. D. et al. (2016). Is decoupling GDP growth from environmental impact possible? *PLoS ONE*, 11(10), e0164733. https://doi.org/10.1371/journal.pone.0164733.

White, M. (2003). Metaphor and economics: The case of growth. *English for Specific Purposes*, 22(2), 131–51. https://doi.org/10.1016/S0889-4906(02)00006-6.

White, M. & Soler, H. (2007). A contrastive view of British and Spanish business press headlines. *Rassegna italiana di linguistica applicata*, 39(1–2), 295–316. Available at: https://www.torrossa.com/en/resources/an/2402479 (accessed 20 September 2022).

Wittgenstein, L. (2009 [1953]). *Philosophical Investigations* (trans. G. E. M. Anscombe, P. M. S. Hacker & J. Schulte). Revised 4th edn by P. M. S. Hacker & J. Schulte. Chichester: Wiley-Blackwell.

Wittmayer, J. M., Backhaus, J., Avelino, F., Pel, B., Strasser, T., Kunze, I. & Zuijderwijk, L. (2019). Narratives of change: How social innovation initiatives construct societal transformation. *Futures*, 112, 102433. https://doi.org/10.1016/j.futures.2019.06.005.

Woodcraft, S., Osuteye, E., Ndezi, T. & Makoba, F. D. (2020). Pathways to the 'good life': Co-producing prosperity research in informal settlements in Tanzania. *Urban Planning*, 5(3), 288–302. https://doi.org/10.17645/up.v5i3.3177.

Zhang, X. & Venkatesh, V. (2017). A nomological network of knowledge management system use: Antecedents and consequences. *MIS Quarterly*, 41(4), 1275–1306. Available at: https://ssrn.com/abstract=3681118 (accessed 20 September 2022).

Žižek, S. (2008 [1989]). *The Sublime Object of Ideology*. New edn. London: Verso.

Žižek, S. (2014). *The Most Sublime Hysteric: Hegel with Lacan* (trans. T. Scott-Railton). Cambridge: Polity.

# 3
# Local meanings and 'sticky' measures of the good life: redefining prosperity with and for communities in east London

Henrietta L. Moore and Saffron Woodcraft

## 3.1 Introduction

In the context of the 'cost-of-living crisis', levelling up 'left-behind' areas and 'building back better' post-Covid and post-Brexit, what it means to prosper is once again at the forefront of political debates in the UK. A version of prosperity that is concurrent with the growth of material wealth has dominated economic and political systems for over two hundred years (Moore, 2015; Cassiers, 2014). As discussed in Chapters 1 and 2, this vision has propelled a singular global development agenda focused on wealth creation driven by economic growth. GDP, as the dominant measure of economic activity, has become the default measure (and metaphor; see Chapter 2) of societal prosperity. The widening gap in quality of life and opportunity between those who benefit from the value created and extracted in our economies and societies and those who do not has resulted in a well-established case for looking for measures of progress beyond economic growth and GDP (Fioramonti, 2017; Jackson, 2017; OECD, 2020; Moore, 2015; Raworth, 2017; Stiglitz, Sen & Fitoussi, 2010; Stiglitz, 2011; World Bank Commission on Growth and Development, 2008, 2010; Spence & Leipziger, 2010).

Describing empirical research undertaken with citizen scientists and communities in east London, we present findings that challenge the orthodox understanding of prosperity as material wealth, as described in the first two chapters. We argue that empirical research in diverse contexts must provide the basis for new theoretical insights if scholars and policy makers are to understand how situated cultural and political imaginaries, local circumstances and systemic interdependencies intersect to enable or inhibit prosperity. From this research we have developed a set of metrics with citizen scientists – the Prosperity Index – that can be used to interrogate prosperity at the local level, to measure progress on policy aimed at improving prosperity for communities, and to provide a tool to hold policy makers to account.

## 3.2 Redefining and localising prosperity

Successive UK governments have perpetuated a crisis of so-called left-behind places (Tomaney & Pike, 2020) with the most recent efforts to tackle the UK 'productivity puzzle' seen in the 2017 Industrial Strategy (Business, Energy and Industrial Strategy, 2017), Local Industrial Strategies (Business, Energy and Industrial Strategy, 2018), City Deals, and rhetorical statements such as 'levelling up' and 'building back better' set out in the government's 'plan for growth' (HM Treasury, 2021). As analysed by Moore and Collins (2021), and further examined in the next chapter, we have shown that these policies constitute a form of trickle-down economics (Dabla-Norris et al., 2015). Nonetheless, a commitment to localising action through such policy documents signals a shift in the way prosperity is conceptualised, opening up avenues for a diversity of context-specific understandings and aspirations to emerge and shape how prosperity is envisaged in policy. These UK policy frameworks reflect a global 'post-GDP' discourse that seeks to broaden debates about what economic activity should return to societies and to expand prosperity measures beyond economic growth and rising household incomes. As a consequence, new measures of subjective wellbeing, happiness, quality of life, and prosperity, have proliferated in recent years, as detailed in Chapter 1. These high-level comparative frameworks provide trends data that can guide macro policy decisions. The most powerful of these is the Legatum UK Prosperity Index (Legatum Institute, 2022), which provides data from 2012 to 2022 at the local authority level across the UK to try to identify constraints on prosperity and where levelling up is taking place. The index is based on existing data sets but does not attempt to gather enhanced knowledge and understanding about prosperity as a lived experience shaped by situated social and cultural values and dynamic, place-specific factors. Despite an emerging discourse that critiques the association of prosperity with material wealth and growth, as discussed in Chapter 1, little research has been done on how prosperity is conceptualised differently across places, cultures and generations, how historical interdependencies and past interventions shape diverse imaginaries of the good life, and how lived experiences of prosperity intersect with, or diverge from, state-led visions and policies.[1] As outlined in Chapter 1, new methodological and theoretical approaches are needed that interrogate questions of power, place, contingency, subjectivity and difference, alongside analyses of material conditions, in order to fully account for the diversity of ideas about what it means to live a prosperous life, the multiple ways people act on these visions, and the situated effects of the systems, frameworks and conditions that shape opportunities.

As a case in point, this chapter examines what prosperity means in a specific context by presenting data from community-based research involving citizen scientists and people living and working in two boroughs in east London. Since 2009, east London has been the focus of a co-ordinated strategic programme by national and local government to close the gap in performance and prospects between the wealthiest and poorest communities (Mayor of London, n.d.) and to deliver shared prosperity as the legacy of London's 2012 Olympic Games. In this chapter, we first situate this research geographically and in relation to London's Olympic legacy policy, which celebrated its tenth anniversary in 2022. Second, we present empirical data about prosperity in east London, which provides the basis for new theoretical and conceptual insights developed in section 3.3. Third, we demonstrate how community-led research generates a context-specific prosperity model, which provides the basis for developing 'sticky measures', new metrics that reflect issues of specific value and concern to individuals and communities in east London. The idea of 'stickiness' refers here to indicators of prosperity that resonate with lived experience and local priorities (Whitby et al., 2014), as opposed to indicators such as GDP and job growth that fail to reflect lived realities of inequality, in-work poverty, and economic exclusion and insecurity.

## 3.3 Prosperity in east London: citizen science and local prosperity pathways

> [T]he facts remain that people in [east London] earn less, have fewer qualifications, are more likely to be unemployed, live in poor and overcrowded housing, be a victim of crime and die younger than an average Londoner. This has been true since Victorian times and

has blighted the lives of successive generations whilst at the same time holding back the performance of the East London economy.

(Growth Borough Partnership, 2016)

East London has a history of poverty, deprivation and disadvantage in relation to the rest of the city that has driven interventions by policy makers and philanthropists for over 200 years (see Figure 3.1). In 2007, London won the bid to host the 2012 Olympic Games on the basis of a legacy promise of social and economic regeneration for east

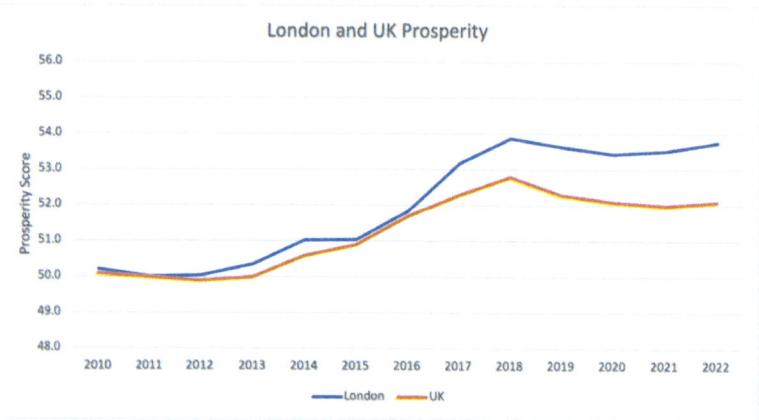

| Local Authority | Rank | Local Authority | Rank |
| --- | --- | --- | --- |
| Richmond upon Thames | 10 | Sutton | 157 |
| City of London | 61 | Tower Hamlets | 160 |
| Harrow | 83 | Kensington and Chelsea | 166 |
| Kingston upon Thames | 90 | Ealing | 178 |
| Barnet | 95 | Southwark | 205 |
| Camden | 101 | Bexley | 212 |
| Islington | 111 | Waltham Forest | 221 |
| Westminster | 112 | Haringey | 233 |
| Hounslow | 116 | Newham | 235 |
| Havering | 118 | Lambeth | 245 |
| Redbridge | 123 | Greenwich | 250 |
| Hammersmith and Fulham | 126 | Lewisham | 263 |
| Bromley | 134 | Brent | 270 |
| Merton | 137 | Enfield | 281 |
| Wandsworth | 150 | Croydon | 292 |
| Hackney | 154 | Barking and Dagenham | 324 |
| Hillingdon | 156 | | |

**Figure 3.1** Differences in prosperity across London.

Source: Legatum Institute, 2022

London (MacRury & Poynter, 2009). The Mayor's Office and London's six Olympic host boroughs[2] adopted the convergence framework as the strategic policy agenda to guide legacy investments. The goal of convergence was to close the gap in prospects and prosperity between people living in the poorest and wealthiest areas of the city within 20 years of the Games (Mayor of London, n.d.).

Development-led regeneration in and around the Olympic Park was conceived as the vehicle to drive this transformation. By 2030, up to ten thousand new homes in five new neighbourhoods, a new cultural and educational quarter and commercial office space to attract major cultural institutions and employers, public realm improvements, schools, shops, community centres and infrastructure will have been provided in the Olympic Park (Olympic Park Legacy Company, 2011). However, patterns of urban development in London and other global cities demonstrate a very uneven distribution of gains from major regeneration investments, with low-income neighbourhoods disproportionately affected by rising land and property prices (Lees & White, 2020; Lees, Slater & Wyly, 2013) and little evidence that development-led regeneration delivers wider socioeconomic benefits to communities (What Works Centre for Local Economic Growth, 2015).

The Olympic Park borders four London boroughs: Hackney, Newham, Tower Hamlets and Waltham Forest. The majority of development related to the Olympic legacy has to date taken place in Hackney and Newham. In 2015, the research team of the IGP designed qualitative field research in three small areas in Hackney and Newham. The Legatum UK Prosperity Index (Legatum Institute, 2022) for Newham and Hackney provides aggregate data for a 10-year period at the local authority level (see Figures 3.2 and 3.3). Both areas appear to have improved their prosperity rankings over time: Hackney ranks 154 out of 374 local authorities in the UK, with a prosperity score that has improved from 49.4 to 54.2 over the period; Newham is ranked 235 with an improved score of 52.7 as compared to 47.5 10 years earlier. While the Legatum Index is the most detailed available compiled from existing data sources, the breakdown of the scores emphasises how complex local conditions are. In Hackney, economic quality has risen from 50.3 to 61.6, and living conditions from 44.3 to 47.8, but safety and security has fallen from 43 to 38.4, social capital from 46.9 to 44.7, and health from 52.1 to 47.9. Comparable figures for Newham show improvements in economic quality from 43.6 to 53.5, in living conditions from 45.7 to 50.8, and in safety and security from 40.9 to 41.1, but declines in health from 56.2 to 48.7. Figures for the natural environment for Hackney show a rise from 41.4

**Figure 3.2**  Prosperity over time: Hackney.

Source: Legatum Institute, 2022

**Figure 3.3**  Prosperity over time: Newham.

Source: Legatum Institute, 2022

to 54.6, but that still leaves the area with a rank of 325 out of 374 across the UK. Newham scores 50.0 for natural environment, up from 39.8, but with an overall UK ranking of 369, which equates to a fall of three points in rank over the 10-year period. These kinds of questions and inconsistencies always arise with aggregate figures (see Chapters 1 and 2), but they underscore the importance of interpreting figures and of understanding the intersections between different dimensions of prosperity as they are assembled in specific locales over time from the point of view of citizens/ residents and other stakeholders.

The aim of the IGP research in the three selected neighbourhoods surrounding east London's Olympic Park (the Prosperity in east London study) was to examine prosperity, as concept, lived experience and policy goal. The object was to assess prosperity in context and to identify if, and how, prosperity strategies developed by policy makers converge, and diverge from lived experience. The research explored three questions. What does prosperity mean to people living and working in east London? What enables and what inhibits prosperity in east London? What would a prosperity model and metrics look like if they were designed by citizens and communities and based on local needs, aspirations and priorities?

### 3.3.1 Research methodology

Data was collected by a team of 10 citizen scientists working with IGP's interdisciplinary academic team in Hackney and Newham. The citizen scientists lived, and sometimes also worked, in the three research sites and were recruited through a publicly advertised process. Selection was based on knowledge of, and interest in, their neighbourhoods and social and economic change in east London. No prior research experience was necessary, as applied research training and support was provided by IGP during the project (including research ethics, research methods, data collection, data management and qualitative data analysis). The citizen scientists were employed by IGP for the duration of the training and research.

The citizen science cohort comprised five women and five men aged between 18 and 60 years old from different cultural, ethnic, social and professional backgrounds. The cohort included a community worker, a learning and inclusion expert, a youth leader, an artist, a self-employed music publicist, a stay-at-home parent, a tailor, and two people who worked in cultural industries. Seven of the citizen scientists had lived or worked in the neighbourhoods for most or all of their lives; the other three had lived or worked locally for between one and three years. The citizen scientists brought diverse forms of local knowledge to the project, including perspectives on the effects and implications of social and economic change based on experiences of growing up or living locally, embodied knowledge of how local space is used, and insights into local decision making. These forms of knowledge added nuance to 'official' accounts of life in the neighbourhood based on public statistics and government reports.

The citizen scientists used a combination of semi-structured interviews and group discussions with people living and working in the three neighbourhoods to collect 256 accounts that explored situated meanings and experiences of prosperity (see Figure 3.4).

A grounded approach to data analysis was adopted by the research team. Citizen scientists were trained in inductive coding and developed thematic data analysis to reflect general categories of understanding and experience of prosperity. Sentiment analysis was then applied to the thematic data to identify whether a single theme, such as social inclusion or the quality of local work, was described in positive, negative or neutral terms, and whether patterns in the distribution of sentiment were observable across the three research sites. Frequency analysis of thematic data was undertaken to identify the most common issues in each research site (Guest, MacQueen & Namey, 2012).

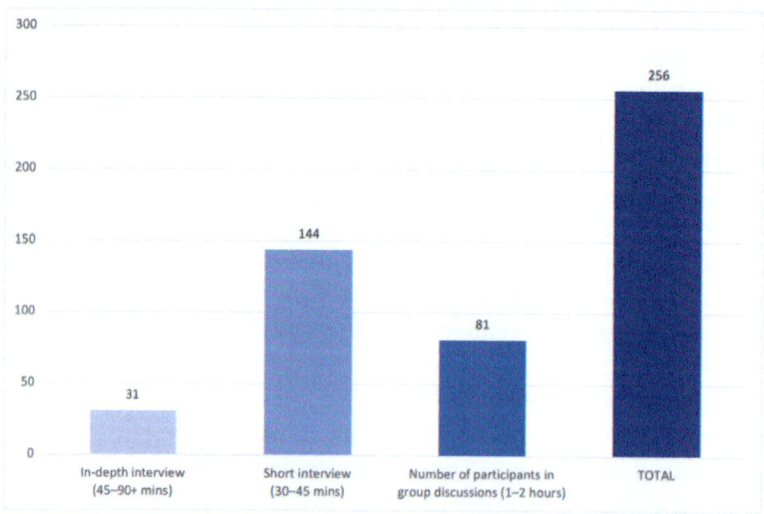

**Figure 3.4** Data points by research method for prosperity in east London.

Source: IGP, 2015

### 3.3.2 Research sites

The Olympic Park borders four London boroughs: Hackney, Newham, Tower Hamlets, and Waltham Forest. Most of the development related to the Olympic legacy has to date taken place in Hackney and Newham. Three small areas in these two London boroughs were selected as research sites: East Village and Stratford in Newham, and Hackney Wick in Hackney (Figure 3.5). Each research site has a different spatial and temporal relationship to the Olympic legacy regeneration programme: East Village is the first new Olympic neighbourhood; Hackney Wick is experiencing considerable residential and commercial development that is attracting new residents and businesses to the area (Hackney Council, 2012; Mayor of London, 2021). Regeneration in Stratford was underway before the Olympics (Westfield Stratford City shopping centre opened in 2011 and Stratford International Station in 2009) but the residential building in the area was accelerated by the Olympics (London Legacy Development Corporation, 2016).

The sites were chosen because they are illustrative of different 'types' of east London neighbourhood. East Village is a new, planned neighbourhood in the Olympic Park, broadly representative of development-led regeneration programmes that are attracting new residents to east London; Stratford and Hackney Wick are established neighbourhood centres with a mix of housing, commercial and public spaces. Hackney Wick has a strong identity as the artistic and creative centre of east

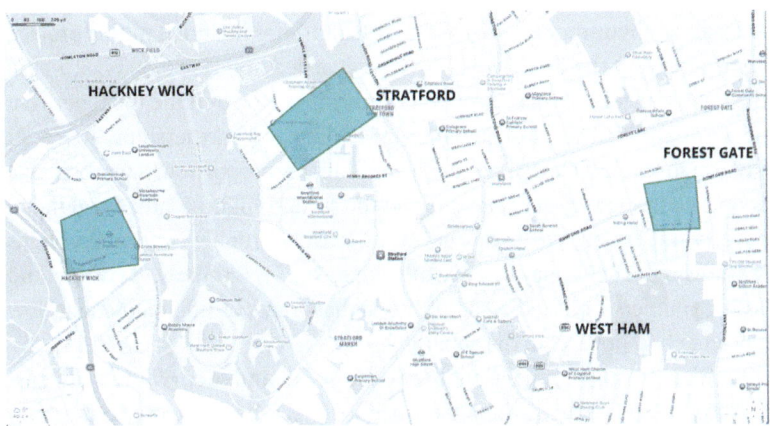

**Figure 3.5** Map of research sites for the prosperity in east London study.

Source: IGP, 2015

London. At the time of the research, the neighbourhood had more than 600 studios and the highest concentration of businesses in the Olympic Park legacy regeneration area.[3] Consequently, the area has distinct population groups: resident artists, employees in creative industries and the remaining light industries, boat dwellers who live on the canals, and people who do not identify as part of the creative or artistic communities living in other areas, including the Trowbridge Estate, one of the largest established areas of residential housing in the neighbourhood.

The three research sites are 'typical' of east London inasmuch as they are superdiverse, reflecting a diversification of diversity (Vertovec, 2007) in terms of ethnicity, country of origin, and a multiplicity of other significant variables, such as legal and socioeconomic status, that affect where and how people live together. These superdiverse communities experience high rates of population change, but they exist alongside long-established communities with more stable populations. 2011 Census data shows that 55 per cent of Newham's population were born outside the UK (Office for National Statistics, 2011), while population data published by Hackney Council shows that 89 different languages are spoken in the borough (Hackney Council Policy and Insight Team, 2019). Each neighbourhood research site has a long history of deprivation linked to processes of deindustrialisation and migration, and each is experiencing rapid social, economic and material changes associated with the Olympic legacy and wider processes of urban development. In 2015, at the time of this research, median household incomes were rising at the borough level, and deprivation levels were falling in Hackney and Newham. However, borough-level data obscures high rates of deprivation and disadvantage that are spatially concentrated in local neighbourhoods such as the research sites included in this project. For example, at the time the research was carried out, Hackney Wick was in the top 2 per cent of most deprived wards in London and the top 5 per cent of most deprived wards in England (LBH Policy and Partnerships, 2015). At a borough level Hackney had the second-highest proportion of working-age people claiming workless benefits and the second-highest rate of childhood poverty in London, yet it was one of the least affordable London boroughs for housing (LBH Policy and Partnerships, 2015). Similarly, Newham and Tower Hamlets reported some of the highest rates of unemployment, low pay and child poverty in the capital.

The strong connection between place and deprivation in east London provided the rationale for using a place-based research methodology rather than examining prosperity in relation to specific population cohorts or cultural groups. A small-area research site – approximately two Census Output Areas, or 250 households, the smallest statistical and administrative geography in England and Wales – was selected in each neighbourhood for the purpose of gathering highly localised data. The rationale for working in small geographical areas was that it would test the hypothesis that different neighbourhoods would have different 'prosperity narratives' that would require different forms of action. There is growing recognition that such localised approaches can help policy makers and citizens to engage effectively with context-specific social challenges such as the ways in which spatial concentrations of advantage and disadvantage intersect with and reinforce forms of inequality. This has become even more crucial for Covid recovery planning for places like Newham, where citizens experience multiple forms of deprivation which are often hidden in aggregate-level data that relates to London generally.

The next section presents empirical accounts of prosperity and focuses on the conceptual distinctions people make between the foundations of prosperity (the conditions that support the *possibility* of a good life) and the actions, practices and aspirations that constitute the lived experience of prosperity.

## 3.4 Prosperity in east London: 'living a good life'

> How can we have a prosperous life for everyone, people of all classes? The situation is precarious for people around here. The combination of unaffordable housing, zero-hours contracts, portfolio careers. ... People have no security. Jobs are not good-quality. ... This is a toxic mix.
>
> (Frances, in her fifties, a professional working in the voluntary sector, who has lived in Hackney for 20 years; interview, July 2015)

This extract from a lengthy conversation with Frances, a long-term resident who owns her Hackney home, articulates a connection between secure livelihoods and inclusion in processes of change and the social and economic life of the city that preoccupied the majority of research participants. When people were invited to discuss what prosperity means to them, and to identify the factors that are most important for their own prosperity, the most common responses were: a secure livelihood, understood as a combination of secure, regular and good-quality work that provides a reliable and adequate income; affordable, secure and good-quality housing in a safe neighbourhood; access to key public services such as childcare and transport; and social and economic inclusion. Livelihood

**Table 3.1** What does prosperity mean to you? Most common responses from research participants.

| | |
|---|---|
| 1 | A secure livelihood, meaning a combination of secure, regular and decent work that provides a reliable and adequate income; access to genuinely affordable housing; access to critical public services like childcare and schools; social, economic and digital inclusion |
| 2 | A good-quality of life, which includes a balance between work and time with family, choice and control, and security |
| 3 | The capacity to remain resident in neighbourhoods experiencing rapid social and economic transformation |
| 4 | Feeling part of the local community, maintaining good relations with neighbours and community cohesion |
| 5 | Having a place in the changes underway in east London, and feeling that local people are included in processes of change |
| 6 | Opportunities for education and self-development |
| 7 | A secure future for young people |
| 8 | Local businesses benefiting from investment in east London |
| 9 | Living in a healthy environment |
| 10 | Living in safe neighbourhoods, with a sense of security when walking at nights and low crime rates |

Source: IGP, 2015

security was the priority, followed by: the capacity to remain resident in neighbourhoods experiencing rapid social and economic transformation; feeling part of the local community; having a place in the changes underway in east London as individuals; feeling that other local people are included in processes of change; access to opportunities for education and self-development; a secure future for young people; knowing that other local people and local businesses benefited from investment in east London; and living in a healthy and safe environment (Table 3.1).

### 3.4.1 Foundations of prosperity

Material security and stability – described by research participants as a secure livelihood – are understood to be vitally important aspects of prosperity. Yet fewer than five people from the 256 accounts this analysis draws on defined prosperity solely in terms of material wealth or the pursuit of wealth. Instead, most people described how a secure livelihood is tightly interwoven with social ties and a broad sense of social and economic inclusion to provide the foundations for a prosperous life. Many individuals distinguished between the foundations for a prosperous life (material security, strong social support and feeling included in the social and economic life of the city), which were discussed as the basis upon which to build a prosperous life, and prosperity as the actions and practices that constitute living a good life, which include the ability to take up opportunities and the confidence to plan for the future.

Trevor, a long-term Stratford resident in his fifties, described this as the difference between 'getting by' and 'doing well'. From Trevor's perspective, having a secure livelihood and an affordable home in a neighbourhood where he had grown up and where he hoped his children would stay provided the basic building blocks for his family. Yet he, like other participants, made a distinction between the satisfaction of basic material and social needs and having the opportunities to 'do well':

> Doing well ... well you know, it's about living the good life ... about being able to choose the job you take – a decent job. Having time to do something in the community, spend time with family and friends, take a break, have a hobby, feel like you're part of what's going on. It's not just about money.

What Trevor describes is a model of prosperity that incorporates a multidimensional imaginary of the good life, which accounts for subjective, social and material conditions and aspirations, and at the same time reflects a dualistic interaction between the foundational conditions that provide the basis for a prosperous life and the opportunities to self-determine and pursue that vision of prosperity. This perspective, which was discussed by research participants of varying ages and social and cultural backgrounds (as the quotes below illustrate), is closely aligned with the concept of prosperity as an ethical project in pursuit of human flourishing and the good life. In contemporary Western thought this perspective is most commonly associated with Aristotle's ethics (Cassiers, 2014; S. A. White, 1992), in which prosperity is derived from states of being (happiness, pleasure, wellbeing, vitality), having (affluence and abundance from access to external material goods), and acting in the world (knowledge, honour and self-esteem originating from civic participation and social relationships) (Walker, 2015; Sardar, 2008; Appadurai, 2004).

> Now I have a family prosperity is about having a healthy, happy child and being healthy myself so I can look after my family. Before it was about me! My car, my phone ... now it's about good community.
> (David, late twenties, lives in Stratford; interview, September 2015)

> Prosperity is feeling safe, knowing your neighbours, having opportunities – London offers better opportunities than other places – and having time for family.
>
> (Maria, early thirties, lives with her partner and daughter in Hackney Wick; interview, September 2015)

> Prosperity is different for everyone but for me it means we can feel at home, the kids can grow and learn, we feel safe, and everyone in the community sort of feeds off each other.
>
> (Ben, early forties, lives with his wife and two children in Hackney; interview, September 2015)

A high proportion of participants felt they were living with multiple forms of insecurity and instability that undermined their opportunities, and those of neighbours and family, to prosper. When describing these conditions, research participants spoke of the localised effects of national and global forces that shape prosperity in ways people have little direct control over. Frances's reference to the 'toxic mix' of casualised labour and rapidly rising housing costs illustrates this point and captures the insecurity experienced by study participants from Hackney Wick. Prosperity in Hackney Wick, as Frances recognises, is shaped by connections to other places and to centres of power involving planning and policy decisions taken by central government, international investments in the UK property market, a globalised trend towards the casualisation of labour that shapes local job markets, and the presence of Europe's largest creative community, which attracts regeneration investment and a new and more affluent population to east London. In this context, opportunities and experiences of prosperity at the individual and neighbourhood levels are configured by the intersection between context-specific conditions – such as east London's post-industrial landscape, history of inward migration, and legacy of social housing provision – and social, economic and political forces operating at different scales (see Chapter 1). Individuals view their prosperity and that of neighbours and local communities through multiple lenses that connect people and places to wider economic and social systems.

### 3.4.2 Local prosperity narratives

Each neighbourhood had observably distinct prosperity narratives. People in Stratford spoke of insecurity in similar terms to those in

Hackney Wick, but they identified how young people in the neighbourhood are disproportionately affected by uncertainty. Insecure work and unaffordable housing make a future in the neighbourhood an unlikely prospect for young people. The possibility of being priced out of neighbourhoods they have grown up in also raises the possibility of losing access to local support networks.

Two prosperity narratives emerged from research in Hackney Wick, reflecting the distinct population groups in the neighbourhood. People who are part of the area's artistic and creative industries connected their feelings of prosperity to a strong sense of identity and belonging derived from the neighbourhood as a creative community with distinct social and economic practices, such as strong community support networks, circular and alternative economies, food growing, entrepreneurialism, and numerous active forms of civic participation. Hackney Wick's post-industrial urban fabric provides scope for fluid spatial practices, including temporary artist and performance space and live/work studios as common modes of dwelling. This group is concerned about neighbourhood regeneration displacing the artists and the creative community, but it also recognises the valuable contribution Hackney Wick's distinct creative identity offers the Olympic Park and is keen to have an active role in shaping decisions about planning, economic and cultural development. Consequently, community life and civic and democratic participation are aspects of prosperity important to people in Hackney Wick's creative communities, who expressed a degree of optimism about their place in future changes, because of their current levels of participation in decision making. People living in other areas of Hackney Wick did not share this optimism or the same sense of identity and belonging to the neighbourhood. Like people living in Stratford, they expressed anxieties about their current and future security and feelings of exclusion from processes of change.

Interviews with people living in East Village also identified a locally specific prosperity narrative, which is shaped in large part by the experience of living in a new community. While East Village residents recognise that the neighbourhood's high-quality environment contributes to their sense of prosperity, it is also widely acknowledged that they are choosing to pay high living costs in return for a good-quality of life. Mark lives with his wife and children in a townhouse. He describes himself as a serial entrepreneur who runs his own businesses and has established several community projects in East Village. Mark's home is classified as affordable housing, but, as he explains, the rent and management charges are high compared to other places he has lived in. He describes the choice to live in East Village as a 'prosperity trade-off':

> I feel like I'm living a prosperous life but it's not sustainable. Personally, it's hard to make it sustainable because I pay such a premium to live here ... If prosperity means saving for holidays and saving for a pension then it is not a prosperous place ... but if prosperity means a first-class education for the kids, healthy food, access to good places for health and wellbeing, somewhere safe ... then you can get on if you can afford to live here.
> (Interview, September 2015)

Mark's perspective is echoed by other people living in East Village, who explain that they are business owners and entrepreneurs, or in well-paid professional jobs, yet find it challenging to afford to live in the neighbourhood. Interviews with Luke and Will, both in their late twenties and living in private rented housing in East Village, reveal the variety of strategies they employ to cope with the costs of living, including subletting bedrooms, sometimes relocating to a neighbour's sofa to let an entire apartment on Airbnb, and in more extreme circumstances changing apartments as often as every six months to take advantage of discounted rental promotions. They describe these practices as widespread among friends and neighbours, who are motivated to trade affordability for the broad sense of prosperity and living well that East Village offers. The viability of this mode of dwelling is questionable for individuals and for the wider community: apart from the inconvenience of moving frequently, people who value the sense of neighbourliness and community in East Village feel it is threatened by a rapidly changing population. East Village is one of London's first large-scale, professionally managed, private-rented-sector (PRS) developments. Institutional PRS, as opposed to PRS offered by small-scale or individual landlords, was identified by the 2010 Coalition Government, and favoured by the then London Mayor Boris Johnson, as a means of improving the quality and security of rental housing in the capital and offering an alternative housing source for people priced out of home ownership. Over the past decade, institutional PRS, or build to rent (BTR), has become a feature of most large-scale new developments in London and the number of homes has grown consistently (Beswick, Imilan & Olivera, 2019). Newham and Tower Hamlets have the highest and third-highest numbers of BTR schemes of all London boroughs. However, the accounts presented here reflect wider challenges experienced by residents living in large-scale new PRS developments, including affordability of housing and centrally provided utilities and management costs (Woodcraft, 2016). Lucy, an East Village resident in her late twenties and an advocate of the high quality of living, sums up the challenge: 'We are buying into a prosperous lifestyle that can't be sustained. It's great but no one still expects to be here in two years' time.'

## 3.5 Local meanings = sticky measures

The perspectives presented in this chapter challenge the orthodox definition of prosperity as material wealth. Furthermore, they demonstrate that prosperity is more than an aggregate of individual wellbeing and individual wealth (Beinhocker & Hanauer, 2014). Wellbeing, as other authors argue (S. C. White, 2015; Gasper, 2010), has come to be defined predominantly as a subjective and psychological state for which individuals are primarily responsible. While it is evident that prosperity has subjective dimensions, the accounts in this chapter demonstrate that prosperity – as outlined in Chapter 1 – connects the individual to known and unknown others through social, political, economic and ecological frameworks and intergenerational obligations that operate on dramatically different scales and temporalities. Visions of what constitutes prosperity and a good life are bound up with the lives, histories and futures of others, and thus bear in material ways on the question of equality within and between societies, for example relationships between individual aspirations and societal needs, prosperity in the present as opposed to that of future generations, and associations between human and ecological systems. Prosperity is better understood as an ethical project that is multidimensional, relational and multiscalar. This observation is significant in expanding the conceptual boundaries of prosperity and delineating between wellbeing as individual and subjective, and prosperity as a multiscalar, relational and collective concept.

These insights demonstrate the importance of new empirical work as the basis for theorising prosperity and raise several implications for both research and policy making. Foremost is the importance of bringing an ethics of diversity to efforts to conceptualise and theorise prosperity, which in turn means that a diversity of pathways to prosperity must also be recognised (Leach et al., 2013). Policies, interventions and investments intent on creating prosperity will change fundamentally if prosperity is recognised as diverse and multiple and approached as a dynamic relation between people and places that takes multiple forms. For this reason, the institutions, public policy frameworks, economic models and investment strategies designed to pursue prosperity, and the metrics used to measure prosperity, need to pay closer attention to situated understandings of prosperity, in terms of what it means and how local outcomes are dynamically shaped by both systemic and locally specific factors.

As other authors have argued in relation to poverty, wellbeing and quality of life (Quick, 2015; Van Staveren et al., 2014; Giuntoli et al., 2014; Satterthwaite & Mitlin, 2014; Satterthwaite, 2003), situated, multidimensional prosperity models must be developed in partnership with local communities. Acknowledging local perspectives that are situated in real-world conditions and constraints will enable policy makers to pay attention to the processes and conditions that enable or inhibit prosperity even when they challenge established ways of thinking. As this research demonstrates, interrogating prosperity as a lived experience through a place-based lens reveals the disconnect between standard prosperity indicators that guide policy making (such as GDP, household income, job growth and employment) and the unintended consequences they create. Indicators are powerful technologies of governance and the wrong measures can lead to misguided policy with high social and economic costs, as Stiglitz, Sen and Fitoussi identify: 'In the quest to increase GDP, we may end up with a society in which citizens are worse off' (2010: xvii). Such an outcome is evident in east London, where gross value added (GVA), household incomes and workforce job growth rose steadily in the years before the Covid pandemic (GLA Economics, 2018). Employment levels reached a new record high of 75 per cent pre-Covid (GLA Economics, 2018), yet in-work poverty, child poverty and income inequality were also increasing. What appears to be rising prosperity in conventional terms is not translating into rising prosperity in local terms. As the experiences and perspectives presented here indicate, people in Hackney Wick and Stratford describe growing pressures from insecure and low-wage work, and residents in each of the three neighbourhoods are affected by rising housing costs, factors that together are putting individuals and communities under considerable stress.

Public confidence and trust in government are casualties of policy making based on indicators that do not resonate with lived experience (Whitby et al., 2014). Deteriorating trust in government is a global trend. In Britain, the proportion of people who say they trust governments 'to place the needs of the nation above the interests of their own political party' declined from 38 per cent in 1986 to 18 per cent in 2013 (NatCen, 2013), and levels of trust in the government remained low throughout 2020 and the Covid-19 pandemic (Davies et al., 2021). In fact, trust in government has diminished in OECD countries since the 2008 financial crisis (OECD, 2017). The OECD calls for greater transparency, more open and inclusive policy-making processes, and more attention to be paid to citizens' perceptions of fairness in decision making as part of efforts to rebuild trust in government (OECD, 2017). It is critical, therefore, that as government attention is focused on 'levelling up' and achieving prosperity for people around the UK, local communities have a voice in identifying what prosperity means in different contexts, shaping targeted responses that support local needs and aspirations, and monitoring progress towards these visions. In this context, 'sticky measures' – prosperity indicators that capture the things that matter in ways that are meaningful and allow for action – will have a crucial role in enabling communities to hold decision makers to account.

## 3.6 Prototyping a new form of citizen-led prosperity index

How do policy decisions change when prosperity measures are co-designed with citizens to reflect lived experience rather than by experts working with universal concepts and frameworks? In this section, we describe the process of working with citizen scientists to translate qualitative research into a conceptual model that represents the factors that support prosperity, and using this model as the basis for developing a new prosperity index. The goal of the prosperity index is to measure what matters for local communities using metrics that meaningfully represent local conditions and aspirations in a way that allows robust measurement and comparison at a hyper-local geography. Furthermore, the goal was to construct an index based mainly on primary survey data collected for the purpose of elucidating local differences in prosperity, rather than aggregate secondary data sources, such as are commonly used in wellbeing indices.

The first step was to translate qualitative research into a conceptual prosperity model. Thematic data was clustered to produce general categories of experience and understanding. Analysis identified 15 categories that participants in all research sites – to varying degrees – described as essential or important to their prosperity and that of their families, neighbours, friends and wider communities (Table 3.2). The 15 categories were organised around five domains and 15 subdomains to reflect the way participants had described interdependencies and overlaps between different aspects of prosperity to produce a prosperity model with five high-level dimensions (see Figure 1.1). This mode of organising the data breaks down the artificial distinctions between social, economic and environmental domains of life that often characterise approaches to public policy.

**Table 3.2** Categorisation of factors that are essential/important for a prosperous life in east London.

| What does prosperity mean? | Explanations from Prosperity in east London pilot study data |
| --- | --- |
| Good-quality and secure jobs | A secure livelihood – secure and well-paid work; work satisfaction; equality at work; scope for career progression; work/life balance; feeling part of the economic life of the neighbourhood/city. |
| Household security and affordability | Secure, affordable and good-quality housing; a mix of housing tenures; likelihood of being able to stay in the neighbourhood; living without financial stress. |
| Inclusion and fairness | Social, financial and digital inclusion; economic fairness; ability to access services, work and education; feeling included and safe in the neighbourhood; access to local support networks and care; feeling part of the economic life of the neighbourhood/city. |
| Local value creation | Strong and inclusive local economies; opportunities for local organisations, businesses and neighbourhoods to share in value generated by wider processes of change; alternative economic models, sharing and circular economies. |
| Healthy bodies and healthy minds | Mental, physical and social health; access to health and care services; access to informal support and care; local support networks; access to open space; civic participation; life satisfaction; personal safety. |
| Healthy, safe and secure neighbourhoods | Decent and secure housing; clean air; safe streets and neighbourhoods; road safety; community safety; access to open and green space. |
| Childhood and adolescence | Early childhood development support; affordable childcare; good-quality education; childhood and adolescent wellbeing and health; support for adolescent transitions; pathways to work, education and training for young people. |
| Good-quality basic education | Access to good-quality basic education for children and young people; informal and community learning; access to space, sports and culture. |
| Lifelong learning | Opportunities for formal and informal lifelong learning for children, young people, adults and older people; volunteering and community participation. |
| Autonomy and freedom | Secure personal freedoms and equalities; access to opportunities; time and space to try new things; work/life balance; lifelong learning and personal development. |

**Table 3.2** (continued)

| What does prosperity mean? | Explanations from Prosperity in east London pilot study data |
|---|---|
| Social relationships | Feeling included in society and social life of the community; time to spend with family and friends; connections with neighbours; involvement in interest groups; access to local support networks. |
| Sense of community | Feeling a sense of belonging to local community; neighbours to talk to; access to support networks in the neighbourhood; feeling pride in the neighbourhood; community safety; feeling people will support each other in times of need. |
| Identities and culture | Feeling secure with cultural, ethnic, religious, personal identities in the neighbourhood; opportunities to participate in the cultural life of the area and to pursue participation in cultural and religious activities; feeling part of the cultural life of the community. |
| Political inclusion | Right to political participation and political representation; feelings of inclusion in political decision making. |
| Voice and influence | Opportunities to influence local decision making; feeling like participation makes a difference; opportunities to make a productive contribution to future of local communities. |

Source: IGP, 2016.

The second step was to identify a robust indicator set that offered the closest fit to the conceptual model and, where possible, to identify indicators and comparative data that could be used to benchmark new survey data about neighbourhood-level prosperity against the average for London. Thirty-two composite indicators, based on 67 metrics, were identified.[4] Of these 67 metrics, 38 are based on new household survey data, and the remaining 29 are constructed from secondary data sources.

The third step was to collect new survey data and construct a prototype prosperity index. Survey data was collected in five neighbourhoods: two of the small-area research sites from the qualitative research stage (Hackney Wick and East Village) and a further three areas undergoing regeneration (Canning Town in Newham, Coventry Cross Estate in Tower Hamlets, and Heath in Dagenham). A random sampling method was used to survey a third of households in each research site. In total, 750 surveys were completed, based on 15-minute face-to-face interviews in June, July and August 2017.

## 3.7 Prosperity Index 2017: headline findings

IGP developed a five-step process to analyse the household survey data and construct a prosperity index, reporting on how well each local area was faring in relation to community priorities. Survey results were standardised to generate composite indicator- and domain-level 'prosperity scores', which were presented on a simple 0 to 10 scale with five-colour red-amber-dark green-light green-yellow colour coding. On the 10-point scale 0 is the worst possible score, 10 is the best possible score, and 5 is the average for London (see Table 3.3).

In the remainder of this section, we draw out some of the headline findings from the 2017 Prosperity Index to give concrete examples of how

Table 3.3  Prosperity Index Dashboard: Foundations of Prosperity Domain.

| DOMAIN 1: FOUNDATIONS OF PROPERITY | OLYMPIC PARK | HACKNEY WICK | HEATH | CANNING TOWN | COVENTRY CROSS |
|---|---|---|---|---|---|
| SUB-DOMAIN 1: GOOD-QUALITY & SECURE JOBS | | | | | |
| Good Jobs | 5.22 | 4.43 | 4.32 | 4.48 | 3.96 |
| Work–Life Balance | 7.01 | 5.35 | 4.01 | 6.60 | 4.34 |
| Commuting | 5.03 | 4.39 | 5.20 | 5.15 | 5.75 |
| SUB-DOMAIN 2: HOUSEHOLD SECURITY & HOUSING AFFORDABILITY | | | | | |
| Real Disposable Household Income | 2.05 | 2.80 | 2.24 | 1.68 | 2.05 |
| Housing Affordability | 4.31 | 3.84 | 3.26 | 1.99 | 0.88 |
| Financial Stress | 6.53 | 5.07 | 8.63 | 7.99 | 8.00 |
| Feeling Secure about the Future | 0.00 | 4.37 | 6.44 | 5.36 | 5.69 |
| SUB-DOMAIN 3: INCLUSION & FAIRNESS | | | | | |
| Access to Financial Services | 6.58 | 6.71 | 7.64 | 6.71 | 7.64 |
| Digital Inclusion | 5.21 | 4.01 | 3.04 | 2.70 | 3.47 |
| Local Income Inequality | 6.35 | 6.77 | 6.91 | 6.35 | 4.87 |

Source: Woodcraft & Anderson, 2019.

'sticky measures' reflecting local priorities and lived experiences offer a different kind of policy-relevant knowledge for action on prosperity. Given the importance people attach to livelihood security as the foundation of a prosperous life, we discuss two composite indicators reporting on factors that underpin a secure livelihood: good-quality and secure work, and household security and housing affordability (see Chapter 4 for more on secure livelihoods). Livelihood security concerns have come to the fore since the data presented here was collected in 2017. At the time of revising and updating this chapter, the UK is experiencing a cost-of-living crisis linked to spiralling energy costs caused by the war in Ukraine and the ongoing effects of Brexit and Covid. The current conditions reinforce the need to align the goals and measures of policy with the lived experiences of citizens who are devising ever more complex strategies to cope with rising costs, in-work poverty, and food and energy insecurity. A key insight from this research is that policy makers should shift away from income growth and employment as key measures of prosperity and adopt livelihood security as the measure of policy success, taking account of the complex intersections between work, income, housing and key public services that people rely on to make a living, and acknowledging the decoupling of employment and living standards, which is obscured by a focus on job growth (see Chapter 4 for a full discussion of IGP's reconceptualisation of livelihood security).

### 3.7.1 Good-quality and secure work

Good-quality and secure work are important components of a secure livelihood. The new Good Jobs indicator in the Prosperity Index reports on the quality and security of work, not solely on employment rates. Quality and security are examined by measuring whether pay and income levels are sufficient for living in London (using the Minimum Income Standard), and whether people who are self-employed or on temporary contracts have chosen these forms of employment.

Four of the five Prosperity Index research sites are ranked below the Greater London average for Good Jobs (see Table 3.3). Ten per cent of those in work were either on temporary contracts or listed as self-employed. Of these, two thirds (65 per cent) reported not being in this type of employment by preference. Qualitative research carried out by citizen scientists at the same time as the household survey found that access to good-quality job opportunities is an issue, in particular for young people and for middle-aged men from working-class backgrounds. Research participants felt that formal pathways to training and education in neighbourhoods like Hackney Wick led to low-paid work with limited opportunities for development. People in Canning Town, Hackney Wick and Coventry Cross acknowledged that major new employers are coming to east London, offering new types of employment in creative industries, technology and financial services. Yet people currently of working age are uncertain how to access new job markets, while young people from these neighbourhoods feel unprepared for both new types of job and how the nature of work is changing.

### 3.7.2 Household security and housing affordability

This composite indicator reports on a new measure of real household disposable income (RHDI), developed from qualitative research that identifies the essential living costs people must meet (Woodcraft & Anderson, 2019), and measures of housing affordability, financial stress, and feelings of security about the future. Two of these metrics – RHDI and housing affordability – are ranked in the Prosperity Index well below the Greater London average for all five sites (see Table 3.3). In all five research sites, 25–30 per cent of respondents reported having less than £200 per month income remaining after taxes, housing costs, utilities and debt repayments. Median RHDI across the five sites was in the £400–499 range, while our analysis, based on data from the Labour Force Survey, shows the London median to be approximately £1,230.

The hyper-local approach to data collection provides new insights into the distribution of income, housing costs and financial stress. For example, East Village in the Olympic Park, which is a new neighbourhood of housing to rent, both private and affordable, has the highest proportion of survey respondents in any type of employment and the highest gross incomes of the five Prosperity Index research sites. Yet the new measure of RHDI shows that households in East Village have some of the lowest levels of disposable income. Qualitative research by the citizen scientists shows that East Village residents attribute this to high housing costs and associated charges, such as estate management fees. In the Coventry Cross research site, 100 per cent of the households surveyed reported incomes lower than the Minimum Income Standard for Inner London, the benchmark used to set the Living Wage and the London Living Wage, which are based on what the public consider to be the minimum income needed to live a socially acceptable life. The median annual household income in the Coventry Cross site was reported as £7,500–9,499.

### 3.7.3 Local social networks are bearing the burden of insecurity

Qualitative research carried out by citizen scientists alongside the Prosperity Index survey identified the crucial role that local social networks – family, friends, neighbours – play in helping people to cope with insecurity. Residents in Canning Town described how neighbours and friends provide informal childcare to enable people employed on zero-hours contracts to take up shifts, and how informal and community-led savings networks operate in the neighbourhood to give people access to financial services. Similar perspectives on the importance of local social networks were discussed in Hackney Wick and Coventry Cross. This picture was reinforced during the Covid pandemic, with neighbourhood-based networks stepping in to fill gaps in public service provision: distributing food, collecting medicines, and checking on elderly and vulnerable neighbours.

The Prosperity Index shows how people in all five sites feel there are strong social networks to draw on and that communities are cohesive, levels of trust are high, and people from different backgrounds get along. However, qualitative research indicates that local social networks are bearing the burden of providing informal support as people live with insecurity. The Prosperity Index shows that sites which reported higher social capital also presented lower levels of financial stress and higher subjective wellbeing than those with lower social capital, despite having similar levels of disposable income. Community networks also provide important social and emotional 'protections' in neighbourhoods that are affected by changes in the economy and disruptions to local social and economic life related to urban development. Strong social networks are a critical protective factor for local prosperity but are under increasing strain after a decade of austerity and disinvestment in local public services and resources such as youth clubs and community and voluntary organisations.

This finding has important consequences for how the dynamics of interaction between individuals, communities and public authorities are understood. Since the late 1990s, the development of local social capital and the enhancement of the collective capacity of communities have been policy priorities under the guise of various urban renewal programmes and now localism. Consequently, local social capital and civic action have become proxies for the 'sustainability' and 'health' of communities (Woodcraft & Anderson, 2019). Measures of local social capital are widely used to inform decision making at the local and national levels for a range of policy domains including community safety, planning and health. IGP has included these standard measures in the Prosperity Index, and all five sites report levels of social capital and wellbeing that are above the London average. However, taking a citizen-led approach to measuring what supports prosperity and what inhibits it reveals the pressure that local communities in east London are experiencing, which conventional indicators disguise.

## 3.8 Conclusion

Taking east London as a case, this chapter demonstrates that locating prosperity as a lived experience in a specific place and time reveals something of the real-world dynamics that create opportunities and constraints to be negotiated as people pursue pathways to prosperity. New empirical data offers conceptual and theoretical insights with significance for research and policy making. This research has shown that prosperity is diverse, multidimensional and multiscalar, characteristics that are significant if prosperity as a national goal is to be coherently and concretely linked to local solutions and theorising by communities, politicians, policy makers and business leaders. Prosperity understood as the pursuit of a good life – a secure livelihood, good-quality work, functioning public services, choice, opportunity, political freedoms, intergenerational justice – is not captured by universal models and frameworks that generate the kind of aggregate data currently available to policy makers. This research demonstrates that taking a holistic, citizen-led approach to theorising and measuring prosperity reveals critical stress points that undermine the capacity of local communities to develop new and alternative pathways for action on prosperity. It is evident, however, that developing visions of prosperity with and for communities, and mapping out pathways to achieving those visions, will bridge the gap between expert-led knowledge and lived experience in ways that are likely to spotlight particular issues and help promote policy change and the accountability of local and national governments. As an increasingly important public issue, 'building back better' 'post-Covid', and mapping, shaping and monitoring pathways to prosperity, should be explored through active deliberation and co-production of knowledge with citizens, as well as renewed academic theorising (Drews & van den Bergh, 2016). Acknowledging that prosperity is diverse and multiple means that how prosperity is defined matters less than which deliberative methods are used to uncover its context-specific meanings.

## Notes

1. A notable exception is Fischer's (2014) ethnographic work exploring how localised notions of the good life shape individual consumption practices and wellbeing in Germany, Guatemala and the United States.
2. London's Olympic host boroughs are Newham, Tower Hamlets, Hackney, Waltham Forest, Barking and Dagenham, and Greenwich. After the Olympic Games the host boroughs were renamed growth boroughs.
3. Hackney Wick contains 448 businesses, 213 of which are in the arts and culture sector, which equates to 98 per cent of all businesses in the arts and culture sector in the Legacy Corporation's development area (London Legacy Development Corporation, 2015).
4. A detailed discussion of the method for selecting indicators and constructing the Prosperity Index can be found in IGP, 2017 (Anderson, 2018; Woodcraft & Anderson, 2019).

## Bibliography

Anderson, B. (2018). Summary of methodology and description of indicators. London: Institute for Global Prosperity. Available at: https://static1.squarespace.com/static/5a0c05169f07f51c64a336a2/t/5d03c68d9c77990001fed537/1560528527980/PIPW_2017_Report_online_ba_140619_update.pdf (accessed 17 December 2022).

Appadurai, A. (2004). The capacity to aspire: Culture and the terms of recognition. In V. Rao & M. Walton (eds), *Culture and Public Action*, pp. 59–84. Stanford, CA: Stanford University Press.

Beinhocker, E. & Hanauer, N. (2014). Redefining capitalism. *McKinsey Quarterly*, 1 September. Available at: https://www.mckinsey.com/featured-insights/long-term-capitalism/redefining-capitalism (accessed 17 December 2022).

Beswick, J., Imilan, W. & Olivera, P. (2019). Access to housing in the neoliberal era: A new comparativist analysis of the neoliberalisation of access to housing in Santiago and London. *International Journal of Housing Policy*, 19(3): 288–310. https://doi.org/10.1080/19491247.2018.1501256.

Business, Energy and Industrial Strategy (2017). *Industrial Strategy: Building a Britain fit for the future*. London: HM Government.

Business, Energy and Industrial Strategy (2018). Local industrial strategies: Policy prospectus. London: HM Government. https://www.gov.uk/government/publications/local-industrial-strategies-policy-prospectus (accessed 17 December 2022).

Cassiers, I. (2014). *Redefining Prosperity*. New York: Routledge.

Dabla-Norris, E., Kochhar, K., Suphaphiphat, N., Ricka, F. & Tsounta, E. (2015). Causes and consequences of income inequality: A global perspective. IMF Staff Discussion Note SDN/15/13. IMF. Available at: https://www.imf.org/en/Publications/Staff-Discussion-Notes/Issues/2016/12/31/Causes-and-Consequences-of-Income-Inequality-A-Global-Perspective-42986 (accessed 17 December 2022).

Davies, B., Lalot, F., Peitz, L., Heering, M. S., Ozkecei, H., Babian, J., Hayon, K. D., Broadwood, J. & Abrams, D. (2021). Changes in political trust in Britain during the COVID-19 pandemic in 2020: Integrated public opinion evidence and implications. *Humanities and Social Sciences Communications*, 8, 166. Available at: https://doi.org/10.1057/s41599-021-00850-6 (accessed 17 December 2022).

Drews, S. & van den Bergh, J. C. J. M. (2016). Public views on economic growth, the environment and prosperity: Results of a questionnaire survey. *Global Environmental Change*, 39, 1–14. https://doi.org/10.1016/j.gloenvcha.2016.04.001.

Fioramonti, L. (2017). *The World after GDP: Politics, business and society in the post growth era*. New York: Wiley.

Fischer, E. F. (2014). *The Good Life: Aspiration, dignity, and the anthropology of wellbeing*. Stanford, CA: Stanford University Press.

Gasper, D. (2010). Understanding the diversity of conceptions of well-being and quality of life. *Journal of Socio-economics* 39(3), 351–60.

Giuntoli, G., Mitchell, B., Sullivan, G. Devins, D. & South, J. (2014). Well-being and poverty. In *Reducing Poverty in the UK: A collection of evidence reviews*, pp. 41–5. York: Joseph Rowntree Foundation.

GLA (2015). GLA household income estimates for small areas (July 2015). Greater London Authority. Available at: https://data.london.gov.uk/dataset/household-income-estimates-small-areas (accessed 17 December 2022).

GLA Economics (2018). *London's Economic Outlook: Spring 2018*. Greater London Authority. Available at: https://www.london.gov.uk/sites/default/files/leo-spring-2018.pdf (accessed 17 December 2022).

GLA Economics (2021). COVID-19 and London's economy: Impacts and economic outlook. Greater London Authority. Available at: https://data.london.gov.uk/dataset/covid-19-and-london-s-economy---impacts-and-economic-outlook (accessed 17 December 2022).

Growth Borough Partnership (n.d.). Convergence framework. http://www.growthboroughs.com/convergence (accessed 17 December 2022).

Guest, G., MacQueen, K. M. & Namey, E. E. (2012). *Applied Thematic Analysis*. Thousand Oaks, CA: SAGE.

Hackney Council (2012). Local Development Framework: Hackney Wick area action plan. Available at: https://www.queenelizabetholympicpark.co.uk/-/media/lldc/planning/cil-09-hackney_wick_area_action_plan_a4_web.ashx?la=en (accessed 17 December 2022).

Hackney Council Policy and Insight Team (2019). Facts & figures leaflet, September. Hackney Council. Available at: https://drive.google.com/file/d/1_KsPGfaHANgewA3YMsmUEyU3H hYzHatX/view (accessed 15 September 2022).

HM Treasury (2021). *Build Back Better: Our plan for growth*. Available at: https://assets.publishing. service.gov.uk/government/uploads/system/uploads/attachment_data/file/969275/PfG_ Final_print_Plan_for_Growth_Print.pdf (accessed 17 December 2022).

Jackson, T. (2017). *Prosperity without Growth: Foundations for the economy of tomorrow*. Abingdon: Routledge.

LBH Policy and Partnerships (2015). Hackney Wick ward profile. London Borough of Hackney. Available at: https://hackney.gov.uk/media/2685/Hackney-Wick-ward-profile/pdf/hackney-wick-ward-profile.pdf?m=635882805259830000 (accessed 17 December 2022).

Leach, M., Raworth, K. & Rockström, J. (2013). Between social and planetary boundaries: Navigating pathways in the safe and just space for humanity, in ISSC & UNESCO (eds), *World Social Science Report 2013: Changing global environments*, 84–9. Paris: OECD Publishing and UNESCO Publishing. https://doi.org/10.1787/9789264203419-10-en.

Lees, L. & White, H. (2020). The social cleansing of London council estates: Everyday experiences of 'accumulative dispossession'. Housing Studies, 35(10), 1701–1722.

Lees, L., Slater, T., & Wyly, E. (2013). Gentrification. Abingdon: Routledge. https://doi.org/ 10.1080/02673037.2019.1680814.

Legatum Institute (2022). The United Kingdom Prosperity Index 2022. Available at: https:// li.com/reports/uk-prosperity-index-2022/ (accessed 17 December 2022).

London Councils (2021). Almost 'one in ten' Londoners to be unemployed by December. Press release. Available at: https://www.londoncouncils.gov.uk/press-release/19-march-2021/almost-%E2%80%98one-ten%E2%80%99-londoners-be-unemployed-december (accessed 17 December 2022).

London Legacy Development Corporation (2015). Hackney Wick Neighbourhood Centre: Local history and heritage. Available at: https://www.queenelizabetholympicpark.co.uk/~/media/lldc/hackney%20wick%20consultation/hackney%20wick%20masterplan%20% 20exhibition%20boards%20(812).pdf (accessed 17 December 2022).

London Legacy Development Corporation (2016). Ten Year Plan 2015/16–2024/25: Draft for board. Available at: https://www.london.gov.uk/moderngovlldc/documents/s55725/ Item22a-Appendix1-TenYearPlan.pdf (accessed 17 December 2022).

London Prosperity Board (2021). *London Prosperity Board*. Available at: https://london prosperityboard.org (accessed 17 December 2022).

MacRury, I. & Poynter, G. (2009). London's Olympic Legacy: A 'thinkpiece' report prepared for the OECD and Department for Communities and Local Government. London East Research Institute, University of East London.

Mayor of London (n.d.). Convergence framework and action plan 2011–2015. Available at: https:// www.london.gov.uk/sites/default/files/gla_migrate_files_destination/Convergence% 20action%20plan%202011-2015.pdf (accessed 17 December 2022).

Mayor of London (2021). Mayor to invest nearly £3m in Creative Enterprise Zones. Press release. Available at: https://www.london.gov.uk/press-releases/mayoral/mayor-to-invest-nearly-3m-in-creative-enterprise (accessed 17 December 2022).

Moore, H. L. (2015). Global prosperity and sustainable development goals. *Journal of International Development*, 27(6), 801–15. https://doi.org/10.1002/jid.3114.

Moore, H. L. & Collins, H. (2020). Towards prosperity: Reinvigorating local economies through Universal Basic Services. Working Paper 01-2020/04. London: Institute for Global Prosperity. https://discovery.ucl.ac.uk/id/eprint/10096789/8/Moore_Towards%20Prosperity_With%20DOI.pdf (accessed 17 December 2022).

Moore, H. L. & Collins, H. (2021). Assembling prosperity in a post-Covid United Kingdom: New approaches to levelling up. Institute for Global Prosperity, London. Available at: https://discovery.ucl.ac.uk/id/eprint/10131207/ (accessed 18 December 2022).

Moore, H. L. & Woodcraft, S. (2019). Understanding prosperity in east London: Local meanings and 'sticky' measures of the good life. *City & Society*, 31(2), 275–98. https://doi.org/10.1111/ciso.12208.

NatCen (2013). British Social Attitudes. 30th edn. Available at: http://www.bsa.natcen.ac.uk/latest-report/british-social-attitudes-30/key-findings/trust-politics-and-institutions.aspx (accessed 18 December 2022).

OECD (2014). Using well-being indicators for policy making: Region of the North of the Netherlands. Available at: http://www.oecd.org/regional/regional-policy/NORTH-OF-THE-NETHERLANDS-CASE-STUDY.pdf (accessed 18 December 2022).

OECD (2017). *Trust and Public Policy: How better governance can help rebuild public trust*. Paris: OECD Publishing. Available at: http://www.oecd.org/gov/trust-and-public-policy-9789264268920-en.htm (accessed 18 December 2022).

OECD (2020). *How's Life? 2020: Measuring well-being*. Paris: OECD Publishing. Available at: https://read.oecd-ilibrary.org/economics/how-s-life/volume-/issue-_9870c393-en#page1.

OECD (n.d.). *Better Life Index*. Available at: www.oecdbetterlifeindex.org/#/11111111111 (accessed 18 December 2022).

Office for National Statistics (2011). 2011 Census Data. Available at: www.ons.gov.uk/census/2011census/2011censusdata (accessed 18 December 2022).

Olympic Park Legacy Company (2011). Legacy Communities Scheme Planning Application. London Legacy Development Corporation. Web APAS (Planning Application Reference 11/90621/OUTODA). Available at: http://planningregister.londonlegacy.co.uk/swift/MediaTemp/3697-54923.pdf (accessed 23 February 2023).

Ostry, J. D., Loungani, P. & Furceri, D. (2016). Neoliberalism: Oversold? *Finance & Development*, June, 38–41. Available at: www.imf.org/external/pubs/ft/fandd/2016/06/pdf/ostry.pdf (accessed 18 December 2022).

Philipsen, D. (2017). *The Little Big Number: How GDP came to rule the world and what to do about it*. Princeton, NJ: Princeton University Press.

Quick, A. (2015). *Inequalities in Wellbeing: Challenges and opportunities for research and policy*. London: New Economics Foundation. Available at: https://kipdf.com/inequalities-in-wellbeing-challenges-and-opportunities-for-research-and-policy_5ab7736e1723dd349c81e3f8.html (accessed 23 February 2023).

Raworth, K. (2017). *Doughnut Economics: Seven ways to think like a 21st-century economist*. London: Cornerstone.

Sardar, Z. (2008). *Prosperity: A transmodern analysis*. Sustainable Development Commission. Available at: https://www.researchgate.net/profile/Ziauddin-Sardar/publication/265067017_Prosperity_A_Transmodern_Analysis/links/5704f10508ae74a08e26d92b/Prosperity-A-Transmodern-Analysis.pdf (accessed 23 February 2023).

Satterthwaite, D. (2003). The Millennium Development Goals and urban poverty reduction: Great expectations and nonsense statistics. *Environment and Urbanization* 15(2), 179–90. https://doi.org/0.1177/095624780301500208.

Satterthwaite, D. & Mitlin, D. (2014). *Reducing Urban Poverty in the Global South*. Abingdon: Routledge.

Social Progress Imperative (2018). 2018 Social Progress Index. Social Progress Imperative. Available at: www.socialprogress.org/static/5c19047de09c3db175c3ffed4ff82b86/2018-social-progress-index-exec-summary.pdf (accessed 23 February 2023).

Spence, M. & Leipziger, D. (eds) (2010). *Globalization and Growth: Implications for a post-crisis world*. Washington, DC: World Bank on behalf of the Commission on Growth and

Development. Available at: https://documents1.worldbank.org/curated/en/180311468174918324/pdf/Globalization-and-growth-implications-for-a-post-crisis-world.pdf (accessed 23 February 2023).

Stiglitz, J. E. (2011). Rethinking macroeconomics: What failed, and how to repair it. *Journal of the European Economic Association*, 9(4), 591–645. https://doi.org/10.1111/j.1542-4774.2011.01030.x.

Stiglitz, J. E., Sen, A. & Fitoussi, J. P. (2010). *Mismeasuring Our Lives: Why GDP doesn't add up*. New York: New Press.

Tomaney, J. & Pike, A. (2020). Levelling up? *Political Quarterly*, 91(1), 43–8. https://doi.org/10.1111/1467-923X.12834.

Van Staveren, I., Webbink, E., de Haan, A. & Foa, R. (2014). The last mile in analyzing wellbeing and poverty: Indices of social development. *Forum for Social Economics*, 43(1), 8–26. https://doi.org/10.1080/07360932.2013.780980.

Vertovec, S. (2007). Super-diversity and its implications. *Ethnic and Racial Studies* 30(6): 1024–54. http://dx.doi.org/10.1080/01419870701599465.

Walker, L. S. (ed.) (2015). *The Good Life and the Greater Good in a Global Context*. Lanham, MD: Lexington Books.

What Works Centre for Local Economic Growth (2015). Estate Renewal – Full Review. Available at: https://whatworksgrowth.org/resource-library/estate-renewal/ (accessed 23 February 2023).

Whitby, A., Seaford, C. & Berry, C. (2014). BRAINPOoL project final report. Beyond GDP: From measurement to politics and policy. World Future Council. Available at: https://www.worldfuturecouncil.org/wp-content/uploads/2016/01/BRAINPOoL_2014_Beyond-GDP_From_Measurement_to_Politics_and_Policy.pdf (accessed 18 December 2022).

White, S. A. (1992). *Sovereign Virtue: Aristotle on the relation between happiness and prosperity*. Stanford, CA: Stanford University Press.

White, S. C. (2015). Relational wellbeing: A theoretical and operational approach. Bath Papers in International Development and Wellbeing, Working Paper no. 43. Centre for Development Studies, University of Bath. Available at: https://www.econstor.eu/bitstream/10419/128138/1/bpd43.pdf (accessed 18 December 2022).

Woodcraft, S. (2016). *Life in East Village*. IGP Working Paper. London: Institute for Global Prosperity.

Woodcraft, S. & Anderson, B. (2019). *Rethinking Prosperity for London: When citizens lead transformation*. London: Institute for Global Prosperity. Available at: https://static1.squarespace.com/static/5a0c05169f07f51c64a336a2/t/5d03c62b56b1ce0001bf6266/1560528440423/LPI_Report_single_140619_update.pdf (accessed 18 December 2022).

Woodcraft, S., Collins, H. & McArdle, I. (2021). Re-thinking livelihood security: Why addressing the democratic deficit in economic policymaking opens up new pathways to prosperity. Institute for Global Prosperity, London. Available at: https://discovery.ucl.ac.uk/id/eprint/10124293/1/Woodcraft_Livelihood%20Security%20WP%20FINAL.pdf (accessed 18 December 2022).

World Bank (2020). *Poverty and Shared Prosperity 2020: Reversals of fortune*. Washington, DC: World Bank. Available at: https://openknowledge.worldbank.org/bitstream/handle/10986/34496/9781464816024.pdf (accessed 18 December 2022).

World Bank Commission on Growth and Development (2008). *The Growth Report: Strategies for sustained growth and inclusive development*. Washington, DC: World Bank. Available at: https://openknowledge.worldbank.org/bitstream/handle/10986/6507/449860PUB0Box3101OFFICIAL0USE0ONLY1.pdf?sequence=1&isAllowed=y (accessed 18 December 2022).

World Bank Commission on Growth and Development (2010). *Post-Crisis Growth in Developing Countries: A special report of the Commission on Growth and Development on the implications of the 2008 financial crisis*. Washington, DC: World Bank. Available at: https://openknowledge.worldbank.org/bitstream/handle/10986/13546/52462.pdf?sequence=1&isAllowed=y (accessed 18 December 2022).

# 4
# Rethinking livelihood security: why addressing the democratic deficit in economic policy making opens up new pathways to prosperity

Saffron Woodcraft, Hannah Collins and Iona McArdle

## 4.1 Introduction

Place-based prosperity has become a policy priority for national, regional and local government in Britain in recent years, in response to growing regional and intra-urban inequalities and social and economic exclusion (Brien, 2020; Business, Energy and Industrial Strategy, 2017a; HM Treasury, 2021; HM Government, 2022). As demonstrated in Chapters 1 and 3 of this volume, new forms of citizen-led research challenge a narrow framing of prosperity as material wealth, offering diverse perspectives on what it means to live a prosperous life that encompass freedom, autonomy, security, social and economic inclusion, healthy environments, belonging and participation (Moore & Woodcraft, 2019; Moore, 2015; Mintchev et al., 2019). Recognising prosperity as diverse and context-specific presents a challenge to conventional ways of understanding the economy and relationships between economic and social life. Making sense of people's experiences of prosperity, and the specific challenges and constraints that limit opportunities to live well, is critical in order to developing policy pathways that align with lived realities.

In this chapter, we examine how citizen-led research in east London offers a new way of understanding livelihood security as a critical determinant of prosperity. Drawing on the qualitative research described in Chapter 3, we develop a conceptual framework to represent the range of assets that people depend on for livelihood security. We demonstrate how conventional policy responses that focus on economic growth and getting people into work can marginalise and undermine other components of this framework. While the empirical research this chapter draws on focuses on individuals and households in five east London neighbourhoods, the findings have broader relevance to place-based policy. The research draws attention to a more general misalignment between concepts of livelihood security and prosperity in economic policy making and the specific challenges that particular communities face. We conceptualise this misalignment as a democratic deficit and argue that knowledge based on lived experience generates fundamentally different ways of understanding how economic and social policy impact on people's lives.

Approaches like the secure livelihoods infrastructure presented in this chapter offer new ways of developing policy-relevant knowledge about the economy, which can be translated to other geographical contexts and policy challenges such as post-Covid recovery planning and levelling up. By applying the secure livelihoods infrastructure to the concept of inclusive growth, the policy framework championed in the post-pandemic 'build back better' context, we draw out these misalignments between policy and lived experience. We do this to demonstrate how new forms of knowledge and collaboration can reveal spaces for action that are currently overlooked by local authorities, public agencies and business, but crucial if pathways to prosperity are to be equitable and achievable.

## 4.2 Secure livelihoods as the foundation of prosperity

Research with citizen scientists in east London, described in the previous chapter, found that secure livelihoods were consistently identified as the most important factor in people's prosperity, providing a foundation for people to build upon and supporting the possibility of a good life (Woodcraft & Anderson, 2019; Moore & Woodcraft, 2019). Respondents described how a secure livelihood depends on several interrelated factors that support or hinder opportunities for a prosperous life. People described secure income and good work, secure and genuinely affordable housing, access to public services, local support networks and belonging to local communities as part of the mix of assets, networks and services they depend on to make a living. The interactions between these different assets were widely discussed. For example, at the time of the research employment in London was at a record high (Office for National Statistics, 2017). However, participants talked about their own experiences of in-work poverty linked to low-paid and insecure work. It was common to hear people discuss the necessity of having more than one job to cope with unpredictable or insecure employment and the high costs of private rented housing:

> How can we have a prosperous life for everyone, people of all classes? The situation is precarious for people around here. The combination of unaffordable housing, zero-hours contracts, portfolio careers … people have no security. Jobs are not good-quality … this is a toxic mix.
> (Frances, Hackney resident; interview, 2015)

People recognised community services and participation in community life as vital to supporting their livelihoods, but in a way that interacts with employment opportunities and social support:

> [T]here is a community spirit here. There is an after-school club in the library and I go and help out there. It's really good and I volunteer there. It's children having help with homework and things like that.
> (Niaja, Heath resident; interview, 2017)

But even the provision of certain services does not necessarily mean they are fully accessible for everyone. As this example demonstrates, it is the intersection of employment opportunities and affordable public services which makes work and caring responsibilities possible:

> There is like a community centre and that's all the way in Dalston and, I mean, if I don't go and pick her up because it's a lot [of money] for transport – it's about a fiver a day just for transport to take her to this place – so we said no, we'll stop that
> (Carer, Hackney; interview, 2017)

The experiences recounted here show there is not a straightforward relationship between having a job or income and livelihood security (see Chapter 3; Moore & Woodcraft, 2019; Moore & Collins, 2021). Good-quality work and a secure income are critical; however, people depend on a range of interconnected services and supports to make a living, which then intersect with other identities in multiple ways to exacerbate insecurity. In this context, it is essential to understand the deeply embedded 'horizontal' forms of inequality (Morris et al., 2018) that co-exist across gender, ethnicity, disability, sexual orientation, trans status and class and are configured in relation to the complex system of formal and informal services and livelihood supports people draw on.[1] A resident of Hackney Wick describes how disability and age intersect with processes of regeneration and change, which results in a lack of accessible public services, which leads to unpaid care:

> Because all of the facilities that were around 20 years ago have now all gone .... Everything's gone. For instance, my mum is disabled, I'm her carer, that's why I'm here, all the places she can go into and be looked after, they're all gone, so I have to ... give up my work so I can look after my mum.

What these examples demonstrate is the misalignment between economic and social policy making and lived experience, which fails to account for the ways multiple identities, services and social supports interact to support or impede people's livelihoods. Next, we outline an infrastructure for secure livelihoods, drawing on citizens' accounts of the interdependencies of assets, services and supports that need to be assembled to build a secure livelihood.

## 4.3 An infrastructure for secure livelihoods

Research data reveals how people in east London depend on a range of interrelated assets for livelihood security: a secure income and good-quality work; affordable, secure and good-quality housing; access to key public services (healthcare, education, care, transport, digital communication); economic, financial, social and digital inclusion; energy security; and access to culturally appropriate food.

We conceptualise these interdependent assets as an *infrastructure for secure livelihoods*, visualised in Figure 4.1. We do this to draw attention to the ways in which people experience the complex interdependencies between, for example, work and housing, and the critical role that services like childcare, schools and public transport play in enabling people to make a living.

## 5 dimensions of secure livelihoods

**Figure 4.1** Infrastructure for secure livelihoods.

Source: IGP, 2022

This is significant, because the assets that constitute this 'infrastructure' cut across different sectors and policy domains, as well as aspects of public and private life. Yet the multisectoral and multidimensional reality of livelihood security described here is rarely addressed holistically; instead, it is tackled through problem-specific responses and siloed decision making. Conventional policy approaches to livelihood security focus on economic growth that drives job creation and employment. In recent years, greater attention has been paid to the quality and security of the jobs being created (Wheatley, 2017; Taylor et al., 2017), but the same attention has not been given to the interactions between labour and housing markets, or to how basic services give people the capacity to seek and maintain work, for example. Because of the interconnected and interdependent nature of these assets, people require all of them if they are to flourish; this contrasts with the conventional view that employment is the only routes to poverty reduction.

Approaching livelihood security in infrastructural terms foregrounds these interactions. It offers decision makers a framework in which to examine the context-specific ways different assets interact with each other, and intersect with inequalities linked to class, race, gender and other identities. This approach provides a nuanced understanding of how the links between services, networks and resources that support livelihood security are configured for particular groups at specific points in time. This draws attention to where a lack of access in one infrastructural component can undermine the ability of others to create insecurity and instability (see Chapter 5). This is the case in east London, where insecure and poor-quality work, low wages, unaffordable housing and diminishing public services generate a spiral of negative interactions. What we see is that local communities carry the burden: social networks of friends, family and neighbours informally provide essential support, such as childcare, as people live with insecurity (Woodcraft & Anderson, 2019).

### 4.3.1 Infrastructures in theory

> [I]nfrastructures – visible and invisible – are deeply implicated in not only the making and unmaking of individual lives, but also in the experience of community, solidarity and struggle for recognition.
> (Amin, 2014: 1)

The secure livelihoods infrastructure framework (Figure 4.1) builds on earlier literature that identifies the social, physical, human, financial and natural assets people draw on to build a livelihood (Chambers & Conway, 1991; Moore & Collins, 2021). This work, often called the Sustainable Livelihoods Approach, succeeded in bringing to the fore asset-based approaches that address people's strengths rather than their vulnerabilities. However, it has been criticised for focusing too much on the individual level at the expense of understanding the way macro-level policy, decisions and power relations impact the assets people have to draw on (Moser & Norton, 2001; de Haan, 2012). By applying a lived-experience approach, upon which the secure livelihoods infrastructure is based, we seek to address this weakness by reframing the building blocks, or assets, necessary for livelihood security, while acknowledging the different scales at which decisions about these assets are made, and how macro-level policy decisions (such as area regeneration, transport prices, care facilities) intersect with everyday lives (see Moore & Collins, 2021).

In policy terms, infrastructure is often framed in either physical or social terms, as 'things', 'spaces', 'services' or 'networks'. Water, power, transport and telecommunications, for example, are frequently seen as material infrastructures, and libraries, pools, schools, playgrounds, community organisations, parks, and even commercial establishments, as social infrastructures (Latham & Layton, 2019). Social capital, trust, civic action and participation are often described in relational terms as intangible aspects of social infrastructure. However, social and urban theorists have recognised that infrastructures are 'social' in every respect (Amin, 2014), functioning as socio-technical systems in which political, cultural, social, economic and physical factors become enmeshed (Latham & Layton, 2019; Klinenberg, 2018), and with which political actors align (Harvey & Knox, 2015). Viewing the secure livelihoods infrastructure in these terms both foregrounds the interaction of assets as experienced at the individual and household levels and draws attention to the wider political and economic systems in which these livelihood supports are imagined, planned and delivered. The secure livelihoods infrastructure encompasses physical assets (transport, communications technology, housing, food, energy), economic assets (policies determining investment in physical assets, shaping labour and housing markets, job quality, minimum income), social assets (education, care and social networks) and political assets (economic and social policy, and investment decisions that frame all of these components from affordable housing to policies on welfare, taxes and the minimum wage).

A failure to understand livelihood security as the outcome of a functioning infrastructure of interrelated assets, which is both local and subject to macro-level economic and political influences, marginalises the critical significance of the relationships between different elements of the systems that influence people's lives (Moore & Collins, 2021). This is how, before the pandemic, we could have record levels of employment in the UK (Office for National Statistics, 2019) alongside record levels of in-work poverty (Bourquin et al., 2019), compounded by the ongoing housing crisis (National Housing Federation, 2019) and the rising costs, due to government cuts, of childcare (Ferguson, 2019). Conventional policy responses that address work and employment in isolation are blind to the ways policies and services can work in conflict with each other to maintain, rather than address, socioeconomic inequalities and to reduce the capacity of people to participate fully in society. The government's strategy for recovering from Covid, outlined in *Build Back Better: Our plan for growth*, once again pursues economic growth, this time through infrastructure, skills and innovation (HM Treasury, 2021). Without focusing on all the elements that contribute to a secure livelihood, it fails to acknowledge how in-work poverty compounds barriers to security beyond that which can be addressed through a focus on productivity via jobs, infrastructural projects and upskilling. This is not to discount the importance of jobs and income in people's lives. We also appreciate the recognition in UK policy of the well-researched intersection between employment and education. However, more attention needs to be paid to less well-researched elements supporting secure livelihoods, which need to be considered equally with fair pay and education if the embedded nature of inequality in society is to be addressed.

We need new ways of thinking and acting. Policy makers must understand lived realities in order to know where and how to intervene if they are to improve quality of life and prosperity; it is not enough to have aggregate, macro-level data forming the basis for local authorities' decision-making processes. The secure livelihoods infrastructure draws directly on the experiences of people living in east London neighbourhoods. The experiences and understanding of prosperity in east London will be different from those in other areas of the country. For example, in Hartlepool, where housing is much more affordable than in east London, children from low-income households are three times less likely to go to university than those in east London (UK2070 Commission, 2019), which increases multidimensional inequality not only within one generation, but for generations to come. An infrastructural way of thinking and framing lived experience provides a way to examine how pathways to prosperity are configured in different places.

We have reviewed research that presents livelihood security as a critical determinant of prosperity for communities in east London. We can conclude from this work that livelihood security depends on more than having a job: it is also about access to an infrastructure of assets, services and networks that support livelihoods. The Covid pandemic has demonstrated the extent and severity of livelihood insecurity around the UK and drawn attention to the necessity of local, and regionally specific, approaches to Covid recovery that take into account diversity and differences within communities. In the next section we problematise the link between secure livelihoods infrastructure and inclusive growth. Inclusive growth is presented as the foundation for policies that underpin many post-pandemic economic recovery strategies which attempt to address insecure livelihoods, but when we subject inclusive growth itself to scrutiny via the secure livelihoods approach presented here a different picture emerges.

## 4.4 Problematising inclusive growth

> Because it is so hard to disagree with the notion of Inclusive Growth, the danger is that it becomes a sort of placebo: helping policy-makers feel they are doing the right thing, but without leading to meaningful change.
>
> (Lee, 2019: 431)

Local government has a critical role in leading post-pandemic recovery planning, and the national 'levelling-up' agenda that seeks to address regional inequalities in Britain (Kruger, 2020; Tomaney & Pike, 2020; HM Government, 2022). Global calls for post-Covid planning to 'build back better' (OECD, 2020; United Nations, 2020) are echoed by growing cross-party support in Britain for economic and social policies that are fair, inclusive, environmentally sustainable and context-specific (Local Government Association, 2020b). Foregrounded even before the pandemic, the scale and severity of livelihood insecurity in the UK has been highlighted by Covid-19, exacerbating the punitive effects of inequalities in income, job security, health, housing, education and digital access, and drawing attention to links between inequalities, poverty and race (Caul, 2020; White & Nafilyan, 2020).[2]

Inclusive growth is the policy framework championed by local government to ensure that all people and places are able to benefit from economic growth (Local Government Association, 2020c, 2020a). Calls for inclusive growth to be the focus of post-Covid renewal strategies have been accompanied by a swathe of resources targeted at local government, setting out the role of local authorities in inclusive growth and mapping the available policy levers.[3] However, evidence that inclusive growth policies can significantly address inequalities is contested (Moore & Collins, 2021). In the next section, we examine this literature through the secure livelihoods infrastructure framework to explore how the gap between 'lived' and 'learned' forms of knowledge exacerbates negative economic and social outcomes for people whose livelihoods are already precarious.

Inclusive growth policies have garnered widespread attention in the UK since 2015 and are increasingly aligned with urban policies that focus on cities as sites of economic transformation and distribution (Lee, 2019; OECD, 2018; Inclusive Growth Commission, 2017; Beatty et al., 2016). These policies are a response to a recognition that the economy, as it is currently constructed, is not delivering for many people even if it evidences GDP and Gross Value Added (GVA) growth. Inclusive growth is concerned broadly with achieving a fairer distribution of the benefits of growth, including between population groups and across areas (Inclusive Growth Commission, 2017). Two models of inclusive growth have been put forward, the most widely adopted of which is known as the 'growth plus' model (Lupton & Hughes, 2016), which acknowledges the need to connect more people to economic growth and the benefits of growth. Second is the 'inclusive economy' model, which proposes a more fundamental change to current economic systems and structures to achieve greater inclusion and more ambitious social goals, such as reducing inequality and poverty, while focusing on the nature of the economy itself rather than just on redistributing the gains of growth (Lupton & Hughes, 2016; Local Government Association, 2020a).

Yet 'inclusion' and 'inclusive growth' lack conceptual precision. In consequence, the terms are used interchangeably with associated concepts like 'social value', 'community wealth building' and 'fair economies' (Tiratelli & Morgan, 2020). Policy frameworks that might make growth inclusive are not clearly defined, or connected to practical action, and inclusion is rarely connected to specific outcomes, such as poverty reduction or the enhancement of livelihood security, but rather is seen as an end in itself (Hughes, 2019; Lee & Sissons, 2016). This weakens the power of inclusive growth as a shared vision with which stakeholders with different objectives and interests can align.

Action on inclusive growth requires a shared vision and efforts co-ordinated across sectors, yet most UK strategies are local-authority-led and lack buy-in from business (Rafferty & Jelley, 2018; Lupton et al., 2019), civil society and other stakeholders. If the term is not clearly understood, it becomes harder to align and integrate the interests of 'growth actors' (such as politicians and officers responsible for economic development, and business leaders) with those of 'inclusion actors' (politicians and officers responsible for public services, and leaders of voluntary, community and other social-economy organisations). Goals of improving both growth and inclusion may co-exist, but in silos. The implication of this misalignment between the interests of 'growth' and the 'inclusion' of actors is that 'inclusion' remains a policy problem and fails to become embedded in mainstream practice (Lupton et al., 2019). In this context, 'inclusive growth' is merely a substitute for 'economic growth', and the use of the term 'inclusive growth' accepts the premise that growth is always desirable and will eventually trickle down (Burch & McInroy, 2018). Consequently, inclusive growth 'practices' remain focused on conventional aspects of economic development: improving job quality, increasing pay and minimum income standards, supporting local supply chains and procurement, improving learning, skills and apprenticeships, and enhancing connections to local labour markets (Lupton & Hughes, 2016; Lupton et al., 2019; Inclusive Growth Commission, 2017).

As described in Chapter 1, the terrain of prosperity is diverse, insecure livelihoods are experienced and understood differently by different communities, and inclusive growth practices fail, linguistically and practically, to account for critical interdependencies between income, work, housing and public services, because of the historical entanglement and association of prosperity with growth rather than with quality of life (see also Moore & Collins, 2021). Inclusive growth thus fails to account for the multidimensionality of interrelationships between elements in specific contexts, as it has no tools with which to recognise different places, voices, ideas or values. Addressing insecure livelihoods requires new conceptualisations and new theories beyond a rehashing of the growth metaphor as inclusive (see Chapter 2 for more on the language, metaphors and narratives of growth).

The failure of inclusive growth reflects a long-established, and taken-for-granted, bifurcation of economic and social 'policy problems' (Lupton & Hughes, 2016). In the context of post-pandemic recovery planning, this bifurcation places severe limitations on the scope for meaningful improvements in livelihood security, resilience, quality of life and 'inclusion' in place-based prosperity. It is difficult to see why interrogating 'inclusion' (such as the impacts of livelihood insecurity on public spending) should be the concern of growth actors, or how economic strategies might produce better social or environmental outcomes, without the kinds of tools and frameworks that draw attention to the gap between lived experience and policy goals, and what lived experience reveals about how 'policy problems' span sectors, scales and challenges. Such frameworks have the potential to increase the range of tools, policy levers and interventions available to deliver place-based prosperity, by connecting 'inclusion' policies to context-specific actions and problems. In the next subsection, we explore how reframing the way inclusion is understood and operationalised in economic policy making is an essential step, which opens up new spaces for action and levers for change on place-based prosperity.

### 4.4.1 Changing how 'inclusion' is operationalised

While inclusive growth as a concept seeks to challenge the nature and distribution of gains (the pace *and* pattern of growth (Lee, 2019)), the question of inclusion is narrowly interpreted by proponents of inclusive growth, as we have argued. Gidley's work mapping the ideological underpinnings of social inclusion theory and policy in the UK and Australia (Gidley et al., 2010) proposes a tripartite, nested schema to explain degrees and effects of social inclusion. This schema proposes that the narrowest interpretation of inclusion, or first domain, emerges from a neoliberal ideology of 'access' with the goal of enhancing human and social capitals and economic productivity. In policy terms, this means access to education, labour markets, skills and training to support global competitiveness and growth potential. The middle domain incorporates ideologies of social justice, which in policy terms translates to concerns with inequalities and forms of engagement and participation. The third and broadest interpretation of social inclusion draws on ideologies of human development, which go beyond questions of social justice to consider diversity, complexity, capacities and empowerment.

Such an approach can usefully be extended to considering problems of economic inclusion and shared prosperity. Current inclusive growth frameworks and practices align with the narrowest interpretation of inclusion as 'access': connecting more people to growth and to the benefits of growth. The focus on growth means that 'inclusion' in this sense is only understood as inclusion in growth, not in a broader place-based prosperity which we know depends on a functioning infrastructure of assets and services that connect citizens to decision making (see Chapter 3; Moore & Woodcraft, 2019). Expanding how inclusion is conceptualised widens the range of policy levers available to local government, and other stakeholders who are shaping places and local economies, by creating space for new forms of collaboration, knowledge generation, and action. For example, thinking about inclusion in relation to questions of participation, social responsibility and empowerment highlights a 'participation gap' or democratic deficit in economics and economic policy making, which we discuss here and which is acknowledged by the RSA's Inclusive Growth Commission (Inclusive Growth Commission, 2017).

In the UK, participatory approaches to framing policy problems and co-designing policy solutions are widely recognised and applied in the contexts of public health (Evans et al., 2010; South, 2015; Local Government Association, 2016c; South et al., 2019) and education (Luff & Webster, 2014; Seal, 2018), and acknowledged but not widely practised in the context of planning policy (Bennett & Roberts, 2004). Participatory approaches have been used in various forms and with differing degrees of participation: to understand poverty (Bennett & Roberts, 2004), in the management of fishing in Marine Protected Areas (Joint Nature Conservation Committee, 2020), for housing and wind farm consultations in Wales (Mills, 2002), participatory budgeting in Govanhill, Glasgow (Local Government Association, 2016a) and Tower Hamlets, London (Local Government Association, 2016b), and in urban renewal projects (such as Gillet Square in east London (Bianchi, 2019)), to name a few. However, citizen participation in shaping local and regional economic development strategies and policies, whether consultative or deliberative or co-produced, is rare, meaning most people have little power over decisions that affect them (Compass, 2020). Even rarer are processes for involving citizens/residents in designing whole-systems approaches to transformations across sectors and services of the kind that are necessary to develop sustainable pathways to prosperity (see Chapter 6).

Yet there is a wide array of evidence that points to the transformative potential of policy that is locally situated and integrates the lived experience and understanding of a community's aspirations to a prosperous life, to enhance their capacities and capabilities and their ability to contribute to a sustainable, fair and inclusive future (Sen, 1999; Nussbaum, 2011; Osuteye et al., 2019). Participatory approaches to policy, planning and design originated in the global South, through development projects meant to empower local communities as an alternative to traditional top-down development projects (Institute of Development Studies, n.d.; Sen, 1999; Chambers, 1994). Done well, participation involves the people directly impacted by a policy or programme as peers, partners or co-designers, from the beginning of the process and actively throughout its development, beyond superficial and tokenistic representation. Local communities, and service users, are viewed as agents of change, and participatory processes act as a means for people to define who they are, what they value, and how they might improve their lives. When embedded in decision-making processes principles of participation work to offer equal standing to a diversity of communities in problem solving, dialogue, planning and collective action and long-term societal change (McCall, 2011).

We argue that expanding 'inclusion' from a model of access (inclusion in growth and connections to the economy) to a model of participation, social responsibility (or fairness) and capacity building creates space for citizens to be included in the processes of knowledge production that are used to frame problems and develop policy responses. The secure livelihoods infrastructure shows how understanding the economy as it is experienced in everyday life illuminates context-specific interactions between macro- and microeconomic factors and generate new kinds of evidence to inform problem-framing and policy responses. As Chapter 3 demonstrates, a grounded approach to examining what constitutes shared prosperity, and pathways towards it, highlights the multiple ways economic structures and activities are enmeshed with social ones. Work, housing, debt, food and public services, for example, are interconnected resources – different aspects of the 'economy', from a household perspective – that are impacted by macro and micro policy decisions with profound effects on social relationships, support networks and possibilities. Furthermore, this work illuminates how policies that pull in opposing directions intersect at the household level to undermine 'inclusion' that focuses only on growth, employment and wages. For example, macroeconomic policies that focus on housing market growth in order to drive employment, planning gains, institutional wealth and household wealth, and to subsidise affordable housing, generate microeconomic effects that undermine claims to inclusion.

Knowledge co-production approaches to policy making that bring citizens and policy makers into dialogue break down arbitrary distinctions that demarcate economic growth and employment from other aspects of life and maintain policy silos. While the economy may be seen in isolation from social life, it is actually embedded within it; it is a social construct, designed for and managed by people (Bourdieu, 2005). An expanded notion of what constitutes the economy and its effects on everyday life creates space for 'inclusive' policy to take into account how intersecting areas of policy can be brought into the debate about 'inclusion', and reconfigured. Expanding how inclusion is conceptualised and operationalised through different forms of citizen and stakeholder collaboration, participation and co-production can be seen as also expanding the range of 'policy levers' open to local authorities and institutions with an interest in place-based prosperity. In the next section, we map out the new spaces and levers that become available.

## 4.5 New levers for action on shared prosperity

In the context of building back better and levelling up, local authorities are inundated with resources that champion inclusive growth (Local Government Association, 2020a, 2020b) in both narrow and wide interpretations (Lupton & Hughes, 2016). This guidance focuses primarily on the strategic functions of local government, and the policy levers (see Figure 4.2) available through public spending, procurement and social value commissioning, coupled with planning policies to drive affordable housing and workspace, and infrastructure investment to drive job growth and improve connections to labour markets (Local Government Association, 2020a). While these resources highlight the importance of political leadership and of innovative approaches like good work charters and community wealth-building initiatives (Local Government Association, 2020a; Lupton & Hughes, 2016), they fail to take account of lessons concerning the impacts of inclusive growth discussed earlier in this chapter. Consequently, while attention to the need for inclusion

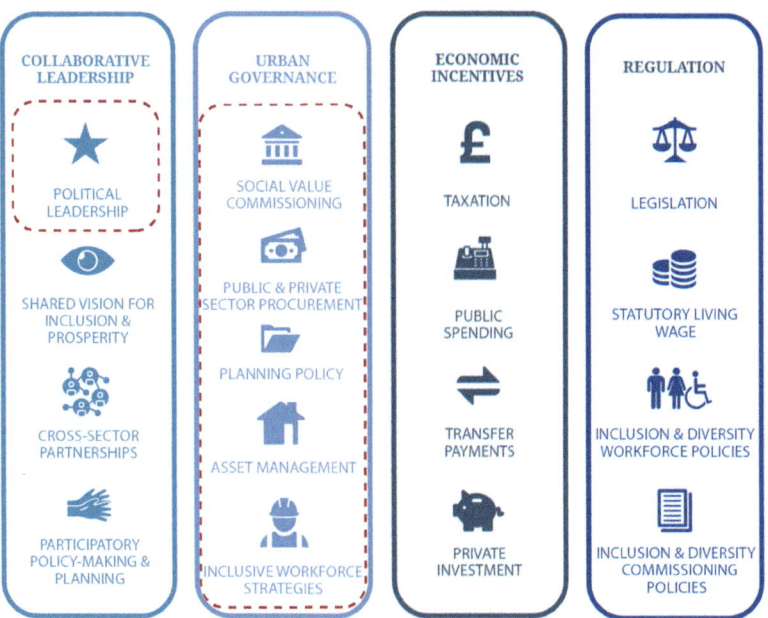

**Figure 4.2**   Local government policy levers for inclusive growth.
Source: IGP 2021

has intensified, policy debates remain focused on a narrow definition of inclusion as access to the benefits of growth, and on traditional markers of economic activity: employment, skills, infrastructure and transport. Important lessons are overlooked, including those that concern connecting inclusion to specific outcomes, such as livelihood security and prosperity, and the need for cross-sector collaborations that engage business in developing a shared vision and strategies for action.

An expanded notion of inclusion, as outlined in the previous section, increases the range of levers available for action in three key ways (see Figure 4.3). The first is inclusion in knowledge-generation processes. As argued throughout this chapter, data, evidence and knowledge based on lived experience generate fundamentally different ways of understanding the economy and the impacts of economic policy on everyday life. The democratic deficit in economic policy making allows few opportunities for understanding and generating actions based on lived experience. The knowledge that is used to frame problems, inform policy, and drive investments intended to level up regional inequalities and place-based policy making, is based on expert-led and macro-level data, missing the nuance of place and knowledge of lived experience. Alternatively,

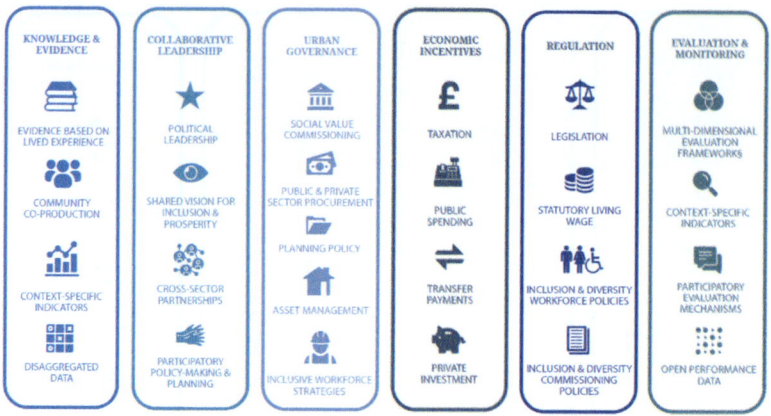

**Figure 4.3** Expanded range of levers linked to broader definition of inclusion.

Source: IGP, 2021

context-specific indicators and disaggregated data, designed and implemented through community co-production of policy, drawing on citizens' own knowledge, can enhance local capacities and capabilities through participation in knowledge-generating processes that contribute to a wider range of livelihood opportunities.

The second lever overlooked in narrow visions of inclusion is collaborative leadership. New approaches to collaborative leadership should focus on cross-sector partnerships that include citizens and businesses, alongside local government, public agencies and third-sector NGOs. An expanded notion of inclusion is operationalised around local priorities, and developed through co-produced forms of knowledge and new forms of partnership that bring citizens into participatory planning and policy making. This shift broadens the range of stakeholders involved in economic decision making, and thereby the scope of plans, policies and practices that can be influenced across sectors.[4]

The third lever in an expanded notion of inclusion is evaluation and monitoring. Taking the case of secure livelihoods in east London in Chapter 3 as an example, we can see the interrelated and multiscalar assets people draw on in daily life. It follows that positioning secure livelihoods as the desired outcome of inclusive-growth policy would require a multidimensional framework for analysis that can incorporate these intersecting assets. This necessitates context-specific indicators and participatory forms of monitoring and evaluation, as well as open-source performance data accessible to citizens, allowing them to hold implementation agencies to account.

An expanded notion of inclusion recognises the need to focus on local lived experience and context-specific pathways to prosperity (which in east London means secure livelihoods), as an outcome of inclusion and economic policy. It works to address the participation gap that currently gives citizens little voice in the research used to frame the problems or in the conversations to contribute to meaningful change through genuinely inclusive policy making.

## 4.6 Conclusion: who shapes economic policy? Addressing the democratic deficit

This chapter argues that there is a misalignment between economic policy making and lived experience – a democratic deficit. We have demonstrated that livelihood security should be at the centre of post-Covid responses in east London, where it has been defined as a critical determinant of prosperity (Chapter 3; Moore & Woodcraft, 2019). Secure income and good-quality work, affordable, secure and good-quality housing, food and energy security, access to key public services, and inclusion in the social and economic life of the city form the assets that people draw on to build a secure livelihood. These are interdependent and intersect with multiple identities, cutting across sectors and policy domains which are commonly siloed in economic decision making. It is evident from the scale of insecurity that the secure livelihoods framework has relevance for other parts of the UK, and this chapter calls for citizen-led knowledge to drive action on strategies and policies for shared prosperity and levelling up in a post-Covid context.

We use secure livelihoods as the framework to examine the inclusive growth/inclusive economies policies currently dominating Covid-19 recovery activities in local government. The current inclusive-growth approach comprises a narrow vision of inclusion as access to the benefits of economic growth. It fails to account for lived realities, and this democratic deficit has contributed to ongoing failures to address rising social and economic inequalities and in-work poverty in the UK. Expanding the notion of inclusion and addressing the democratic deficit creates new policy levers for local government which account for context-specific interactions between macro- and microeconomic factors to generate effective policy making. New policy levers for action on place-based prosperity can fundamentally shift not only the spheres within which local government operates, but the way the economy is understood.

## Notes

1. For example, London Prosperity Index analysis shows that Black, Asian and minority ethnic groups not only suffer from lower household disposable income than white ethnic groups, but also feel less safe in public spaces, feel dissatisfaction with local environmental and health services, and experience a lack of autonomy and ability to change their lives (Charalambous, 2020). Most people experience an intersection of the identities (Crenshaw, 1991) and realities that contribute to their ability to make a living and live a good life, which cannot be understood through macroeconomic analysis alone.
2. People in the poorest areas of England and Wales have been twice as likely to die from Covid-19 than those in less deprived areas (Caul, 2020). People from Pakistani, Bangladeshi and black and minority ethnic backgrounds have a significantly higher risk of death than people from white backgrounds, which is partly a result of socioeconomic deprivation (White & Nafilyan, 2020).
3. Policy levers, or styles of action, are instruments available to policy makers to direct, manage and shape services (Steer et al., 2006).
4. The London Prosperity Board (LPB) is an example of collaborative leadership in action. It is an innovative cross-sector partnership between the IGP, UCL, London government, public agencies, businesses, the third sector, and local communities in east London. Its goal is to develop new ways of thinking, generate new forms of evidence and test new ways of working that make sustainable and inclusive prosperity a reality for people living and working in London (London Prosperity Board, 2020).

## Bibliography

Amin, A. (2014). Lively infrastructure. *Theory, Culture & Society*, 31(8), 137–61. https://doi.org/10.1177/0263276414548490.

Beatty, C., Crisp, R. & Gore, T. (2016). *An Inclusive Growth Monitor for Measuring the Relationship between Poverty and Growth*. York: Joseph Rowntree Foundation. Available at: https://www.jrf.org.uk/report/inclusive-growth-monitor (accessed 20 December 2022).

Bennett, F. & Roberts, M. (2004). *From Input to Influence: Participatory approaches to research and inquiry into poverty*. York: Joseph Rowntree Foundation. Available at: https://www.jrf.org.uk/sites/default/files/jrf/migrated/files/1859351786.pdf (accessed 20 December 2022).

Bianchi, M. (2019). Renewing the city through public participation and cultural activities: The case study of Gillet Square, a community-led urban regeneration project. *Journal of Entrepreneurial and Organizational Diversity* 8(1), 1–21. https://doi.org/10.5947/jeod.2019.001.

Bourdieu, P. (2005). *The Social Structures of the Economy* (trans. C. Turner). Cambridge: Polity.

Bourquin, P., Cribb, J., Waters, T. & Xu, X. (2019). Why has in-work poverty risen in Britain? IFS Working Paper W19/12. Institute for Fiscal bStudies, London.

Brien, P. (2020). The UK Shared Prosperity Fund. House of Commons Library. Available at: https://commonslibrary.parliament.uk/research-briefings/cbp-8527/ (accessed 20 December 2022).

Burch, D. & McInroy, N. (2018). *We Need an Inclusive Economy Not Inclusive Growth*. Manchester: Centre for Local Economic Strategies. Available at: https://cles.org.uk/wp-content/uploads/2018/12/Policy-Provocation_We-need-an-inclusive-economy-not-inclusive-growth_191218.pdf (accessed 20 December 2022).

Business, Energy and Industrial Strategy (2017a). Industrial strategy: Building a Britain fit for the future. White Paper. London: HM Government. Available at: https://assets.publishing.service.gov.uk/government/uploads/system/uploads/attachment_data/file/664563/industrial-strategy-white-paper-web-ready-version.pdf (accessed 24 February 2023).

Business, Energy and Industrial Strategy (2017b). Industrial strategy: The 5 foundations. Policy paper. London: HM Government. Available at: https://www.gov.uk/government/publications/industrial-strategy-the-foundations/industrial-strategy-the-5-foundations (accessed 20 December 2022).

Caul, S. (2020). Deaths involving COVID-19 by local area and socioeconomic deprivation: Deaths occurring between 1 March and 31 May. ONS. Available at: https://www.ons.gov.uk/people populationandcommunity/birthsdeathsandmarriages/deaths/bulletins/deathsinvolving covid19bylocalareasanddeprivation/deathsoccurringbetween1marchand31may2020 (accessed 20 December 2022).

Chambers, R. (1994) The origins and practice of participatory rural appraisal. *World Development*, 22(7), 953–69. https://doi.org/10.1016/0305-750X(94)90141-4.

Chambers, R. & Conway, G. (1991) Sustainable rural livelihoods: Practical concepts for the 21st century. IDS Discussion Paper 296, Institute of Development Studies, Brighton.

Charalambous, E. (2020). Same storm, different boats: How racial inequalities impact prosperity. Institute for Global Prosperity. Available at: https://seriouslydifferent.org/igp-stories/same-storm-different-boats-how-racial-inequalities-impact-prosperity (accessed 20 December 2022).

Compass (2020). Participation at 45°: Techniques for citizen-led change. Available at: https://www.compassonline.org.uk/publications/participation-at-45%CB%9A-techniques-for-citizen-led-change/ (accessed 20 December 2022).

Crenshaw, K. (1991). Mapping the margins: Intersectionality, identity politics, and violence against women of color. *Stanford Law Review*, 43(6), 1241–99. https://doi.org/10.2307/1229039.

de Haan, L. J. (2012). The livelihood approach: A critical exploration. *Erdkunde*, 66(4), 345–57. https://doi.org/10.3112/erdkunde.2012.04.05.

Evans, D., Pilkington, P. & McEachran, E. (2010). Rhetoric or reality? A systematic review of the impact of participatory approaches by UK public health units on health and social outcomes. *Journal of Public Health*, 32(3), 418–26. https://doi.org/10.1093/pubmed/fdq014.

Ferguson, D. (2019). Parents in England face shock rise in childcare costs as government cuts bite. *The Observer*, 21 March. Available at: https://www.theguardian.com/money/2019/mar/31/childcare-fees-rocket-lack-of-early-years-funding-nurseries-close.

Gidley, J., Hampson, G., Wheeler, L. & Bereded-Samuel, E. (2010). Social inclusion: Context, theory and practice. *Australasian Journal of University–Community Engagement*, 5(1), 6–36.

Harvey, P. & Knox, H. (2015). *Roads: An anthropology of infrastructure and expertise*. Ithaca, NY: Cornell University Press.

HM Government (2022). *Levelling Up the United Kingdom*. London. Available at: https://assets.publishing.service.gov.uk/government/uploads/system/uploads/attachment_data/file/1054769/Levelling_Up_the_United_Kingdom__accessible_version_.pdf (accessed 21 December 2022).

HM Treasury (2021). *Build Back Better: Our plan for growth*. London. Available at: https://assets.publishing.service.gov.uk/government/uploads/system/uploads/attachment_data/file/969275/PfG_Final_print_Plan_for_Growth_Print.pdf (accessed 21 December 2022).

Hughes, C. (2019). How could inclusive growth policies reduce poverty at local level? Joseph Rowntree Foundation and University of Manchester. Inclusive Growth Analysis Unit, Briefing Paper no. 9. Available at: https://documents.manchester.ac.uk/display.aspx?DocID=42550 (accessed 21 December 2022).

Inclusive Growth Commission (2017). *Inclusive Growth Commission: Making our economy work for everyone*. London: Royal Society of Arts. Available at: https://www.thersa.org/globalassets/pdfs/reports/rsa_inclusive-growth-commission-final-report-march-2017.pdf (accessed 21 December 2022).

Institute of Development Studies (n.d.). About participatory methods. Available at: https://www.participatorymethods.org/page/about-participatory-methods (accessed 21 December 2022).

Joint Nature Conservation Committee (2020). Developing a participatory approach to the management of fishing activity in UK offshore Marine Protected Areas. Available at: https://jncc.gov.uk/our-work/mpa-adaptive-management/ (accessed 21 December 2022).

Klinenberg, E. (2018) *Palaces for the People: How social infrastructure can help fight inequality, polarization, and the decline of civic life*. New York: Crown.

Kruger, D. (2020). Levelling up our communities: Proposals for a new social covenant. Available at: https://www.dannykruger.org.uk/files/2020-09/Kruger%202.0%20Levelling%20Up%20Our%20Communities.pdf (accessed 21 December 2022).

Latham, A. & Layton, J. (2019). Social infrastructure and the public life of cities: Studying urban sociality and public spaces. *Geography Compass*, 13(7), e12444. https://doi.org/10.1111/gec3.12444.

Lee, N. (2019). Inclusive growth in cities: A sympathetic critique. *Regional Studies*, 53(3), 424–34. https://doi.org/10.1080/00343404.2018.1476753.

Lee, N. & Sissons, P. (2016). Inclusive growth? The relationship between economic growth and poverty in British cities. *Environment and Planning A*, 48(11), 2317–39. https://doi.org/10.1177/0308518X16656000.

Local Government Association (2016a). Govanhill, Glasgow. Available at: https://www.local.gov.uk/govanhill-glasgow (accessed 21 December 2022).

Local Government Association (2016b). Tower Hamlets, 'You decide!'. Available at: https://www.local.gov.uk/tower-hamlets-you-decide (accessed 21 December 2022).

Local Government Association. (2016c) Case study: NHS England Citizens' Assembly. Available at: https://www.local.gov.uk/case-study-nhs-england-citizens-assembly (accessed 21 December 2022).

Local Government Association (2020a). Building more inclusive economies: Full report. Available at: https://www.local.gov.uk/publications/building-more-inclusive-economies-full-report (accessed 21 December 2022).

Local Government Association (2020b). Post-COVID-19 recovery strategies that will contribute to a fairer, cleaner, and more sustainable economy. Available at: https://www.local.gov.uk/parliament/briefings-and-responses/post-covid-19-recovery-strategies-will-contribute-fairer-cleaner (accessed 21 December 2022).

Local Government Association (2020c). The role of councils in building inclusive economies. Available at: https://www.local.gov.uk/inclusive-economies (accessed 22 December 2022).

London Prosperity Board (2020). London Prosperity Board. Available at: https://londonprosperityboard.org/ (accessed 21 December 2022).

Luff, P. & Webster, R. (2014) Democratic and participatory approaches: Exemplars from early childhood education. *Management in Education*, 28(4): 138–43. https://doi.org/10.1177/0892020614547317.

Lupton, R. & Hughes, C. (2016). Achieving inclusive growth in Greater Manchester. What can be done? Joseph Rowntree Foundation and University of Manchester. Available at: https://hummedia.manchester.ac.uk/institutes/mui/igau/IGAU-Consultation-Report.pdf (accessed 21 December 2022).

Lupton, R., Hughes, C., Macdougall, A., Goldwyn-Simpkins, H. & Hjelmskog, A. (2019) Inclusive growth in Greater Manchester 2020 and beyond: Taking stock and looking forward. Joseph Rowntree Foundation and University of Manchester. Available at: https://documents.manchester.ac.uk/display.aspx?DocID=46396 (Accessed 22 September 2022).

McCall, E. (2011). Communication for development: Strengthening the effectiveness of the United Nations. UNDP, New York. Available at: https://unsdg.un.org/resources/communication-development-strengthening-effectiveness-united-nations (accessed 24 February 2023).

Mills, J. (2002) Participatory techniques for community development work. Cardiff University. Available at: https://blogs.cardiff.ac.uk/schep/wp-content/uploads/sites/413/2017/06/PC-PRA-community-booklet-final.pdf (accessed 21 December 2022).

Mintchev, N., Baumann, H., Moore, H. L., Rigon, A. & Dabaj, J. (2019) Towards a shared prosperity: Co-designing solutions in Lebanon's spaces of displacement. *Journal of the British Academy*, 7(s2), 109–35. https://doi.org/10.5871/jba/007s2.109.

Moore, H. L. (2015) Global prosperity and sustainable development goals. *Journal of International Development*, 27(6), 801–15. https://doi.org/10.1002/jid.3114.

Moore, H. L. & Collins, H. (2020). Towards prosperity: Reinvigorating local economies through Universal Basic Services. IGP Working Paper 01-2020/04. London: Institute for Global Prosperity. Available at: https://discovery.ucl.ac.uk/id/eprint/10096789/ (accessed 21 December 2022).

Moore, H. L. & Collins, H. (2021). *Assembling prosperity in a post-Covid United Kingdom: New approaches to levelling up*. IGP Working Paper Series. London: Institute for Global Prosperity. https://doi.org/10.14324/000.wp.10131207.

Moore, H. L. & Woodcraft, S. (2019). Understanding prosperity in east London: Local meanings and 'sticky' measures of the good life. *City & Society*, 31(2), 275–98. https://doi.org/10.1111/ciso.12208.

Morris, S., Patel, O., Stainthorp, C. & Stevenson, O. (2018). Structurally unsound: Exploring inequalities: Igniting research to better inform UK policy. Report. Resolution Foundation and UCL. Available at: https://www.ucl.ac.uk/grand-challenges/sites/grand-challenges/files/structurally-unsound-report.pdf (accessed 21 December 2022).

Moser, C. & Norton, A. (2001). *To Claim Our Rights: Livelihood security, human rights and sustainable development*. London: Overseas Development Institute. Available at: https://cdn.odi.org/media/documents/1816.pdf (accessed 21 December 2022).

National Housing Federation (2019). 1 in 7 people in England directly hit by the housing crisis. National Housing Federation. Available at: https://www.housing.org.uk/news-and-blogs/news/1-in-7-people-in-england-directly-hit-by-the-housing-crisis/ (accessed 24 February 2023).

Nussbaum, M. C. (2011). *Creating Capabilities: The human development approach*. Cambridge, MA: Harvard University Press.

OECD (2016). The Inclusive Growth in Cities Campaign. Available at: https://www.oecd.org/inclusive-growth/Inclusive%20Growth%20in%20Cities_Flyer_ENG.pdf (accessed 21 December 2022).

OECD (2018). *Opportunities for All: A framework for policy action on inclusive growth*. Paris: Organization for Economic Cooperation and Development. Available at: https://www.oecd.org/economy/opportunities-for-all-9789264301665-en.htm (accessed 21 December 2022).

OECD (2020) Building back better: A sustainable, resilient recovery after COVID-19. Available at: https://www.oecd.org/coronavirus/policy-responses/building-back-better-a-sustainable-resilient-recovery-after-covid-19-52b869f5/ (accessed 30 January 2023).

Office for National Statistics (2017). UK labour market: October 2017. Available at: https://www.ons.gov.uk/employmentandlabourmarket/peopleinwork/employmentandemployeetypes/bulletins/uklabourmarket/october2017 (accessed 21 December 2022).

Office for National Statistics (2019). Employment in the UK: September 2019. Available at: https://www.ons.gov.uk/employmentandlabourmarket/peopleinwork/employmentandemployeetypes/bulletins/employmentintheuk/september2019 (accessed 21 December 2022).

Osuteye, E., Ortiz, C., Lipietz, B., Castán Broto, V., Johnson, C. & Kombe, W. (2019). Knowledge co-production for urban equality. KNOW Working Paper Series no. 1, Knowledge in Action for Urban Equality, London. Available at: https://www.ucl.ac.uk/bartlett/development/sites/bartlett/files/know_workingpaper-no1_vf.pdf (accessed 21 December 2022).

Rafferty, A. & Jelley, R. (2018). Understanding business behaviour that supports inclusive growth. Joseph Rowntree Foundation and University of Manchester. IGAU Responsible Business Report 1 of 2. Available at: https://hummedia.manchester.ac.uk/institutes/mui/igau/IG-Responsible-Business-Report-1.pdf (accessed 21 December 2022).

Seal, M. (2018). *Participatory Pedagogic Impact Research: Co-production with community partners in action*. Abingdon: Routledge.

Sen, A. (1999). *Development as Freedom*. New York: Anchor Books.

Sissons, P., Green, A. E. & Broughton, K. (2018) Inclusive growth in English cities: Mainstreamed or sidelined? *Regional Studies*, 53(3), 435–46. https://doi.org/10.1080/00343404.2018.1515480.

South, J. (2015). A guide to community-centred approaches for health and wellbeing. Public Health England, London. Available at: https://assets.publishing.service.gov.uk/government/uploads/system/uploads/attachment_data/file/768979/A_guide_to_community-centred_approaches_for_health_and_wellbeing__full_report_.pdf (accessed 21 December 2022).

South, J., Bagnall, A., Stansfield, J. A., Southby, K. J. & Mehta, P. (2019) An evidence-based framework on community-centred approaches for health: England, UK. *Health Promotion International*, 34(2), 356–66. https://doi.org/10.1093/heapro/dax083.

Steer, R., Spours, K., Hodgson, A., Finlay, I., Coffield, F., Edward, S. & Gregson, M. (2006). 'Modernisation' and the role of policy levers in the learning and skills sector. *Journal of Vocational Learning and Training*, 59(2), 175–92. https://doi.org/10.1080/13636820701342574.

Taylor, M., Marsh, G., Nicol, D. & Broadbent, P. (2017). Good work: The Taylor review of modern working practices. HM Government. Available at: https://www.gov.uk/government/publications/good-work-the-taylor-review-of-modern-working-practices (accessed 21 December 2022).

Tiratelli, L. & Morgan, C. (2020) *Cultivating Local Inclusive Growth in Practice*. London: New Local Government Network. Available at: https://barrowcadbury.org.uk/wp-content/uploads/2020/02/Cultivating-Local-Inclusive-Growth_final.pdf (accessed 22 December 2022).

Tomaney, J. & Pike, A. (2020). Levelling up? *Political Quarterly*, 91(1), 43–8. https://doi.org/10.1111/1467-923X.12834.

UK2070 Commission (2019). Fairer and stronger: Rebalancing the UK economy. Execute summary. Available at: https://uk2070.org.uk/wp-content/uploads/2019/05/FIRST-REPORT-UK-2070-EXECUTIVE-SUMMARY.pdf (accessed 21 December 2022).

United Nations (2020). A UN framework for the immediate socio-economic response to COVID-19. Available at: https://unsdg.un.org/resources/un-framework-immediate-socio-economic-response-covid-19 (accessed 21 December 2022).

Wheatley, H. (2017). New research: More than half of self-employed not earning a decent living. Press release. Available at: https://neweconomics.org/2017/08/self_employed_not_earning/ (accessed 21 December 2022).

White, C. & Nafilyan, V. (2020) Coronavirus (COVID-19) related deaths by ethnic group, England and Wales: 2 March 2020 to 10 April 2020. Office for National Statistics. Available at: https://www.ons.gov.uk/peoplepopulationandcommunity/birthsdeathsandmarriages/deaths/articles/coronavirusrelateddeathsbyethnicgroupenglandandwales/2march2020to10april2020 (accessed 21 December 2022).

Woodcraft, S. & Anderson, B. (2019) *Rethinking Prosperity for London: When citizens lead transformation*. London: Institute for Global Prosperity. Available at: https://discovery.ucl.ac.uk/id/eprint/10080172/ (accessed 21 December 2022).

# 5
# Building co-designed infrastructures in Lebanon's spaces of displacement

Hanna Baumann, Joana Dabaj, Nikolay Mintchev, Henrietta L. Moore and Andrea Rigon

## 5.1 Introduction

What does it take to bring people together in socially fragmented and culturally diverse urban settings? How can communities affected by displacement and compounded crises establish a sense of shared prosperity? In what follows, we address these questions within the Lebanese context of large-scale displacement. Lebanon has a long history of receiving refugees and migrants. Over the past century, it has been the recipient of multiple waves of displaced people, including Armenians, Palestinians, Iraqis and, more recently, a large number of Syrians. At the time of writing, with approximately 1.5 million Syrian refugees, Lebanon has the highest number of refugees per capita in the world: approximately a quarter of its population (UNHCR, 2021).

The arrival of Syrians in Lebanon is often portrayed as exerting 'pressure' or 'strain' on the country's economy, services and infrastructure (Abid et al., 2017; see also Baylouny, 2020). But even if such claims are true in some circumstances and contexts, they do not tell the whole story, and they raise important questions about what opportunities there are to create pathways to livelihood security and sustainable prosperity in the context of large-scale displacement. Solutions to the challenges presented by displacement and migration must be approached on multiple levels simultaneously. On one level, national policies and humanitarian or development interventions that generate incomes, an effective educational system and decent public infrastructure are crucial for dealing with the effects of mass displacement. A primary focus on this level, however, runs the risk of relying on aggregate outcomes, as well as on narrow conceptions of prosperity and progress, without considering if and how these outcomes translate into good-quality of life for people on the ground. On a second level, we argue that solutions must be locally driven and locally adapted in ways that prioritise the concerns that are relevant to people and the spaces they inhabit; crucially, this includes displaced people themselves as well as host populations.

This chapter focuses on possibilities for creating solutions at this second level through the co-design and community-engaged construction of urban interventions in a socially inclusive manner, whereby both host and refugee populations play an active role in the co-creation process and take ownership of the results. We illustrate the long-term and multifaceted value of urban co-design with the example of a participatory spatial intervention built in the town of Bar Elias in 2019, and evaluated in 2021. The aim of the evaluation was to understand how the intervention – with its specific history of being co-created with the community – affects people's experience of the built environment, including their experiences and feelings of belonging to that environment and their relation to the people with whom they co-inhabit it.

Prosperity, as the chapters in this volume make clear, is a concept and a phenomenon that ought to be understood in a context-specific fashion. In the case of Lebanon, the incomplete recovery from the Civil War (1975–90), the wave of displacement from Syria since 2011, and the multiple recent political and economic crises, shape the local parameters of how prosperity is understood. Infrastructure is an important element in this context, because of longstanding deficits that the country has faced in infrastructure and in the provision of electricity, water, waste management, housing and open public spaces (see Chapter 6 for more on electricity infrastructure).

Even before the current economic crisis, the quality of Lebanon's infrastructure was ranked among the lowest in the world (Harake & Kostopoulos, 2018). The infrastructural rebuilding and recovery after the Civil War was partial and insufficient (Chalcraft, 2009: 155), and closely bound up with sectarian politics and regimes of power that directly link service provision to private economic and political interests (for a review of the infrastructural vulnerabilities in Lebanon, see Baumann & Kanafani, 2020). The Beirut post-war recovery process has been heavily criticised for exacerbating inequalities, displacing local residents, failing to improve community relations, and destroying heritage architecture to build luxury tower blocks (e.g., Bou Akar, 2018; Fawaz, 2009; Harb el-Kak, 2000; Hourani, 2015; Khechen, 2018; Krijnen & Fawaz, 2010; Sawalha, 2010). Part of the problem is that the planning and development of the reconstruction projects have shown little regard for the needs, experiences and aspirations of local residents. As Aseel Sawalha's (2010) ethnography of Beirut's seaside neighbourhood of Ain al-Mraiseh shows, when the post-war reconstruction process excluded residents and their views from decision making, the result was resentment and disillusionment towards the state and the Solidere company in charge of reconstruction. People felt that a vision of reconstruction was imposed on them without any regard or concern for them and their views, especially when it came to the needs of the most vulnerable members of the community. Within the post-war recovery process, Sawalha claims, 'development and modernity meant creating a cosmopolitan global city, in the hope of attracting investors and tourists, but at the same time it excluded its vulnerable residents from its future urban plans' (2010: 131; see also Makdisi, 1997). Here, the vision of prosperity embodied in the process of reconstruction was a vision of diversity, cosmopolitanism and inclusion, but with a neoliberal twist: it was a vision of a welcoming cosmopolitan city, but only for those with enough money to fuel an economy of high-end consumption. All other residents – whether they are low-income Lebanese, Syrian migrant workers, refugees, or domestic workers tied to the callous and exploitative *kafala* sponsorship system[1] – are marginal to this vision of prosperity, despite the fact that it is through their labour that the city's activities and services, including the reconstruction process, are able to continue.

## 5.2 Prosperity in the context of urban displacement

To rethink or redefine prosperity, as this volume argues, means to engage in depth with locally specific experiences, and to do so in an inclusive way that values the voices of people of all social and national backgrounds. In contexts of displacement and migration, what must also be attended to is the question of how the Other – the refugee, the displaced person, the migrant, the stranger – fits within the project of building a better future. One response to displacement and migration that has become all too familiar is the populist, protectionist response that focuses on protecting the prosperity of those who have it by keeping others out, either physically, or socially and economically. Within this model, the inclusion of foreigners in national life is seen as an impingement or as an obstacle to building a better society. Recent critiques of this argument have pointed out that the presence of refugees can lead to economic benefits for host communities (for example, Betts & Collier, 2017; Betts et al., 2017; Fawaz. et al., 2018; Yassine & Al-Harithy, 2021), and that migration can also lead to vibrant and cohesive urban communities, as the case of London has shown (Mintchev & Moore, 2017, 2018). This means that diversity can become the foundation of a prosperous society, and not an obstacle to it as proponents of the nationalist protectionist response often assume. But the question of whether (and how) countries, cities and communities can build shared prosperity depends on multiple variables such as the scale of migration, the educational levels and cultural backgrounds of newcomers, and, not least, the public services which have the potential to enhance everyone's capacities by covering their basic needs.

The question of how particular visions of prosperity come about and how they become embedded within societies needs to be examined across different scales, from governance to quotidian urban interactions. Top-level decisions about anything from legal rights for refugees and migrants to job creation strategies and funding for urban infrastructure are decisive for determining what kind of society people co-inhabit, but equally important is the way in which people manage their urban environments at the local level in everyday life. Attentiveness to subjectivity and agency is key to understanding how inclusive prosperity can be achieved in contexts of displacement. The way people relate to one another on a day-to-day basis depends on a range of subjective factors, including psychic representations and affective orientations towards others; it also depends on the kinds of practices that communities engage in, and the spatial and infrastructural conditions they inhabit and share. As Ash Amin writes,

> urban infrastructure (layout of public spaces, physical infrastructure, public services, technological and built environment, visual and symbolic culture) [has] resonance as a 'collective unconscious' working on civic feelings, including those towards the stranger. … [I]nterventions in the urban infrastructure guided by principles of multiplicity and common access have an important part to play in an urban politics of living with difference.
> 
> (Amin, 2012: 63)

In the Lebanese context of displacement, refugees are embedded in the urban fabric of large cities and small towns across the country. Unlike Jordan and Turkey (the other two main hosts of displaced Syrians), Lebanon has a policy of non-encampment, which means that the majority of Syrians have settled in and near cities, seeking job opportunities and access to services (Sanyal, 2017; Turner, 2015). This, though, does not make refugees' lives and livelihoods any less precarious and uncertain. Syrians who are able to find employment are usually poorly paid, with no job security, long working hours and limited time for rest or leisure. Since 2020, the economic crisis has made this situation worse for Syrians and for Lebanese. Precarity has expanded to the majority of the population, including Lebanese in middle-class professional occupations, and pushed a huge number of people into poverty, energy insecurity and food insecurity, with Syrian refugees and poor people being disproportionately affected (for example, UNICEF, 2021; United Nations Economic and Social Commission for Western Asia, 2021).

Tensions between refugees and hosts are also an issue in some areas, either because of sectarian and political differences, or as a result of competition over resources such as housing, jobs and services. Although Syrians were received with hospitality in the early days of the conflict in Syria (Christophersen et al., 2013), this dynamic soon changed, and the dominant narrative became one of 'hosting fatigue': refugees were said to be overstaying their welcome and becoming 'a burden' on the country's already strained infrastructure (Fakhoury, 2017: 686; Knudsen, 2017: 136). The result was an increasingly tense environment, culminating in fear of harassment and abuse in public spaces, as well as social disengagement from the public realm (Harb & Saab, 2014; DeJong et al., 2017; Knudsen, 2018: 108–9).

However, despite these circumstances, there are opportunities to develop spaces and practices that lead towards a shared vision of prosperity. One way to do this, as we argue in this chapter, is through co-designed and inclusive interventions. Such interventions must be inclusive in the sense that they embody principles of diversity, openness and accessibility. They must also be co-designed in a way that invites local residents, both short- and long-term, to make key decisions about what is needed to meet local priorities. The practice of co-design has a number of significant benefits: it ensures that interventions are responsive to locally relevant issues; it presents an opportunity for people from diverse cultural and social backgrounds to collaborate; and it supports people's agency by ensuring that local residents make important decisions and take ownership of the final outcomes. This approach is fundamentally different from large-scale top-down projects of infrastructural development, because it generates specific forms of affective engagement, not just between the people involved in the co-design, but also between the participants and the urban environment.

The participatory spatial intervention (PSI) presented in this chapter exemplifies how the process of co-design amplifies the impact of infrastructural recovery. The intervention was led by Andrea Rigon (Bartlett Development Planning Unit) and involved Hanna Baumann (IGP), and Joana Dabaj and Riccardo Conti (CatalyticAction). The PSI is a relatively small initiative that was created as part of a wider academic research project led by Henrietta Moore. As such, the scale of its impact can hardly compete with that of big infrastructural projects funded by states or private companies. The fact that the PSI was co-designed, however, has meant that this relatively modest initiative has been embraced, maintained and further developed by the Bar Elias community in a way that has led to transformations of the urban environment as well as to experiences of sociality when people engage with one another. As the post-implementation evaluation reveals, the participatory approach and its focus on social diversity and inclusion supported Bar Elias residents in engaging positively with one another and with local infrastructures during and beyond the intervention. These new forms of engagement and their effects on the quality of urban life demonstrate the potential of collaborative development to improve public spaces and services and align them with new visions of shared urban prosperity.

## 5.3 Co-design in Bar Elias

Bar Elias is a refugee-hosting town in the Beqaa Valley, near Lebanon's border with Syria. Since 2011, the town has seen its population nearly double as a result of displacement. At the start of the project in 2018, the town was home to approximately 65,000 Lebanese citizens, 6,000 Palestinian refugees, 31,500 registered Syrian refugees and up to 15,000 unregistered Syrians (UNHCR, 2018; Ullrich, 2018; Haddad et al., 2018). This ratio of refugees to hosts places Bar Elias in a category that the UN classifies as 'high pressure' in terms of the potential for social instability (Inter-Agency Coordination Lebanon, 2015). And indeed, while Bar Elias has been welcoming towards Syrians, there are reports of tensions, in particular because the presence of the displaced has altered public spaces such as street-side markets (Ullrich, 2018). As a result, UN-funded projects have been targeting locations like Bar Elias with large-scale infrastructure projects in the hope of alleviating the social pressure and potential for political instability (United Nations Development Programme, 2018). While the infrastructural issues that preceded the arrival of Syrian refugees continue in the area, the town has seen significant infrastructural investment from a variety of international donors, including a new Médecins Sans Frontières (MFS) hospital at the entrance road to the town (where the PSI was focused), as well as a football stadium and a recycling plant.

However, as some UN representatives acknowledged in interviews, the technocratic assumption that increased infrastructural investment will automatically lower the potential for conflict between refugees and hosts is somewhat simplistic. The problem with this view is that it treats everyday urban politics as a zero-sum game in which residents fight over scarce resources, without duly acknowledging that living with difference requires civic feelings anchored in joint aspirations and collaborative actions. The PSI was designed to embody a fundamentally different approach, one based on citizen social science as a mechanism of involving members of the community in the research process while capitalising on opportunities to bring people together to make joint contributions to the future of their town. Citizen social science, as we practise it, is a research methodology in which members of the community are recruited, trained in research and integrated into the research team, where they play an active role in all project activities, from research design and data collection to presentation and publication of findings and development of interventions (for more detail on citizen social science see Jallad & Mintchev, 2019; Jallad et al., 2022; Mintchev et al., 2022).

The research leading up to the physical intervention focused on the manner in which vulnerabilities created by public services (or the lack thereof) are shared, and how they can be jointly addressed to create solutions that benefit both refugees and hosts (for a detailed documentation of the PSI process and its outcomes, see Dabaj et al., 2020). The PSI began with the recruitment and training of local citizen scientists who subsequently carried out research over the course of 10 months, beginning with a one-week workshop in August 2018, to identify the town's public spaces, their uses and their users. The entrance road to the city was identified as the site for the physical intervention, because it is the only space used by all groups residing in and visiting Bar Elias. This was followed by a seven-day participatory design workshop with citizen scientists and other residents (Figure 5.1). The latter, like the citizen scientists, were recruited to reflect the diversity of Bar Elias's communities in terms of nationality, gender, age and class.

This attention to diversity was crucial, as participatory research and design often risks privileging the input of local elites and consequently reproducing entrenched power relations and inequalities (Mansuri & Rao, 2013; Rigon, 2014; see also Dabaj & Conti, 2020; Rigon et al., 2021). Our deliberate inclusion of residents from different backgrounds was intended to act as a countermeasure to this challenge. And indeed, some of the participants noted that the PSI was the first time that 'locals' (understood here as Lebanese and Palestinians, most of whom have lived in the town for decades) and displaced Syrians worked on a common project. The content of the discussion during the workshops also made a difference to cross-cultural conversation. The dialogues helped residents to engage with various points of view about the infrastructural challenges of the town, including the ones faced by all communities as well as those particular to certain groups or neighbourhoods. The dialogue highlighted the way in which local concerns were often shared, and gave

**Figure 5.1** Bar Elias residents at the Participatory Planning Workshop, October 2018.

Source: Hanna Baumann

expression to a narrative that was in stark contrast to the commonly voiced allegations that others overstretch local services. By focusing the discussion on the interdependence of everyone in the town, participants' narratives centred on the need to construct an infrastructure to manage and improve the town's shared spaces and resources.

Within this framework of interdependence, participants and researchers studied and learned about the infrastructural conditions of the town and the various, intersectional vulnerabilities that these conditions generated. They brainstormed the underlying causes of local vulnerabilities and began to formulate potential solutions that would address them through small-scale interventions. A number of potential solutions were then proposed as a way to address residents' vulnerabilities, while contributing to a vision of the city that was shared by different social groups. Proposals included various types of urban provision: improved safety mechanisms such as traffic lights, pedestrian crossings and access ramps; improvements to the main road, where different communities meet, including street shading, benches and greenery to increase the hours of use and provide protection from summer sun and winter rain; beautification measures and signage intended to encourage a sense of shared identity and responsibility; and proposals for bigger centralised projects such as the creation of a park with a playground that would serve as an inter-communal meeting space. All of these proposed solutions were centred around a vision

**Figure 5.2** A child playing on the circular bench.

Source: CatalyticAction

of improving opportunities for inter-group relations, fostering pride in the town, and improving the experience of diverse groups of users of the road, including children and people living with disabilities. These proposals were subsequently translated into designs, which were presented to the residents for feedback and consultation in December 2018.

The research and consultation process produced a series of designs that were implemented and built in May 2019. One of the designs was a large circular concrete seating area that was installed on a wide section of the pavement in front of the local polyclinic (Figure 5.2). Previously, this space was either blocked by cars parked on the pavement or, when this was not the case, used by waiting patients, who were forced to sit on the ground. The bench was covered by a shade under which patients and other users could rest and socialise. The bench was also designed to encourage children to play.

The aluminium panels that provided shade were laser-cut in a way that spelled out Arabic phrases on the pavement. The slogans reflected participants' values and aspirations of co-existence (for example, 'Bar Elias, the mother of strangers, cleanliness and togetherness'). Another key initiative of the PSI was the rehabilitation of a previously dilapidated green space behind the MSF hospital, which had been earmarked to become a parking lot. The space was cleaned up, planted and turned into a park with benches, with a specially added access path from the main road (Figure 5.3). All along the entrance road to the town, newly

**Figure 5.3** The green space behind the MSF hospital after clean-up and planting.

Source: CatalyticAction

**Figure 5.4** Access ramp onto high pavement.

Source: CatalyticAction

installed shades and seating encouraged people to sit and gather, while floor games invited children to play and use the pavements. Speed bumps were installed to calm traffic and pavement ramps to enable easier access for pushchairs and wheelchairs. Murals and signage pointing out local sites were added to enhance the aesthetics of the public realm and to make the town easier to navigate for visitors (Figures 5.4, 5.5 and 5.6).

**Figure 5.5** Shade incorporating laser-cut phrases and recycled materials above newly installed seating. A sign in the background points passers-by to the revitalised garden.

Source: CatalyticAction

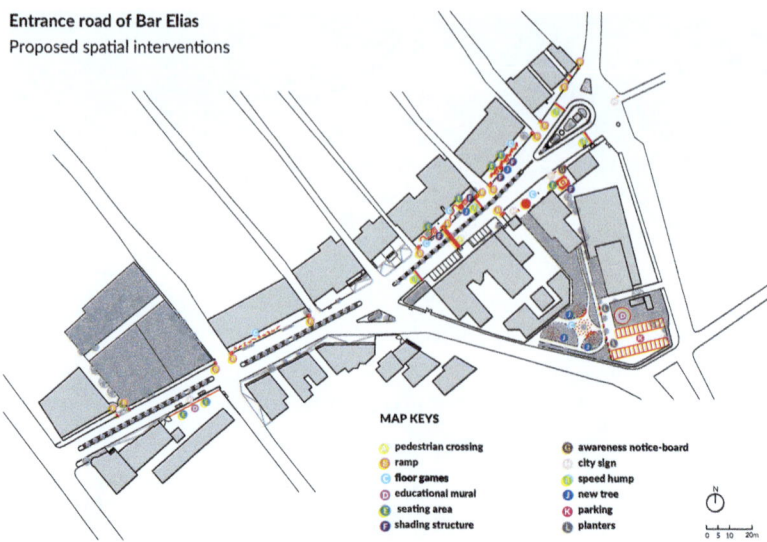

**Figure 5.6** Overview of Participatory Spatial Intervention.
Source: CatalyticAction

## 5.4 Social impacts of co-designed infrastructures

Two years after the completion of the PSI, in September 2021, our team designed an evaluation programme to assess the intervention's impact over time. The preceding period had been one of disruption and crisis. In October 2019, a revolution erupted across the country, with mass protests that eventually ousted the government. This was followed by a massive currency depreciation, which led to unemployment, rising poverty rates and a surge in the cost of living. In the spring of 2020, the Covid-19 pandemic hit Lebanon hard, especially since there was no social safety net to support people during lockdown. In August 2020, one of the largest ever non-nuclear explosions destroyed vast swathes of Beirut, killing over 200 people, injuring thousands, and displacing hundreds of thousands.

These successive and compounding crises were felt in Bar Elias. There had been over 250 deaths from Covid-19 in the town at the time of the evaluation, according to local reports (see Lebanese Ministry of Health, 2022). At the same time, the economic crisis resulted in a decline of the public realm, with shortages of money and basic goods leading to a proliferation of theft of anything that could be of value, from cars to pieces of hard infrastructure such as manhole covers. The relationship between long-term residents (Lebanese and Palestinian) and displaced Syrians also deteriorated during this period. Negative rumours were spread about refugees and there were occasional conflicts in the ubiquitous queues for health services at the polyclinic or for fuel at the petrol station. The acute economic crisis also meant that the municipality could not afford to maintain the built environment beyond the most essential services.

The evaluation of the PSI took place in this context of recession and the incapacity of the public sector. Like the research that preceded it, the evaluation was carried out in collaboration with citizen scientists, with four members of the original citizen science group taking the lead in monitoring and documenting the impact. The evaluation team observed and recorded residents' interactions with all elements of the PSI over six days and conducted short interviews with users and passers-by. The findings suggested that the majority of residents saw the PSI as having a positive impact on the town and the community. The PSI's focus on making the town centre a space where it is easier for people to socialise fostered inter-group interactions and a stronger sense of collective identity, while opening up new spaces to previously marginalised groups.

The most notable impact of the PSI was generated by its key design feature – the shaded seating area with play elements and mosaic decorations – which had transformed the town both physically and socially by encouraging social interactions. In fact, the space had become known locally as 'the new town square', a new landmark in the town which served as a gathering point for all residents and visitors across differences of nationality, class and age. It was used by children and caregivers waiting for doctor's appointments throughout the day, and by young men who needed a place to socialise in the evenings. The space was also the site for large gatherings, public demonstrations and communal celebrations: protests of up to 2,000 people during the October 2019 revolution; gatherings on the Palestinian national day (officially known as Independence Day) and protests against the Israeli attacks on Gaza in 2021; celebrations on Muslim holidays such as Ramadan, Hijri New Year and the Prophet's Birthday. All of these activities were now taking place at the newly developed space (Figures 5.7 and 5.8).

As one citizen scientist explained, the PSI transformed the landscape of the town and the way in which residents expressed their collective identity: the PSI, he said, was *'wajhet al mantaqa'* (the face of the area), and was comparable to Beirut's bustling Hamra Street. The space, he elaborated, had become a local landmark, and people would frequently say, 'Let's meet at the *saha* (square)', referring to the bench outside the polyclinic.

**Figure 5.7** Gathering around the seating area during the Lebanese revolution, October 2019.

Source: Moayad Hamdallah, citizen scientist

**Figure 5.8** Gathering to celebrate the Prophet's Birthday, 2019.

Source: Moayad Hamdallah, citizen scientist

But with increased use, prime location and a sequence of crises came increased securitisation. As the economic situation worsened, shortly after the construction of the PSI, the police placed a temporary police station (a container) next to the bench, in order to observe the main road and reduce theft. This blocked the flow of people and inhibited access to a drinking fountain, and also made the area aesthetically and socially less welcoming. The looming presence of police officers made people – and especially women – less comfortable in the space. Nevertheless, a young man who regularly sat on the bench said that, despite the police presence, the installation was hugely beneficial: 'The space has been used a lot more in the past two years, and it benefits everyone, but especially the Syrians who come here because their houses are too small.' Initially, residents had expressed worries that creating a seating area in a public square would attract 'thugs', but this prediction did not come true; instead, the installation became a 'place for all groups', as another citizen scientist put it, and it also brought a sense of pride to the town, particularly among those who had taken an active part in the research, design and implementation.

In comparison with the circular bench, the rehabilitated green space was less successful in its goal of providing a safe and inclusive public space. This was because it required a significant amount of maintenance, which the municipality did not have the capacity to deliver in a time of crisis. During the design phase of the PSI project, CatalyticAction had negotiated with the municipality that only a small part of the park would be used for car parking, and that the municipality would water and care for the greenery in the park. Two years on, however, much of the space was used for parking, especially by the polyclinic staff, and the municipality only watered the plants when a member of the citizen science team followed it up with them. The newly installed wooden benches had been stolen six months after completion (with numerous unsubstantiated rumours circulating that refugees were to blame and that polyclinic staff stole the benches for their homes). Furthermore, the space was used for very limited periods during the day: in the daytime, the space was barely visited by anyone, because of the strong sun and lack of shade; at night, the absence of lighting meant that hardly anyone would visit, save for the occasional couple looking for a quiet date spot. The only time when the space was busy was in the evenings when it was cooler and still bright: children played football in the green area for several hours every evening, and families visited the space around sunset to let small children run around. As Moayad Hamdallah (one of the most active citizen scientists on the team) explained, this small green area holds enormous potential for improving residents' wellbeing in the future: 'If the park is maintained and a playground installed, it could create a peaceful spot for children who are badly impacted by the stressful economic situation and allow them to play in a safe area set back from the road.'

The smaller elements of the PSI that were placed along the main road (for example, seating, access ramps, speed bumps, trees) also led to mixed outcomes in terms of impact. Initial worries about young men loitering on the seats did not materialise, but other issues came to the fore. Some of the newly installed shaded seating was claimed by shop owners, causing tensions with other residents who were also interested in using

**Figure 5.9** One of the trees planted as part of the PSI providing shade to a street seller, 2021.

Source: CatalyticAction

it. The seating installed for the local taxi stand also ran into problems: the fact that it was built for short waits meant that it was not comfortable enough for the longer periods that taxi drivers spent waiting for customers. This, combined with the lack of shade, meant that drivers preferred to bring their own chairs and sit on the tree-lined central reservation (median) of the road. The trees were well looked after by shop owners and daily street users, and they thrived, while providing much-needed shade (Figure 5.9).

The 16 ramps designed to enable access for wheelchair and pushchair users were successful at improving access to the pavement. A major problem – one that was correctly anticipated during the design phase – was that the ramps were used by motorcycles and tuk-tuks to drive onto the pavement. In response, one local butcher had removed the ramp near his shop because he felt that the exhaust from small vehicles affected the quality of his meat. The colourful floor games painted on the pavement proved to be particularly successful. They were regularly used by children, especially in the cooler summer evenings, and the murals and signage were generally well maintained. The speed bumps that were put in place to slow down some of the traffic had to be removed because of lack of maintenance, but the citizen scientists have committed to having them reinstalled once the municipality raises the necessary funds.

Another key part of the post-implementation impact was the way in which members of the Bar Elias community treated, maintained and built on the different elements of the PSI. As we suggested earlier, one of the benefits of co-design and community-engaged implementation is that residents of the community take ownership of the project and maintain a strong investment in its long-term maintenance and use. As the findings of the impact evaluation revealed, Bar Elias residents did in fact assume ownership of the PSI installations and took a number of actions on their own initiative to preserve and enhance them. Several people even replicated parts of the PSI. For example, about a month after the PSI's completion, staff from the aforementioned polyclinic added additional concrete benches with planters and a sign for disability access along the path to the rehabilitated garden. In another example, a local activist from the organisation Moltaka Shabab Bar Elias (Bar Elias Youth Meeting Point) installed murals in the different neighbourhoods of the town.

When maintenance could not be carried out by the municipality, members of the community were able to step in to maintain the intervention. A staff member from the polyclinic took on the responsibility of watering the trees in front of the building, while an employee of the MSF hospital watered the trees on the opposite side of the street. The citizen scientists also took an active role in the long-term maintenance of the PSI's different elements. In particular, one team member – Moayad Hamdallah – expressed a keen sense of responsibility to ensure that the installations remained in good shape: he notified CatalyticAction of any changes or need for repairs; he continuously negotiated with the municipality and local politicians about maintaining the positive changes despite the economic crisis; and he stored removed parts of the PSI, such as some of the speed bumps, at his home in the hope that they will be reinstalled at a later point. Hamadallah also co-ordinated several small maintenance works directly with the team and took part in the works while they were carried out.

While this chapter has focused on the impacts on the urban environment and residents' sociality of the co-designed social infrastructure, the participatory approach created a human infrastructure of trained and mobilised residents able to act for their town across boundaries of nationality, gender, age and religion (Rigon et al., 2021). Some of the citizen scientists who were initially recruited for this project went on to work on other research initiatives, where they were able to apply the training and experience they had gained while working in the IGP team. For others, the experience of working in a diverse group enhanced their understanding of their community. One citizen scientist, for example, said that taking part in the PSI helped him to think from the perspective of other groups and consider their needs with greater awareness. Another member of the team made a similar statement about awareness, understanding and acceptance across social divides: 'Working with colleagues from different backgrounds gave me more confidence and openness to accept people with different thoughts and ideas.' Furthermore, being able to take ownership of the intervention and its outcomes helped participants to adopt new roles in their communities. One citizen scientist noted that the spaces enhanced by the intervention are known to her friends and neighbours as spaces she created, while another citizen scientist said that the team members who participated in the project were now 'well known in the community' for the work that they had done. Such recognition was always welcomed by the people who made a contribution, but it was particularly significant for refugees, whose participation in the improvement of their town meant that they could 'give back' to their hosts, as one Syrian citizen scientist put it. Within the context of displacement and often strained host–refugee relations, the process of the PSI, from research to implementation, was an opportunity to challenge the stereotype of refugees as passive recipients of aid and to highlight their ability and willingness to contribute to their town and community. Refugees were denied the rights of national citizenship (in the legal sense of the term), but they were both capable of exercising and willing to exercise urban citizenship (in the participatory sense of the term) by demonstrating a duty of care towards the town that they lived in and the people with whom they co-inhabited it (Rigon et al., 2021). Finally, citizen scientists used the skills and social networks they acquired to engage in a variety of other independent initiatives, including building a group with the aim of running for political office, student activism, involving neighbours in planning a better use of an empty space near their dwellings, and advocacy with the municipality.

## 5.5 Conclusion

The participatory spatial intervention presented in this chapter illustrates how collaborative creation of social infrastructures in which members of the public are involved in research, design and implementation can amplify impact and generate social value beyond the materiality of the infrastructures themselves (Rigon et al., 2021). This, we argue, has important implications for thinking about economic and infrastructural recovery, especially in the Lebanese context of displacement, where tensions between hosts and refugees, competition over resources, and narratives about refugees as a burden persist. Investment in infrastructures is much needed at the moment, but it is important to question what that investment is used for, how it is implemented, who will benefit from it, and with what consequences. There is good reason to anticipate that the impact of infrastructural recovery will be not only very limited, but also fraught with a range of social and political challenges, if it is conducted in a top-down manner without any input or engagement from local community members. In order to achieve adequate delivery of services, as Fawaz (2018) suggests, infrastructural projects must build on existing informal arrangements and localised support systems.

Furthermore, efforts to improve quality of life are impossible to separate from efforts to address displacement-related challenges. This is because hosts and refugees inhabit the same spaces, and use (and contribute to) overlapping infrastructures, services and social support systems. But contrary to claims that hosts and refugees are in continuous competition over scarce resources in a zero-sum game, the experience of Bar Elias shows that it is both possible and beneficial to view refugees and hosts as interdependent actors who can support one another and work together towards shared goals. Future initiatives and interventions, regardless of their scale, should thus account for the value of partnership with communities and uphold principles of dialogue and inclusion, with the right mechanisms in place to embed these principles into practice.

If infrastructural projects aspire to delivering prosperity as it has been redefined in this volume, they need to include the intended beneficiaries in the process of creation. This means giving people the opportunity to express their voices, whether this is done through consultation and co-design of policy action, or, as in the case of the PSI discussed here, through participation in the building and implementation of the project. As our example from Bar Elias shows, this approach is beneficial for both the residents and the built environment: it gives people a chance to create an urban environment they want to live in, it strengthens feelings of belonging, it encourages people to care for their public spaces and, not least, it transforms social relations towards pathways to collaboration for meaningful change.

## Note

1. Migrant domestic workers are excluded from the country's labour laws and are instead governed by the *kafala* sponsorship system whereby workers' rights to work and live in the country are tied to their employer. This frequently results in exploitation and abuse.

# Bibliography

Abid, R. Z., Manan, S. A. & Rahman, Z. A. A. A. (2017). 'A flood of Syrians has slowed to a trickle': The use of metaphors in the representation of Syrian refugees in the online media news reports of host and non-host countries. *Discourse & Communication*, 11(2), 121–40. https://doi.org/10.1177/1750481317691857.

Amin, A. (2012). *Land of Strangers*. Cambridge: Polity.

Baumann, H. & Kanafani, S. (2020). *Vulnerability and Public Services in the Lebanese Context of Mass Displacement: A literature review*. RELIEF Working Paper. Available at: https://discovery.ucl.ac.uk/id/eprint/10116036/1/Baumann_RELIEF%20WP_%20Vulnerability%20and%20Public%20Services%20in%20the%20Lebanese%20Context%20of%20Mass%20Displacement_.pdf (accessed 21 December 2022).

Baylouny, A. M. (2020). *When Blame Backfires: Syrian refugees and citizen grievances in Jordan and Lebanon*. Ithaca, NY: Cornell University Press.

Betts, A., Bloom, L., Kaplan J. & Omata, N. (2017). *Refugee Economies: Forced displacement and development*. Oxford: Oxford University Press.

Betts, A. & Collier, P. (2017). *Refuge: Transforming a broken refugee system*. London: Allen Lane.

Bou Akar, H. (2018). *For the War Yet to Come: Planning Beirut's frontiers*. Stanford, CA: Stanford University Press.

Chalcraft, J. T. (2009). *The Invisible Cage: Syrian migrant workers in Lebanon*. Stanford, CA: Stanford University Press.

Christophersen, M., Thorleifsson, C. M. & Tiltnes, Å. A. (2013). *Ambivalent Hospitality: Coping strategies and local responses to Syrian refugees in Lebanon*. Oslo: Fafo. Available at: https://reliefweb.int/report/lebanon/ambivalent-hospitality-coping-strategies-and-local-responses-syrian-refugees-lebanon (accessed 24 February 2023).

Dabaj, J. & Conti, R. L. (2020). Placemaking in Lebanese cities hosting displaced communities. *Journal of Public Space*, 5(1), 219–46. https://doi.org/10.32891/jps.v5i1.1259.

Dabaj, J., Rigon, A. & Baumann, H. (2020). Participatory Spatial Intervention: How can participatory design and a diversity lens help address vulnerabilities in Bar Elias, Lebanon? Beirut: CatalyticAction & UCL. Available at: https://www.catalyticaction.org/wp-content/uploads/2020/06/PSI-Report_Digital_FINAL_low.pdf (accessed 22 December 2022).

DeJong, J., Sbeity, F., Schlecht, J., Harfouche, M., Yamout, R., Fouad, F. M., Manohar, S. & Robinson, C. (2017). Young lives disrupted: Gender and well-being among adolescent Syrian refugees in Lebanon. *Conflict and Health*, 11(Suppl. 1), 25–34. Available at: 10.1186/s13031-017-0128-7 (accessed 22 December 2022).

Fakhoury, T. (2017). Governance strategies and refugee response: Lebanon in the face of Syrian displacement. *International Journal of Middle East Studies*, 49(4), 681–700. https://doi.org/10.1017/S0020743817000654.

Fawaz, M. (2009). Neoliberal urbanity and the right to the city: A view from Beirut's periphery. *Development and Change*, 40(5), 827–52. https://doi.org/10.1111/j.1467-7660.2009.01585.x.

Fawaz, M. (2018). CEDRE aid: An integrated infrastructure development plan, not a random laundry list. Lebanese Center for Policy Studies. Available at: https://www.lcps-lebanon.org/articles/details/1866/cedre-aid-an-integrated-infrastructure-development-plan-not-a-random-laundry-list (accessed 22 December 2022).

Fawaz, M., Gharbieh, A., Harb, M. & Salamé, D. (2018). For a different kind of refugee talk. In M. Fawaz, A. Gharbieh, M. Harb & D. Salamé (eds), *Refugees as City-Makers*, pp. 4–9. Beirut: Issam Fares Institute for Public Policy and International Affairs, American University of Beirut.

Haddad, S., Aliaga, L. & Attree, L. (2018). *Building Peace into Refugee Responses: Syrian refugees in Lebanon*. London, Beirut: Saferworld, Lebanese Center for Policy Studies. Available at: https://www.saferworld.org.uk/downloads/building-peace-into-refugee-responses-26-4.pdf (accessed 22 December 2022).

Harake, W. & Kostopoulos, C. (2018). Strategic assessment: A capital investment plan for Lebanon – investment opportunities and reforms. Working paper, 6 April. Washington, DC: World Bank Group.

Harb, C. & Saab, R. (2014). Social cohesion and intergroup relations: Syrian refugees and Lebanese nationals in the Bekaa and Akkar. Save the Children, AUB. Available at: https://www.researchgate.net/publication/319178524_Social_Cohesion_and_Intergroup_Relations_Syrian_Refugees_and_Lebanese_Nationals_in_the_Bekaa_and_Akkar (accessed 22 December 2022).

Harb el-Kak, M. (2000). Post-war Beirut: Resources, negotiations, and contestations in the Elyssar project. *Arab World Geographer*, 3(4), 272–88. https://doi.org/10.5555/arwg.3.4.8q0284022441228v.

Hourani, N. B. (2015). People or profit? Two post-conflict reconstructions in Beirut. *Human Organization*, 74(2), 174–84. https://doi.org/10.17730/0018-7259-74.2.174.

Inter-Agency Coordination Lebanon (2015). Most vulnerable localities in Lebanon. Map. Available at: https://data2.unhcr.org/en/documents/download/45715 (accessed 22 December 2022).

Jallad, M. & Mintchev, N. (2019). Too close for comfort: Citizen social science and methodological innovation in Hamra, Beirut. *Jadaliyya*. Available at: https://www.jadaliyya.com/Details/40376/Too-Close-for-Comfort-Citizen-Social-Science-and-Methodological-Innovation-in-Hamra,-Beirut (accessed 24 February 2023).

Jallad, M., Mintchev, N., Pietrostefani, E., Daher, M. & Moore, H. L. (2022). Citizen social science and pathways to prosperity: Co-designing research and impact in Beirut, Lebanon. *International Journal of Social Research Methodology*, 25(6), 769–82. https://doi.org/10.1080/13645579.2021.1942664.

Khechen, M. (2018). The remaking of Ras Beirut: Displacement beyond gentrification. *City*, 22(3), 375–95. https://doi.org/10.1080/13604813.2018.1484643.

Knudsen, A. (2017). Syria's refugees in Lebanon: Brothers, burden, and bone of contention. In R. Di Peri & D. Meier (eds), *Lebanon Facing the Arab Uprisings: Constraints and adaptation*, pp. 135–54. Basingstoke: Palgrave Macmillan.

Knudsen, A. (2018). The great escape? Converging refugee crises in Tyre, Lebanon. *Refugee Survey Quarterly*, 37(1), 96–115. https://doi.org/10.1093/rsq/hdx018.

Krijnen, M. & Fawaz, M. (2010). Exception as the rule: High-end developments in neoliberal Beirut. *Built Environment*, 36(2), 245–59. http://dx.doi.org/10.2148/benv.36.2.245.

Lebanese Ministry of Health (2022). Monitoring of COVID-19 infection in Lebanon – 30/6/2022 – cases by cazaa. Available at: https://www.moph.gov.lb/en/Pages/127/43750/monitoring-of-covid-19- (accessed on 4 July 2022).

Makdisi, S. (1997). Laying claim to Beirut: Urban narrative and spatial identity in the age of Solidere. *Critical Inquiry*, 23(3), 661–705. https://doi.org/10.1086/448848.

Mansuri, G. & Rao, V. (2013), *Localizing Development: Does participation work?* Washington, DC: World Bank.

Mintchev, N., Daher, M., Jallad, M., Pietrostefani, E., Moore, H. L., Ghamrawi, G., Harrache, A., Majed, A. & Younes, Y. (2022). Sustained citizen science from research to solutions: A new impact model for the social sciences. *International Journal of Qualitative Methods*, 21, 1–16. https://doi.org/10.1177/16094069221133232.

Mintchev, N. & Moore, H. L. (2017). Community and prosperity beyond social capital: The case of Newham, East London. *Critical Social Policy*, 37(4), 562–81. https://doi.org/10.1177/0261018316683461.

Mintchev, N. & Moore, H. L. (2018). Super-diversity and the prosperous society. *European Journal of Social Theory*, 21(1), 117–34. https://doi.org/10.1177/1368431016678629.

Rigon, A. (2014). Building local governance: Participation and elite capture in slum-upgrading in Kenya. *Development and Change*, 45(2), 257–83. https://doi.org/10.1111/dech.12078.

Rigon, A., Dabaj, J. & Baumann, H. (2021). Participatory design and diversity: Addressing vulnerabilities through social infrastructure in a Lebanese town hosting displaced people. In A. Rigon & V. Castán Broto (eds), *Inclusive Urban Development in the Global South: Intersectionality, inequalities, and community*, pp. 198–212. Abingdon: Routledge.

Sanyal, R. (2017). A no-camp policy: Interrogating informal settlements in Lebanon. *Geoforum*, 84, 117–25. https://dx.doi.org/10.1016/j.geoforum.2017.06.011.

Sawalha, A. (2010). *Reconstructing Beirut: Memory and space in a postwar Arab city*. Austin: University of Texas Press.

Shehabi, A. & Al-Masri, M. (2022). Foregrounding citizen imaginaries: Exploring just energy futures through a citizens' assembly in Lebanon. *Futures*, 140, art. no. 102956, 1–16. https://doi.org/10.1016/j.futures.2022.102956.

Turner, L. (2015). Explaining the (non-)encampment of Syrian refugees: Security, class and the labour market in Lebanon and Jordan. *Mediterranean Politics*, 20(3), 386–404. https://doi.org/10.1080/13629395.2015.1078125.

Ullrich, L. (2018). *Below the surface: Results of a WhatsApp survey of Syrian refugees and host communities in Lebanon*. Beirut: UNDP.

UNHCR (2018). Map: Syria refugee response. Lebanon, Bekaa & Baalbek-El Hermel Governorate: Distribution of the registered Syrian refugees at the cadastral level, as of 31 July 2018. https://data.unhcr.org/en/documents/details/66241 (accessed 24 February 2023).

UNHCR (2021). Lebanon Fact Sheet. September. Available at: https://reporting.unhcr.org/document/963 (accessed 22 December 2022).

UNICEF (2021). Water supply systems on the verge of collapse in Lebanon: Over 71 per cent of people risk losing access to water. Press release. Available at: https://www.unicef.org/press-releases/water-supply-systems-verge-collapse-lebanon-over-71-cent-people-risk-losing-access (accessed 22 December 2022).

United Nations Development Programme [2018]. Lebanon Host Communities Support Programme: 2017 Annual report summary. Available at: www.lb.undp.org/content/lebanon/en/home/library/poverty/LHSP-2017-Annual-Report-Summary.html (accessed 22 December 2022).

United Nations Economic and Social Commission for Western Asia (ESCWA) (2021). Multidimensional poverty in Lebanon (2019–2021): Painful reality and uncertain prospects. E/ESCWA/CL3.SEP/2021/POLICY BRIEF.2. Available at: https://www.unescwa.org/publications/multidimensional-poverty-lebanon-2019-2021 (accessed 22 December 2022).

Yassine, B. & Al-Harithy, H. (2021). Entrepreneurial systems of Syrian refugees as stimulators of host economy: Case of Ouzaii (Lebanon). *Refugee Survey Quarterly*, 40(1), 1–29. https://doi.org/10.1093/rsq/hdaa013.

# 6
# Decentralised renewable energy: a pathway to prosperity for Lebanon?

Henrietta L. Moore, Hannah Collins and Diala Makki

## 6.1 Introduction

Lebanon is embroiled in five major crises simultaneously: an economic crisis, a refugee crisis, a climate crisis, a post-Covid crisis and the aftermath of the port of Beirut explosion. Since 2021 these crises have been compounded by ongoing government failures, the Ukraine war and rocketing prices for food and energy. There is widespread agreement that policy inaction is fuelling an economic and social catastrophe, underpinned by sustained distrust between government and citizens/residents. The capture of resources by the elite, sectarian politics and regional conflict have ensured long-term fragility and dysfunction and are continuing to drive political unrest. The lack of consensus on an alternative economic vision for Lebanon further erodes trust, and sidelines and marginalises community efforts and initiatives.

Multiple intersecting crises have affected people's quality of life, diminishing job opportunities and reducing the provision of public services in education, health, clean water, waste management and energy. Weakened public services are undermining wellbeing and human capital development and putting the social contract at further risk. According to the Human Capital Index (HCI), a next-generation Lebanese worker will only achieve 52 per cent of the productive potential she would have had if she had had a complete education and full health. This figure is below the average for both upper-middle-income countries and the MENA region (World Bank, 2020). It underscores the point that Lebanon is not allocating sufficient resources to key public services to build the necessary capacities and capabilities of its citizens/residents (World Bank, 2022).

The future prosperity of Lebanon is closely linked to improved public services, and at the core of these is the question of energy (Ahmad, 2020; Moore & Collins, 2019). A reliable, sustainable, affordable and accessible energy supply would significantly improve the wellbeing, employability, safety, health and education of Lebanon's population. It is becoming increasingly evident that energy policy in Lebanon should focus on hybrid systems, with decentralisation, sustainability and enhanced renewable energy (RE) provision, informed by Lebanon's residents, who are already engaging in multifaceted responses to crumbling energy infrastructure, rising prices and government failures. In this chapter, we draw on the IGP's work in Lebanon since 2017 under the RELIEF Centre in order to look beyond macroeconomic questions and the cost of infrastructure development, and examine potential transformations in energy systems in terms of people's quality of life and the role public services play in building capacities and capabilities (IGP, 2019a, 2019b; Moore & Collins, 2019; RELIEF Centre & UN-Habitat Lebanon, 2020; Pietrostefani et al., 2022; Shehabi et al., 2021; Shehabi & El-Masri, 2022; Zaher, 2022).[1]

## 6.2 Challenges for energy policy in Lebanon

Climate change impacts the entire economy of Lebanon and all aspects of the environment, which is vulnerable to rising sea levels and heatwaves (Ministry of Foreign Affairs of the Netherlands, 2018). The Lebanese population has been subject to severe water shortages for decades. Water service delivery is substandard and intermittent. This has particular consequences for the poor, who spend up to 15 per cent of their total household income on alternative water supplies, which are not themselves sustainable (World Bank, 2020). In July 2021 more than four million people were at risk of losing access to safe drinking water, as the country's main power plants ran out of fuel (UNICEF, 2021). Water shortages and heatwaves add strains to a struggling energy system. Projections for temperature rises of between 1°C and 3°C by 2040 are estimated to lead to an annual increase in electricity consumption for cooling of between 9.04 and 28.55 per cent (Kabakian et al., 2011). The Lebanese economy loses about $800 million per year in agricultural and food costs that can be traced directly and indirectly to climate change (USAID, 2019). Alarming levels of environmental degradation are the consequence of ongoing mismanagement and political stasis. Levels of pollution and the degradation of natural resources pose significant risks to economic and social sustainability, and to the health and wellbeing of citizens/residents. UNDP has estimated the cost of environmental degradation at

4.4 per cent of the country's GDP (World Bank, 2020: 48). There is an urgent need to shift towards a green economy based on collaborative, transparent and inclusive engagement with municipalities, business, civil society, and communities.

In Lebanon, as around the world, there is a mixed response to the changing landscape of the IPCC (2018, 2021, 2022) deadlines on climate change and how these might connect to energy reform, innovation, investment and participation. Further constraints for an RE transition for Lebanon are the vested interest throughout the economy in oil imports and the entrenched nature and power of the private generator owners who provide back-up power when blackouts occur. The prospect of natural resource discovery has generated a great deal of investment interest and political debate (Fattouh & Mahadeva, 2016). Domestic gas could reduce import dependence and emissions. The gas market is expected to be dominated initially by gas imports that will eventually be partly replaced by indigenous gas. Gas streams will enter the Lebanese market at different geographical locations and on different contractual terms, but there is no developed legal or physical infrastructure to manage market ownership and structure. The AUB Policy Institute (2018) suggests that the government of Lebanon needs to play a central role in regulating the gas market. There is potential for a hybrid-energy system here that allows for private sector investment in gas and RE technologies, but it needs to be connected to a broader agenda and policies for long-term prosperity in Lebanon (Ahmad, 2020).

While Lebanon is searching for oil and gas reserves (without significant success), it has set a target of 30 per cent renewable energies by 2030. An earlier target of 12 per cent of its primary energy source to be renewable by 2020 was missed because of the ongoing political and financial crises in the country. Lebanon has had one of the biggest increases in greenhouse gas (GHG) emissions since 1990, and the energy sector, including transport, is responsible for 79 per cent of the country's total GHG emissions (USAID, 2019). Power generation is the main contributor here, because 88 per cent of imported fuel and 53 per cent of diesel and gas are used for thermal power generation (Shehabi et al., 2021). However, as one participant in the research pointed out, change needs to begin with the phasing out of fossil fuels.

> The focus should be on starting to phase out of our current conventional fossil fuel dependency on heavy fuel oil instead of being blinded by this frenzy of this clean gas coming our way without even knowing if we actually have gas.
> (Participant, IGP/Chatham House workshop, IGP, 2019b: 17).

Electricité du Liban (EDL) holds the monopoly of energy supply in Lebanon. It is a vertically integrated national utility accountable to the Ministry of Energy and Water (MoEW) which is responsible for policy formulation for the electricity, fuel and water sectors. The Lebanese Center for Energy Conservation (LCEC) is the national energy agency for Lebanon and acts as the technical arm of the MoEW (LCEC, 2018). Overall responsibility rests with the Council of Ministers (CoM) chaired by the Prime Minister, and includes ministries that represent the major political parties in the country (World Bank, 2019). EDL is a highly politicised entity, with government appointment boards chosen through opaque processes based on sectarian quotas.

The electricity sector is a huge financial burden on Lebanon's public finances. In 2020 the energy minister claimed that losses from the electricity sector cost about USD 1.6 billion in public funds each year (Chehayeb, 2021), or 3 per cent of GDP, while others suggest it is as much as USD 2 billion, or 4.5 per cent of GDP (Hatoum, 2020). Since 1992, subsidies and spending in the electricity sector have accounted for around 40 per cent of government debt (Ayat et al., 2021). The government of Lebanon estimates that more than a quarter of Lebanon's debt – currently more than $90 billion – results from EDL's deficit (Snaije, 2022). The debt-to-GDP ratio in 2019 was approximately 170 per cent, and this debt continues to grow while GDP does not (Snaije, 2022).

EDL's tariffs are still based on a 1997 fuel cost of around USD 20 per barrel of oil (World Bank, 2022), which in 2018 covered only 37 per cent of average operating costs, representing a substantial subsidy. The challenge for MoEW is to reduce transfers to EDL to cover its deficits while keeping tariffs low to mitigate the adverse effects of rising prices on citizens/residents. In May 2021, the tariff was around USD 0.01 per kWh, but the cost of each kWh generated by EDL was USD 0.11–0.18, representing less than 10 per cent of the total cost of the service (Ahmad, Mahmalat & Saghir, 2021). Low electricity tariffs that do not reflect the cost are a barrier to deployment of RE because of the long amortisation period. EDL cannot increase the tariffs until the infrastructure and the grid are reliable, but at the same time EDL does not have the finances to improve the system's reliability (Vallvé et al., 2019). EDL will be the main customer for all large-scale RE projects, but their financial deficit and bankability problems increase the risk of investment. There is no dedicated department within EDL for incorporating RE into the national grid, and no grid codes exist internationally that could be adopted (UN ESCWA, 2018).

Despite such large subsidies, electricity supply is insufficient to meet demand. Inadequate energy infrastructure and supply have resulted in endemic power outages. The power gap is estimated at about 1 GW (and is likely much higher than this), leading to daily cuts for three hours in Beirut and up to 17 hours in the Beqaa Valley (World Bank, 2019). Following the Covid pandemic, the economic crash and the Beirut port explosion in 2020, the Lebanese currency has fallen fifteenfold in value. Hyperinflation means food staples are out of reach for many, essential medicines are out of stock, and there has been even less fuel to supply the overburdened energy infrastructure. The war in Ukraine and massive hikes in food and energy prices have exacerbated the situation further. Over half the Lebanese population is now living in poverty, and extreme poverty has risen threefold since 2019, with many people unable to afford basic services (UN, 2021). In 2020, the World Bank termed Lebanon's economic and financial crisis a 'deliberate depression' (World Bank, 2020), and in 2022 a Ponzi scheme (World Bank, 2022).

Lebanese residents in 2021 witnessed an increase in severe electricity shortages and corresponding blackouts, compounded by a reduction in the foreign currency reserves necessary for fuel imports, and the expiry in 2020 of the contract with Sonatrach, the largest heavy fuel supplier for EDL (World Bank, 2022). Power rationing increases dependency on expensive private diesel generators, but their fuel is also dependent on imports and the availability of foreign currency (Shehabi et al., 2021). In October 2021 electrical power was cut completely for 24 hours when both of the country's main power plants ran out of fuel.

The unreliability of the energy services is an inherent feature of everyday life in Lebanon. Informal connections to private diesel generators, to maintain the electricity necessary to meet the basic requirements of households and businesses, have been normalised (Abi Ghanem, 2018, 2021). The large number of 'illegal' connections to the grid results in a financial burden on the national economy that exceeds USD 330 million per year (AEMS, 2017). In 2017, 66 per cent of Lebanon's households relied on diesel generators to back up power supply, with over 46 per cent of households paying 8.4 per cent of their income to secure electricity (Harajli & Chalak, 2018). Residents pay a double electricity bill: one to EDL and the other for back-up generation, almost twice that of EDL, which results in the highest electricity bills in the region (Fardoun et al., 2012). Neighbourhoods are allocated one private energy provider, with the backing of politicians and municipal officials. These energy providers do not face competition and can set their own fees. They are further legitimised through local tariffs aimed at them. New housing blocks are built with space for generators, so new tenants have little choice but to accept this informal arrangement (Verdeil, 2016; Abi Ghanem, 2018). In 2018, the total private generator market was estimated at USD 1.1 billion, serving 1.08 million customers whose electricity purchase was estimated at 4 terawatt hours (TWh). In total, when fuel imports and distribution, generator sales and maintenance services are considered, the value of the market is estimated at around USD 2 billion. The total size of the labour force linked to these operations is thought to be around 13,200 persons (World Bank, 2022). This contractual and physical entanglement of private generators in daily life reflects a process of long-running adaptation to the fragility of energy as a key public service, but while some argue that it impedes innovation (Dziadosz, 2018), others suggest that this informal sector provision will need to be woven into the process of transformation towards renewables and more sustainable energy provision (Abi Ghanem, 2021; Ahmad, 2020; and see below).

## 6.3 Renewable energy technology and policy in Lebanon

The landscape of energy policy in Lebanon is complex, incorporating different actors and drivers (Ahmad, 2020; Moore & Collins, 2019; IGP, 2019a). A transition towards a green energy system involves widespread deployment of RE technology at different scales, the development of enabling infrastructure, public and private investment, the implementation of appropriate regulatory frameworks, and the creation of new value chains, markets and industries (Ersoy et al., 2021).

Initial steps have been taken to develop Lebanon's energy sector towards renewable sources, starting more than a decade ago and developed through the National Energy Efficiency Action Plan (NEEAP) 2011–2016 and the National Renewable Energy Action Plan (NREAP) 2016–2020. Environmentally, full implementation of the NREAP would have reduced Lebanon's yearly carbon dioxide emissions by 11.25 per cent (UN ESCWA, 2018). By 2020, total installed RE power capacity amounted to 350 MW, including 286 MW from hydropower, 7 MW from landfill and 56.37 MW from solar (IRENA, 2020). This was far short of the targets set. A subsequent NREAP, 2021–2025, with updated targets, has not been developed (LCEC, 2021).

There is recognition within different sections of government (through the 30 per cent target goal, NREAP 2016–2020, the National Energy Efficiency and Renewable Energy Action (NEEREA) loan scheme, and the Capital Investment Plan) and from the public (through the uptake of solar water heaters (SWHs) and photovoltaics (PVs)) and the private sector (through private bank loans for domestic installation and the financing of wind farms in rural areas and the Beirut River Solar Snake (BRSS)) that RE is the way forward. While there is some co-ordination between the big players in RE in Lebanon, it is apparent that a lack of legal framework is inhibiting the sector from flourishing, and limiting its development. In addition to Covid-19, the financial crash and government paralysis, the main barriers to full deployment of RE technologies are a lack of components and a lack of clarity within the existing, outdated institutional and legal frameworks. Regulations are based on industrial traditions and codes; they are not up to date with sector developments. Delays to the implementation of a legal framework to privatise, liberalise and unbundle the sector have meant that only one wind power programme signed a purchase power agreement (PPA), under a law that is now defunct (UN ESCWA, 2018). This means that decrees that give EDL a monopoly in generation, transmission and distribution are still being applied. A legal regulator to set prices and liaise between government and private power producers has not been appointed. It is not clear which legal process the Lebanese government will deploy, and this uncertainty is delaying major investments in utility-scale RE. A critical challenge for Lebanon will be managing governance and transparency in the energy sector (Ahmad, Mahmalat & Saghir, 2021).

The solar photovoltaic sector is now well established in Lebanon, and growth since 2020 has been particularly rapid, as residents desperately try to avoid blackouts and expensive generator bills. Solar PV energy production is in abundant supply in Lebanon, which has around 300 days of sunshine per year, for eight to nine hours each day (Berjawi et al., 2017). Given that most electricity rationing in Lebanon occurs during the day, solar energy offers a sustainable alternative to cuts and diesel generators. Solar PV plants can be complemented with wind power. Initially, SWHs were the most developed RE technology in Lebanon, gaining momentum since 2010 with the aim of achieving 'a solar water heater for every household' (Bassil, 2010). The NEEAP 2011–2015 laid out a financing scheme for the SWH market (LCEC, 2016). Private banks, supported by the Lebanese Central Bank (BDL), offered five-year, interest-free loans for residential SWHs (that do not exceed $5000), and the MoEW contributed $200 to cover capital costs. SWH projects that exceeded $5000 could apply for a NEEREA loan. These loan schemes created momentum in the Lebanese SWH market, which more than doubled in 2010–2020 (LCEC, 2019b). Thirty-eight per cent of the SWH systems installed in Lebanon were partially or totally manufactured in Lebanon (UNDP/GEF, 2014), showing potential for market development in other RE systems. However, since 2019, financing schemes have no longer been available for renewable energy projects (residential, commercial or industrial), and the Covid pandemic, currency devaluation and the global energy crisis have resulted in volatility in costs and the flooding of the market with lower-quality solar panels, inverters and other necessary equipment. A new scheme announced in 2022 by the Banque de l'Habitat in conjunction with LCEC is intended to provide financial support for household PV systems through a list of LCEC-approved qualified installers, but is yet to be rolled out.

In 2011, EDL adopted a net-metering policy to support the expansion of solar energy to households; extending the policy to community grids in 2016. Net-metering allows for a two-directional flow of energy, from the grid to the customer and from the customer's RE facility to the grid, using a bidirectional meter (Berjawi et al., 2017). EDL does not pay for the net production of consumers, but credits the excess production to the next bill. More than 50 projects are connected to the net-metering network, but because of the lack of meters at EDL net amounts must be calculated manually, which limits the effectiveness of the policy (UN ESCWA, 2018).

From 2010 to 2017 solar PV capacity rose from around 0.35 megawatt peak (MWp) to over 35 MWp, averaging an annual equivalent growth of 100 per cent (Amine & Rizk, 2018). Solar PV generation increased from 35,000 MWh in 2016 to 53,000 MWh in 2017, constituting 0.35 per cent of the annual electricity generation by EDL (Amine & Rizk, 2018). By 2017, a total of 1417 solar PV projects had been implemented in Lebanon, but most were small in terms of capacity. It has been calculated that residential installations make up around 17 per cent of the sector, with industry comprising 30 per cent of capacity and the commercial sector accounting for 17 per cent (Ahmad, 2020). One estimate suggests that solar PV alone could cover the daily power peak load, far outreaching the LCEC 2020 target, improving energy security, reducing energy bills and reducing the impact of fossil fuels for electricity generation (Berjawi et al., 2017). The International Renewable Energy Agency (IRENA) predicts that Lebanon could cost-effectively obtain 30 per cent of its electricity supply from renewable sources by 2030, if proper plans were implemented (IRENA, 2020), and a large number of research studies have supported both the feasibility and the potential of solar energy in the context of hybrid systems (Mannah et al, 2021; Haddad, 2021; Kassem et al., 2021, 2022; Arnaout et al., 2021; Çamur et al., 2021; Dobeissi et al., 2021; Abou Brahim, 2020).

Analysts are well aware that to scale up energy from renewable resources will require the expansion of solar farms and mini-grids. The first solar farm, the Beirut River Solar Snake (BRSS), with a total planned output of 10 MW, came as part of the NEEAP 2016–2020 plan to install 200 MW of solar farms by 2020. The private sector designed and built the RE generation plant with government support. The idea of the BRSS was to take advantage of the 'unused' space above the Beirut River to supply energy and raise awareness of the potential of solar energy (Nasr, 2020). It opened in 2016, but only the first stage of the project has been completed, adding an extra 1 MW of electricity to the grid (Machnouk et al., 2019). A second phase, involving a six-kilometre extension, has been indefinitely postponed.

An obstacle to the high penetration of RE is land availability in Lebanon. Tfail, an inland region in the eastern Baalbek District on the border with Syria, has been shown to include around 13 $km^2$ of elevated flat lands with high levels of solar irradiation (Ayoub & Boustany, 2019). An examination of the technical and economic feasibility of a 300-MW solar PV plant in Tfail demonstrates robust technical and financial incentives with levellised cost-of-electricity ranges between 4.2 and 5.3 cents/kWh of electricity produced. The average annual energy generation over the project's lifetime is around 600 GWh per year. Given the location, such a project could play a role in potential electricity swap deals and trading with the Syrian grid in the future (Ayoub & Boustany, 2019). This pre-feasibility research is important, as it provides information for potential investors, and it has been reported that the European Bank for Reconstruction and Development is seeking consultants for a feasibility study for the project (Bellini, 2019).

Solar farms, mini-grids and community initiatives have all been tried in Lebanon (IGP, 2019a, 2019b), but the repeated pattern is of great ambition followed by paralysis. In 2018 CEDRO launched the 'Village 24' initiative, the first community-led RE system in Lebanon (UNDP/CEDRO, 2018). Approximately a hundred households in Kabrikha in Southern Lebanon signed up to the scheme, which was entirely powered by 250-kWp solar PV coupled with diesel generators. The intention was that this should be the first community initiative to utilise the net-metering policy.

Electricity costs have dropped by 30 per cent and the village no longer experiences power cuts. Through this initiative, in the event of a power cut a community-scale RE power plant can plug into the separate local grid that is owned and operated by the municipality, and then plug back into the utility network when national power is restored (UNDP/CEDRO, 2018). When the initiative was launched, it was hoped that this hybrid model would lead to the implementation of other community-led RE systems (whether solar, wind or bioenergy) that provide energy security, environmental benefits, community co-operation and economies of scale (UNDP/CEDRO, 2018).

Mini-grids are emerging as potential solutions in blocks of flats in cities in Lebanon, and also in local communities, but all are currently tied into back-up use of diesel generators. The Baaloul project, funded by USAID and supported by Caritas, makes use of a community mini-grid of 80-kWp PV panels, some EDL supply, and diesel generators. The aim was to ensure supply, but also to protect the local environment from pollution by diesel generators. The profits are directly distributed to inhabitant shareholders, and energy bills for inhabitants have dropped by 50 per cent. By involving the local community in decision making, project financing, and then redistribution of profits, this project has strengthened social solidarity and built local capacity. This is a feature of community-run RE projects noted elsewhere in Lebanon (Chaplain, 2022), as the following quote makes clear:

> We installed a PV system on a women's cooperative in the south of Lebanon. This cooperative needed a lot of machines to run their operations. They only had a very little generator but after installing the PV system for them their condition improved. They had less manual labour so less physical pain, more time spent with their family, more diversified products, more income and so forth. So, this highlighted that decentralized renewable energy is not only a good solution for the environment but also for the social aspects; for woman and power, etc.
> (Participant, IGP/Chatham House workshop, IGP, 2019b)

Other forms of community/collective provision involve supply by municipalities, such as the Menjez municipal project, which uses a similar hybrid system and is run by the municipality's energy committee; profits are not redistributed to residents, but reinvested in other local projects.

## 6.4 A comparison of energy infrastructure and use in Hamra, Ras Beirut and El Mina

As part of the IGP's work on prosperity gains and inclusive growth in Lebanon under the RELIEF Centre, we explored what prosperity means for local residents and how it can be achieved. The approach is based on three fundamental principles: context-specific measures of prosperity, a commitment to collaboration and co-design, and a focus on data. The IGP's work begins with the proposition that the notion of prosperity must include a foundational economy of goods and services that improves the collective wellbeing and quality of life of local residents, as well as important individual and community assets relating to belonging, history, identity, culture, and hope and optimism for the future (see Introduction and Chapters 1 and 2). Designing and envisaging prosperity and pathways towards it are particularly challenging when jobs, housing and basic services (energy, water and waste management, among others) are failing or non-existent. The research investigated multiple issues relating to quality of life, and results from the development of a citizen/resident-led prosperity model show that good-quality housing and infrastructure, as well as affordable and reliable utilities and public services, contribute to what Lebanese residents describe as the foundations of a prosperous life (Figure 6.1).

Between 2017 and 2021 research was undertaken in Hamra, Beirut (RELIEF Centre & UN-Habitat, 2020), Ras Beirut (Zaher, 2022) and El Mina, Tripoli (Pietrostefani et al., 2022). Fine-grained analysis of the three projects is beyond the scope of the present chapter, but insights gained from the Lebanese context and opportunities for RE futures can be used to compare energy-related findings. There is a chronic lack of data on energy use and demand in Lebanon (IGP, 2019b). Consequently, energy infrastructures and livelihoods were investigated through a mixed-method approach of qualitative and quantitative data gathered using systematic questionnaires and geographic information system (GIS)-based mapping, and interviews.[2]

What the findings from the two neighbourhood studies underscore is the context-specific energy landscapes that contribute to residents' ability to get by, which highlights the fact that locally specific knowledge is necessary to address the unique energy circumstances each locale faces. For example, residents in El Mina pay less for energy (44.4 per cent of them paid LL 1,500–30,000 per month for public electricity in 2020) than those in Hamra (42.4 per cent paid LL 150,000–300,000

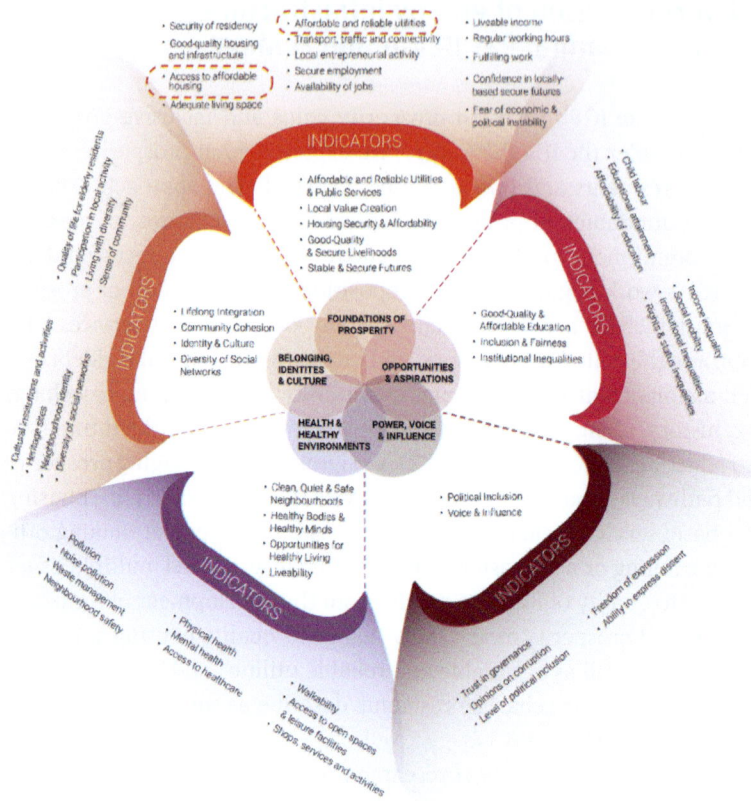

**Figure 6.1** The Hamra Prosperity Model highlighting affordable and reliable utilities and public services, such as electricity, as a foundation of prosperity.

Source: IGP, 2022

per month for public electricity in 2019), but rely more on generators: of the households surveyed in Hamra 59.2 per cent are connected to private generators (Figure 6.2), while in El Mina the proportion is 84.6 per cent (Figure 6.3). In terms of RE options, El Mina has installed more solar panels (63) than Hamra (30), and, unsurprisingly, neighbourhoods with higher income levels in El Mina have installed more rooftop solar panels than neighbourhoods with lower income levels.

Results from both surveys demonstrated the intersections between energy services/infrastructure, housing and education levels, as well as the role ethnicity plays in accessing electricity. The older the buildings, the worse the electricity supply; the electricity supply is dependent on the condition of the buildings. In El Mina 40 per cent of the buildings

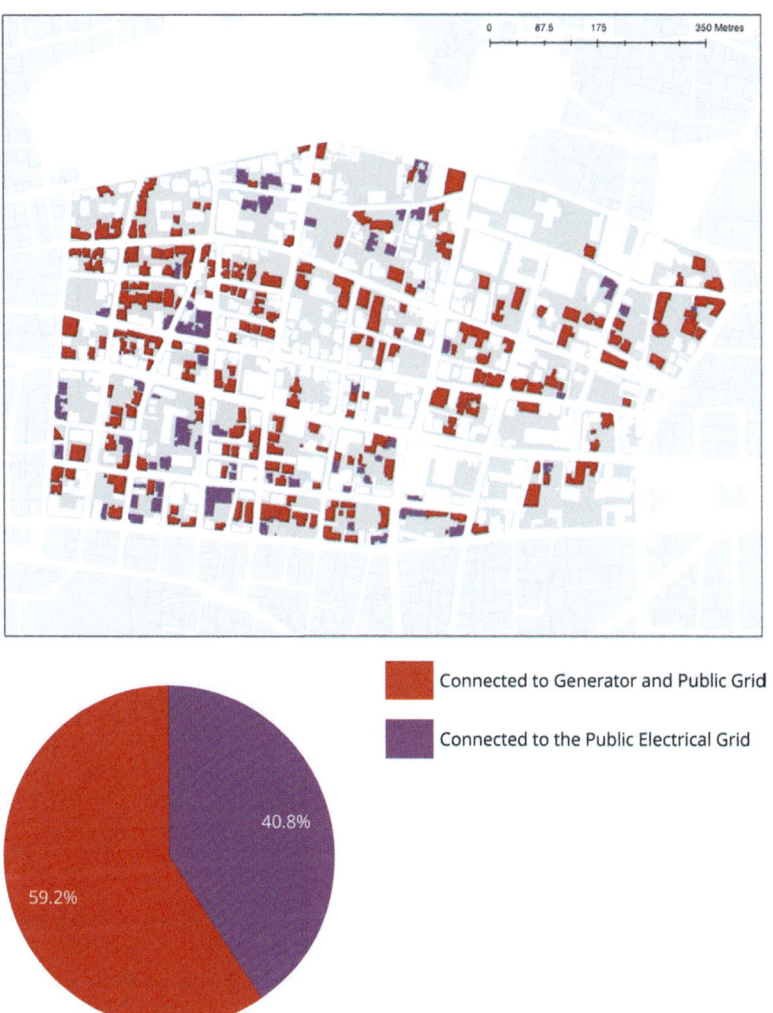

**Figure 6.2** Household survey results from Hamra showing 59.2 per cent of households are connected to private generators.

Source: RELIEF Centre & UN-Habitat, 2020

connected to the grid had major defects in need of repair, while this number was 10 per cent in Hamra. The majority of the buildings with major or critical defects in connection date back to between 1976 and 2000 in El Mina, and to the years before the civil war in Hamra (Figure 6.4). Similarly, buildings with highly precarious or potentially life-threatening structural or architectural elements, amounting to 57.6 per cent in El Mina and 66.7 per cent in Hamra, needed major or emergency intervention

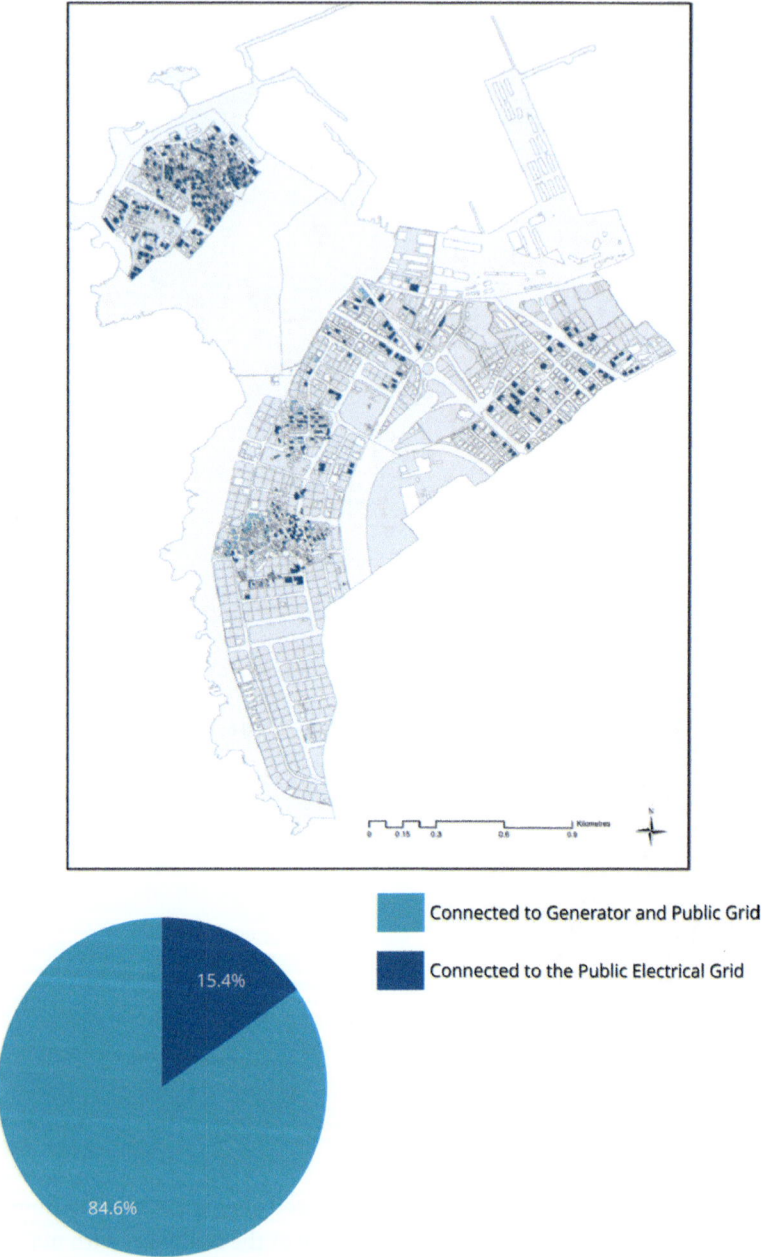

**Figure 6.3** Household survey results from El Mina showing 84.6 per cent of households are connected to private generators.

Source: Pietrostefani et al., 2022

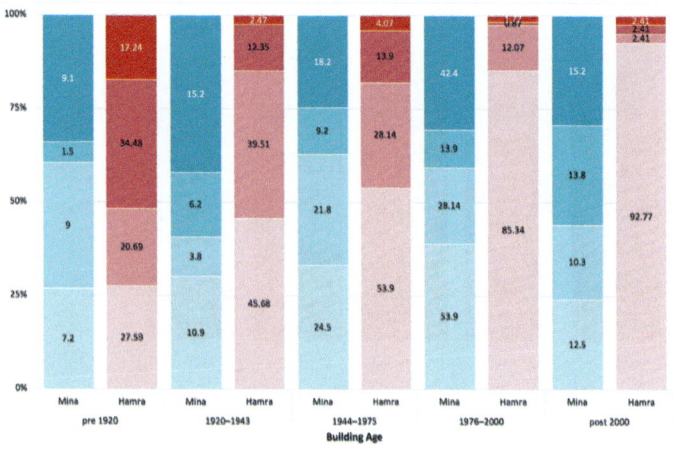

**Figure 6.4** Building survey results from El Mina and Hamra showing buildings' connection to electricity versus building age.

Source: Pietrostefani et al., 2022

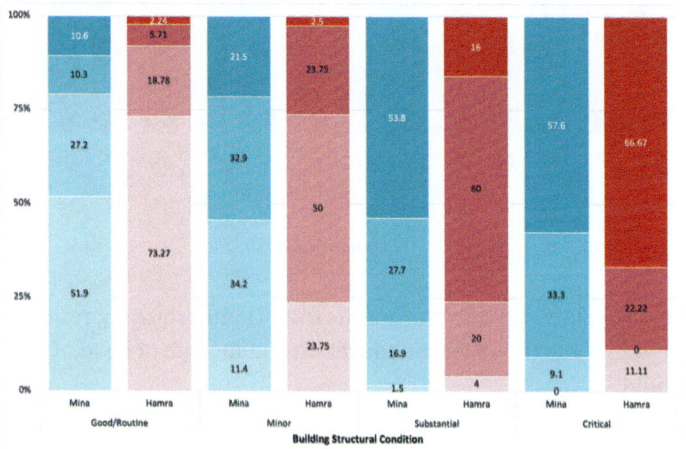

**Figure 6.5** Building survey results from El Mina and Hamra showing buildings' connection to electricity versus structural condition of buildings.

Source: Pietrostefani et al., 2022

for their electrical connection (Figure 6.5). Connection to a generator increases with income and the education level of the household head in both Hamra and El Mina (Figures 6.6 and 6.7). Lebanese households were nearly twice as likely to be connected to a private generator as Syrian

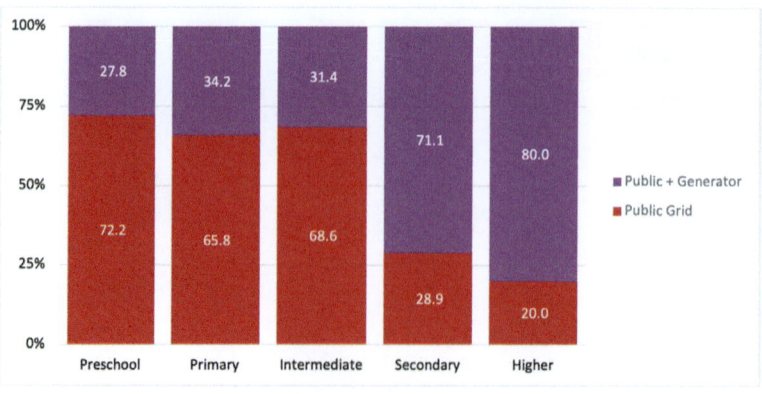

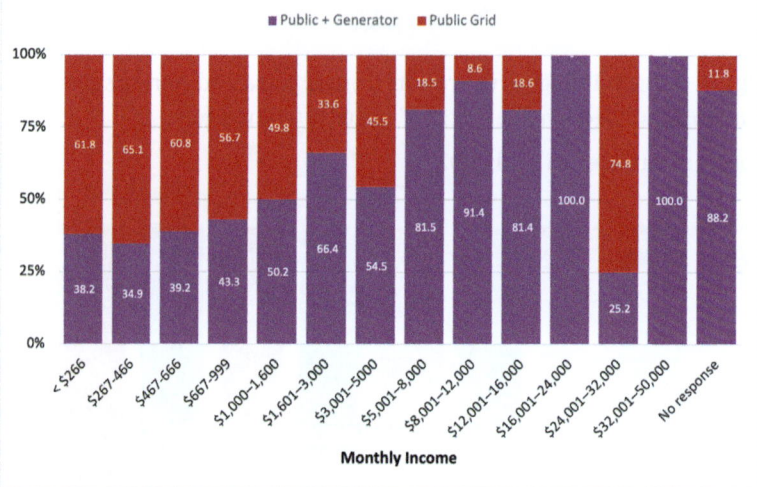

**Figure 6.6** Household survey results from Hamra showing residents' connection to electricity versus education and income of head of household.

Source: Pietrostefani et al., 2022

households in Hamra, and three times as likely in El Mina (Figure 6.8). However, Lebanese households in El Mina pay much more (more than LL 150,000) than Syrian households in El Mina (LL 1,500–50,000) and Lebanese households in Hamra (LL 1,500–LL37,500) (Figure 6.9).

Investigating prosperity and its relationship to energy supply at the community level (see Chapter 1) shows realities and nuances very different from those revealed by aggregate data gathered at larger scales, as these two cases demonstrate. For example, the biggest barrier to RE supply in El Mina may be infrastructure access, whereas in Hamra it

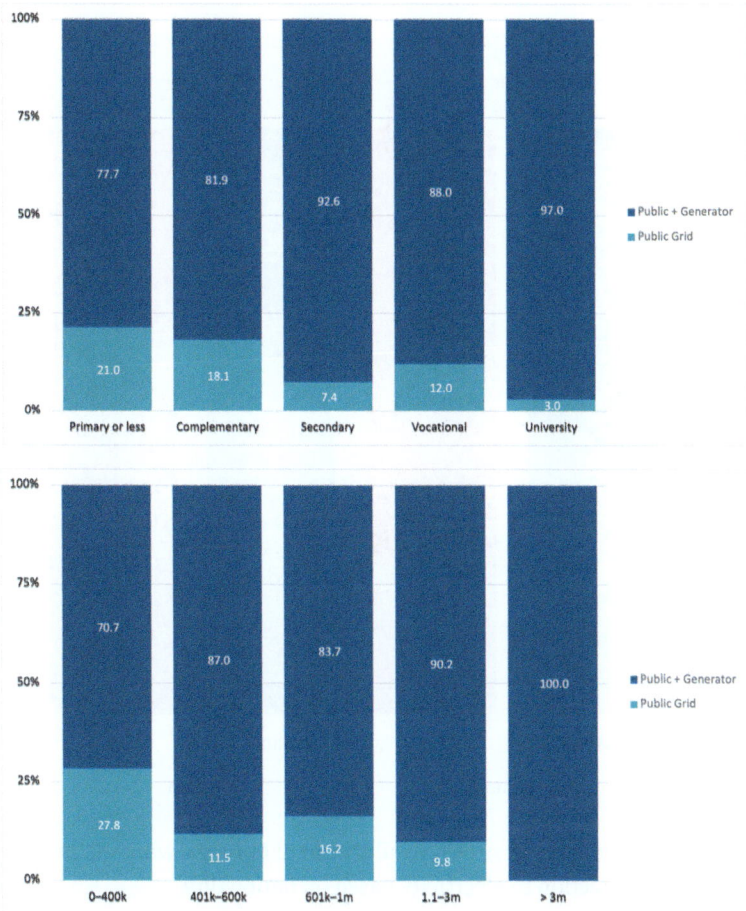

**Figure 6.7** Household survey results from El Mina showing residents' connection to electricity versus education and income of head of household.

Source: Pietrostefani et al., 2022

could be dependence on private generators. These factors need further interrogation to carve out pathways to prosperity that are locally specific but that also contribute to reducing national GHG emissions and reaching the 2030 UN Sustainable Development Goals. Further ethnographic research carried out in Ras Beirut highlights how energy failures are experienced and linked in everyday contexts to fragility in livelihoods, and the intersections between food, water, waste and health.

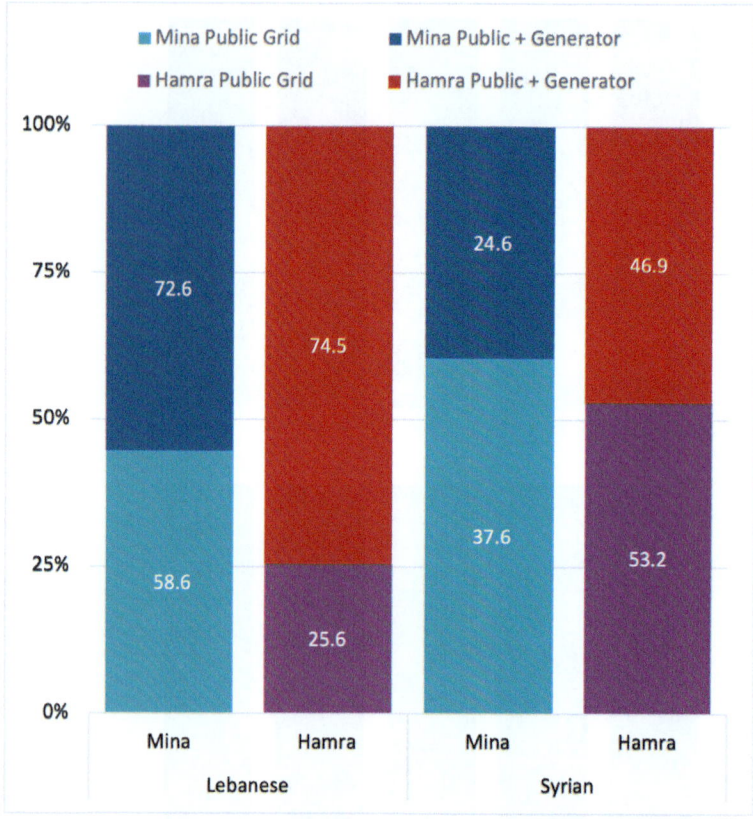

**Figure 6.8** Household survey results from El Mina showing the rate of residents' connection to electricity based on nationality.

Source: Pietrostefani et al., 2022

> One time it is the unavailability of fuel, another it is the need to buy the fuel from the black market. One time it is the unavailability of medicine, another it is the availability at ridiculously high prices of medicine. Let alone the days we spent in blackouts and had to throw away everything in our fridges, which is also not cheap anymore!
> (Rami, physiotherapist and security guard, in Ras Beirut, interviewed in 2021; Zaher, 2022: 7)

When asked about the impact of electricity cuts and rising energy prices, another informant replied:

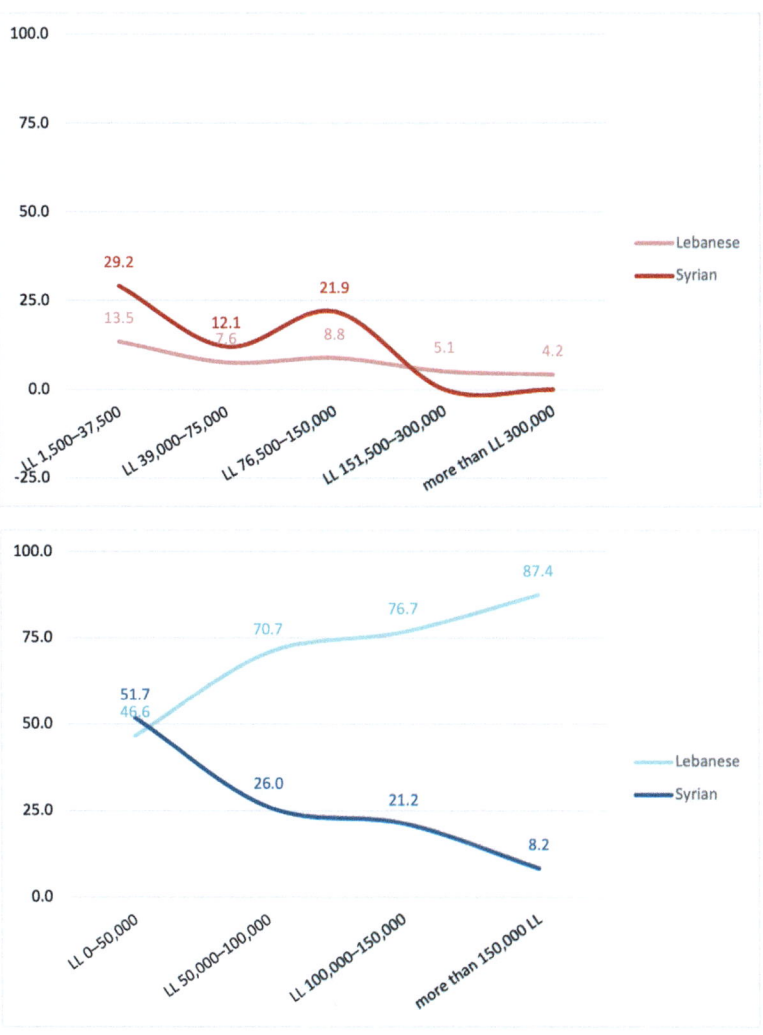

**Figure 6.9** Household survey results from El Mina showing Lebanese and Syrian expenditure on 5 amperes of private electricity.

Source: Pietrostefani et al., 2022

> Oh many, many things. The area used to be so full of life and light, it has been dead for months now. People do not have fuel to do anything, there is no electricity for light, even the beautiful soul and love for life that the Lebanese had has disappeared.
>
> (Diana, mother in Ras Beirut, interviewed in 2021; Zaher, 2022: 12)

And a shop owner angrily described the impact on his business:

> Besides, the electricity bills have become very high also and there are hours that pass when there is no light or air conditioning in the shop. Who would come in and choose something to wear if it is hot and there is no light inside?
>
> (Zaher, 2022: 16)

Multiple intersecting crises are experienced not just as a collapse in infrastructure and rising prices, but as an assault on belonging, identity, livelihoods, enjoyment and future opportunities.

## 6.5 Narrating futures: a citizens' assembly

> An informed public debate about the challenges and issues related to electricity sector reform is largely absent from the Lebanese public sphere. This is a result of limited access to details about proposed policy measures and lack of understanding of those among citizens. Citizens effectively lack direct, first hand information about the objectives and details of the electricity reform. The relevant legislation is not available in electronic form, the website of the Ministry of Energy and Water is not updated, and the information provided through the media does not encompass all the details of the proposed initiatives. There are no institutionalized channels for public consultation, and it does not take place on a regular basis.
>
> (Hasbani, 2011: 30)

Public participation and energy literacy are crucial components in RE transitions, and green transformations more generally (Chodkowska-Miszczuk et al., 2021; Mehmood et al., 2022; Adams et al., 2022). In 2020, the IGP's RELIEF Centre ran the first citizen assembly (CA) on energy in the MENA region in Hamra, Beirut (Shehabi et al., 2021). The aim was to tackle five main questions from residents' perspectives: How did we get to where we are? What is energy justice to us? What is the energy mix we would like to have? What do we need to be doing as individuals and communities to achieve a better energy future? How should we move forward with our decisions on the above questions?

Design of the CA began with the importance of developing mechanisms for public participation in RE transitions (Droubi et al., 2022) and explored issues of energy justice and energy citizenship (Olawuyi,

2021; Wahlund & Palm, 2022). The aim was to make such narratives (Durdovic, 2022; Miller et al., 2015) publicly accessible and to link them to the scientific, technical, economic and political dimensions of a just energy transition. This background information was essential for participants to begin a process of co-designing and co-producing an energy system that might better serve the public interest by setting the ground for pathways to prosperity involving better health outcomes, decent and stable employment, greener public spaces and transport, and new public, private and civic institutions (see Chapters 1 and 2). The advantage of a CA is that it offers a deeper and more meaningful opportunity for residents, researchers and other stakeholders to understand local contexts and the conditions needed to build people-centred visions of energy futures. Democratic deficits and public distrust, as well as alienation from formal politics, are particularly acute in Lebanon, and this situation highlighted for all participants questions of governance, accountability and trust, making evident the tension and the trade-offs between what is desirable, and what is practical and possible. Participants on the CA expressed grave misgivings about the possibility of delivering genuine transformation in a context of dysfunctional and sectarian politics, but through the unfolding of the CA became increasingly engaged with the relevance and value of citizen/resident deliberation and participation (Shehabi & Al-Masri, 2022).

Shehabi and Al-Masri noted that four imaginaries began to emerge over time: (i) a state-led fossil fuel-dependent imaginary, (ii) a techno-economic-environmental imaginary dependent on renewable energy, (iii) a decentralised and privatised regional imaginary of private sector-led solutions or subregional grids, (iv) a dystopic – but realistic – citizen imaginary that sought circular or interconnected solutions that are autonomous from the central government (Shehabi & Al-Masri, 2022). They were clear that although none of these imaginaries emerged as fully articulated visions, they surfaced from the debates and the process of co-design and critical reflection. The citizen imaginary drew on lived experience in that it envisaged an integrated system where energy provision, waste management and clean water would all be provided, using new waste-to-energy technologies discussed in the CA, which appealed to the participants. Participants also emphasised the importance of thinking about reconstruction and transformation in integrated ways, and not as disconnected sectors, drawing on their own experience of collapsing infrastructures and systemic interconnections (Shehabi & Al-Masri, 2022). In her analysis of the energy transition in Lebanon, Haddad (2021) underlined the potential in taking a whole-systems approach, and incorporating this mindset into stakeholder engagement. She further noted that the value of such an approach is not just one of stressing interconnecting systemic issues, but of using the insights derived from such an approach to create spaces that allow for experimentation and for innovative procedural practices to grow. The research presented in this chapter underscores that point and also emphasises the key importance of locale-based approaches to drive transformation.

## 6.6 Conclusion: looking to the future

A long-term solution to the energy crisis will need to come with wider economic and political restructuring, likely against the interests of the majority of Lebanon's ruling elite (Ahmad et al., 2021). There is now a need to look beyond recalibration of the Lebanese energy system in the form of institutional reforms which are slow to implement, to the way decentralised, local production of energy can potentially provide the population with a higher standard of reliable, affordable and renewable energy as part of a whole-systems approach to sustainable prosperity (Moore & Collins, 2019; Ahmad, 2020; Haddad, 2021).

For an RE transition to be successful people must also be willing to modify their lifestyle through reducing and adapting power consumption (Khoury et al., 2016). This is not just a Lebanese problem; changing mindsets in the age of consumption is a significant hurdle for RE transitions worldwide (Loveday et al., 2008; Von Borgstede et al., 2013; Shi et al., 2019). Fully grounded, well-researched and localised insights into energy options must be made available to citizens/residents so they can make informed decisions for themselves and the environment.

With new generations coming of age there is a global shift in the social contract decisions that must be made to acknowledge and account for the planet's finite resources. The millennial generation constitutes approximately 20 per cent of the Lebanese population (Youth Policy, n.d.). Lebanese young people are challenging the status quo (Kastrissianakis et al., 2019). They have already played an essential role in the growth in Lebanese civil society (AbiYaghi et al., 2017) and are set to become decision makers in the region in the next 15 years. The millennial generation have grown up with power cuts as a daily presence and are finding creative ways to solve the energy crisis, utilising the potential for RE technology. Lebanese-based social enterprises which offer RE solutions are contributing to the growth in the solar energy industry. For example, millennial-run OTB Consult partnered with Greenpeace to train young Lebanese and refugees living in Lebanon in the skills to enter the solar energy market (Greenpeace, n.d.). Lebanon's entrepreneurs have the capability to contribute to RE provision, supporting the rebuilding of communities, the regeneration of water and soil, and the next transformation phase, which will be fuelled by the rise of data, robotics and artificial intelligence.

Historically, Lebanon has been known for its support for entrepreneurial activity (Ahmed & Julian, 2012). Data from the Global Entrepreneurship Monitor (2019) shows that 21.6 per cent of 18–64-year-olds are established business owners, 24.08 per cent are either nascent entrepreneurs or owner-managers of new businesses, and 42.01 per cent see good opportunities to start a business in the place they live in. But entrepreneurs in Lebanon are constrained by high electricity costs and unstable supply, as well as by a sectarian political order that can channel entrepreneurial talent into bribery and lobbying (Stel & Naudé, 2016). The reinforcement of family-owned business and entrepreneurs with connections to government (Stel & Naudé, 2016) limits the potential for new RE entrepreneurs by limiting the diversity of ideas and knowledge.

By looking to existing RE successes in Lebanon, future energy systems will likely need a combination of on- and off-grid hybrid technology, will be decentralised, and will come from the ground up. Not only will they create a reliable energy network, but they will have knock-on benefits through new value chains and forms of employment, benefiting the education, health and safety of communities. Unemployment in Lebanon is subject to a wide range of estimates with an absence of reliable data, but in 2018–19 less than 50 per cent of the working-age population were participating in the labour force (ILO, 2019). A study by IRENA and UN ESCWA found strengths for local manufacturing in Lebanon, where industries related to electronics, steel, aluminium and plastics are well developed and could play a role in stimulating the RE industry. Furthermore, university programmes associated with RE research mean that the technical know-how is available and there is good potential for local integration and manufacturing of RE technology in Lebanon (IRENA & UN ESCWA, 2018). Analysis of the RE technology value chain in Lebanon estimates that 20,000 jobs could result from the deployment of RE technologies, the bulk being in the solar PV sector (Vallvé et al., 2019).

A hybrid model of local ownership could help redefine energy citizenship and encourage people to engage with issues of energy access and payment. Community ownership is already a common model in Lebanon, with buildings collectively buying generators to share, indicating there are traction for change and opportunities for decentralised approaches (IGP, 2019a, 2019b). Decentralisation of RE systems changes the dynamic of how we think about energy and may help to change the way we use it. New forms of localism are taking hold around the world that are an opportunity for RE transitions. There needs to be policy recognition and research into the entanglement of renewable energy provision in shaping people's lives in the future, and its contribution to sustainable pathways to prosperity. Electricity provision drives people's quality of life and impacts everything from agriculture to transport, water, waste, education and health. It is deeply embedded in people's ability to build a secure livelihood. Therefore, tackling the energy crisis requires a whole-systems approach that recognises electricity as the driver of the emergence of prosperity as an assemblage (see Chapter 1), bringing new energetics in a place-based system to drive positive change.

## Notes

1. The RELIEF Centre aims to speed up transitions to sustainable, prosperous societies in the context of mass displacement, in order to improve the quality of people's lives. The centre focuses on the prosperity of Lebanon in particular, but is also part of a larger agenda for developing sustainable ways to improve the quality of life of people throughout the world (see www.relief-centre.org). It is funded by the Economic and Social Research Council of the UK.
2. Based on visual inspection that is guided by structured questionnaires and conducted by local citizen scientists, the building and infrastructure surveys involve assessments of building conditions and basic urban services (water and sanitation, solid waste management, electricity and mobility), and population identification by nationality in each building for all sampled buildings. Questions within the field surveys were based on the UN-Habitat–UNICEF Neighbourhood Profile methodology, but El Mina Neighbourhood questionnaires were heavily modified by RELIEF–CatalyticAction staff in consultation with citizen scientists to reflect El Mina's buildings and infrastructure and to collect more accurate data.

## Bibliography

Abi Ghanem, D. (2018). Energy, the city and everyday life: Living with power outages in post-war Lebanon. *Energy Research & Social Science*, 36, 36-43. https://doi.org/10.1016/j.erss.2017.11.012.

Abi Ghanem, D. (2020). Infrastructure and the vulnerability of Palestinian refugees in Lebanon: The story of Shatila camp's 'electricity martyrs'. Jadaliyya/جدلية., 2 January. Available at: https://www.jadaliyya.com/Details/40397 (accessed 22 December 2022).

Abi Ghanem, D. (2021). Insights from an assemblage perspective for a (better) understanding of energy transitions: Facing the challenge of sustainability in Lebanon's energy crisis. In A. Kumar, J. Höffken & A. Pols (eds), *Dilemmas of Energy Transitions in the Global South: Balancing urgency and justice*, pp. 18–38. Abingdon: Routledge.

AbiYaghi, M.-N., Catusse, M. & Younes, M. (2017). From *isqat an-nizam at-ta'ifi* to the garbage crisis movement: Political identities and antisectarian movements. In R. Di Peri & D. Meir (eds), *Lebanon Facing the Arab Uprisings: Constraints and adaptation*, pp. 73–92. London: Palgrave Macmillan.

Abou Brahim, R. (2020). Introducing micro-grids in Lebanon: Opportunities and challenges – The case-study of Rashayya. MSc thesis, American University of Beirut. Available at: https://scholarworks.aub.edu.lb/bitstream/handle/10938/21947/IntroducingMicro-gridsinLebanonOpportunitiesandChallengesTheCaseStudyofRashayya_AbouBrahimR_2020.pdf?sequence=1 (accessed 23 December 2022).

Adams, J., Kenner, A., Leone, B., Rosenthal, A., Sarao, M. & Boi-Doku, T. (2022) What is energy literacy? Responding to vulnerability in Philadelphia's energy ecologies. *Energy Research & Social Science*, 91, 102718. https://doi.org/10.1016/J.ERSS.2022.102718.

AEMS (2017). The impact of the Syrian crisis on the Lebanese power sector and priority recommendations. Ministry of Energy and Water/UNDP. https://www.undp.org/lebanon/publications/impact-syrian-crisis-lebanese-power-sector-and-priority-recommendations (accessed 23 December 2022).

Ahmad, A. (2020). Distributed power generation for Lebanon: Market assessment and policy pathways. World Bank. Available at: https://documents1.worldbank.org/curated/en/353531589865018948/pdf/Distributed-Power-Generation-for-Lebanon-Market-Assessment-and-Policy-Pathways.pdf (accessed 23 December 2021).

Ahmad, A., Mahmalat, M. & Saghir, J. (2021). Lebanon's independent electricity regulator: Avoiding the 'political economy trap'. Available at https://www.lcps-lebanon.org/articles/details/2386/lebanon%E2%80%99s-independent-electricity-regulator-avoiding-the-%E2%80%98political-economy-trap%E2%80%99 (accessed 25 February 2023).

Ahmad, A. McCulloch, N., Al-Masri, M. & Ayoub, M. (2020). From dysfunctional to functional corruption: The politics of reform in Lebanon's electricity sector. Available at https://www.aub.edu.lb/ifi/Documents/publications/working_papers/2020-2021/20201218_from_dysfunctional_to_functional_corruption_working_paper.pdf (accessed 25 February 2023).

Ahmed, Z. U. & Julian, C. C. (2012). International entrepreneurship in Lebanon. *Global Business Review*, 13(1), 25–38. https://doi.org/10.1177/097215091101300102.

Amine, J. & Rizk, S. (2018). *2017 Solar PV Status Report for Lebanon*. MoEW, LCEC, UNDP & GEF. Available at https://lcec.org.lb/sites/default/files/2021-03/2017%20Solar%20PV%20Status%20Report%20for%20Lebanon.pdf (accessed 25 February 2023).

Arnaout, M., Ismail, H., Jaber, H., Koubayssi, A., Rammal, R. & Noun, Z. (2021). Study and review on the renewable energy potential in Lebanon, in *2021 International Conference on Microelectronics (ICM)*, pp. 199–202. Available at: https://ieeexplore.ieee.org/document/9664917 (accessed 25 February 2023).

AUB Policy Institute (2018). Lebanon's gas market development and the role of FSRU. Energy Policy and Security Program at the Issam Fares Institute for Public Policy and International Affairs at AUB. Policy Brief no. 5/2018. Available at https://www.aub.edu.lb/ifi/Documents/publications/policy_briefs/2018-2019/20181018_lebanon_gas_market_development.pdf (accessed 24 December 2022).

Ayat, C., Haytayan, L., Obeid, J. & Ayoub, M. (2021). Keeping the lights on: A short-term action plan for Lebanon's electricity sector. Issam Fares Institute for Public Policy and International Affairs at AUB, Konrad-Adenauer-Stiftung and Natural Resource Governance Institute. Available at: https://www.aub.edu.lb/ifi/news/Pages/20210310-keeping-the-lights-on-a-short-term-action-plan-for-lebanon-electricity-sector.aspx (accessed 24 December 2022).

Ayoub, M. & Boustany, I. (2019). Bankability of a large-scale solar power plant in the Tfail-Lebanon. Issam Fares Institute for Public Policy and International Affairs at AUB and Lebanese Foundation for Renewable Energy. Policy Brief no. 5/2019. Available at https://www.aub.edu.lb/ifi/news/Pages/20190522-bankability-large-scale-solar-power-plant-tfail-lebanon.aspx (accessed on 24 December 2022).

Bassil, G. (2010). Policy paper for the electricity sector. Ministry of Energy and Water, Lebanese Republic. https://rise.esmap.org/data/files/library/lebanon/Lebanon_final/Energy%20Efficiency/EE%201.1.pdf (accessed 24 December 2022).

Belaid, F., Boukrami, E. & Amine, R. (2021). Renewable energy in the MENA region: Key challenges and lessons learned. In S. Goutte, K. Guesmi, R. H. Boroumand & T. Porcher. (eds), *Advances in Managing Energy and Climate Risks*, pp. 1–22. Cham: Springer. https://doi.org/10.1007/978-3-030-71403-1_1.

Bellini, E. (2019). Lebanon's Tufail region may host planned 500 MW solar plant. *PV Magazine*, 23 May. Available at https://www.pv-magazine.com/2019/05/23/lebanons-tufail-region-may-host-planned-500-mw-solar-plant/?utm_source=dlvr.it&utm_medium=twitter (accessed 24 December 2019).

Berjawi, A. H., Najem, S., Faour, G., Abdallah, C. & Ahmad, A. (2017). Assessing solar PV's potential in Lebanon. Working Paper. Issam Fares Institute for Public Policy and International Affairs, AUB, Lebanon. https://www.aub.edu.lb/ifi/Documents/publications/working_papers/2016-2017/20170808_solar_pvs.pdf (accessed 24 December 2022).

Çamur, H., Kassem, Y. & Alessi, E. (2021). A techno-economic comparative study of a grid-connected residential rooftop PV panel: The case study of Nahr El-Bared, Lebanon. *Engineering, Technology & Applied Science Research*, 11(2), 6956–64. https://doi.org/10.48084/etasr.4078.

Chaplain, A. (2022). Strategies of power and the emergence of hybrid mini-grids in Lebanon. *Jadaliyya*, 8 March. Available at: https://www.jadaliyya.com/Details/43932 (accessed 24 December 2022).

Chehayeb, K. (2021). Lebanon electricity crisis: 'Disaster in the making'. *Aljazeera*, 11 June. Available at https://www.aljazeera.com/news/2021/6/11/lebanon-electricity-crisis-disaster-in-the-making (accessed 24 December 2021).

Chodkowska-Miszczuk, J., Kola-Bezka, M., Lewandowska, A. & Martinát, S. (2021). Local communities' energy literacy as a way to rural resilience: An insight from inner peripheries'. *Energies*, 14(9), 2575. https://doi.org/10.3390/en14092575.

Council of Ministers (2018). Summary of the electricity sector in Lebanon. Presentation by Minister of Energy and Water to the Lebanese Council of Ministers, Beirut, Lebanon.

Dobeissi, R. E., Vanin, A., Nasyrov, R. & Sharov, Y. (2021). Assessment of the potential for power deficit reduction using renewable energy sources: The case of Lebanon. In *3rd International Youth Conference on Radio Electronics, Electrical and Power Engineering*, pp. 1–5. https://doi.org/10.1109/REEPE51337.2021.9387971.

Droubi, S., Heffron, R. J. & McCauley, D. (2022). A critical review of energy democracy: A failure to deliver justice? *Energy Research & Social Science*, 86, 102444. https://doi.org/10.1016/j.erss.2021.102444.

Durdovic, M. (2022). Emergent consequences of narrating futures in energy transitions. *Futures*, 138, 102930. https://doi.org/10.1016/j.futures.2022.102930.

Dziadosz, A. (2018). Can green energy beat Lebanon's 'generator mafias?' *Bloomberg UK*, 26 February. Available at https://www.bloomberg.com/news/features/2018-02-26/can-green-energy-beat-lebanon-s-generator-mafias (accessed 25 December 2022).

Ersoy, S. R., Terrapon-Pfaff, J., Ayoub, M. & Akkouch, R. (2021). Sustainable transformations of Lebanon's energy system. Friedrich-Ebert-Stiftung. Available at: https://www.aub.edu.lb/ifi/Documents/publications/research_reports/2020-2021/20211216_sustainable_transformation_of_lebanon_energy_system_report.pdf (accessed 25 December 2022).

Fardoun, F., Ibrahim, O., Younes, R. & Louahlia-Gualous, H. (2012). Electricity of Lebanon: Problems and recommendations. *Energy Procedia*, 19, 310–20. https://doi.org/10.1016/j.egypro.2012.05.211.

Fattouh, B. & Mahadeva, L. (2016). Managing oil and gas revenues in Lebanon. Lebanese Center for Policy Studies. Available at https://api.lcps-lebanon.org/content/uploads/files//1472126663-fattouh-lavan-management-paper-eng.pdf (accessed 25 February 2023).

Global Entrepreneurship Monitor (2019). Entrepreneurial behaviours and attitudes. Available at https://www.gemconsortium.org/data (accessed 29 August 2019).

Greenpeace. (n.d). *Greenpeace Solar Technician Program*. Available at https://www.greenpeacearabic.solutions/en-solartechnicians (accessed 25 December 2022).

Haddad, C. (2021). Current barriers and future outlooks for renewable energy in Lebanon: An exploratory analysis in environmental governance. Dalhousie University School for Resource & Environmental Studies. Available at: https://www.lebanesechamber.ca/wp-content/uploads/2021/04/CaseStudy_RenewableEnergyLebanon_vFinal.pdf (accessed 26 December 2022).

Harajli, H. & Chalak, A. (2018). Energy efficient home appliances: Perspectives from Lebanese consumers. UNDP/CEDRO, Beirut. https://www.cedro-undp.org/Library/Assets/Gallery/PDFfiles/CEDRO%20%20%20Report%20Draft%209.pdf (accessed 27 December 2022).

Hasbani, K. U. (2011). *Electricity Sector Reform In Lebanon: Political Consensus in Waiting* (Working Paper No. 124). Stanford Center on Democracy, Development, and the Rule of Law. Available at: https://cddrl.fsi.stanford.edu/arabreform/publications/electricity_sector_reform_in_lebanon_political_consensus_in_waiting (Accessed 17 October 2022)

Hatoum, L. (2020, June 15). Why Lebanon's electricity crisis is so hard to fix. *Arab News*, 14 June. Available at: https://www.arabnews.com/node/1689841/middle-east (accessed 23 December 2022).

IGP (2019a). Transitions to Renewable Energy and Sustainable Prosperity in Lebanon: A people-centred approach to equitable energy supply. Institute for Global Prosperity, Chatham House, UN ESCWA. Available at: https://static1.squarespace.com/static/5d89ee82afad6b391d45c37d/t/5dbab2d767dcb450208ea7ea/1572516568288/IGP_Report_pages7B%2B%283%29.pdf (accessed 25 February 2023).

IGP (2019b). Transitions to Renewable Energy and Sustainable Prosperity in Lebanon: Why democratic infrastructure supports innovative energy projects. Institute for Global Prosperity, Chatham House, UN ESCWA. Available at: https://static1.squarespace.com/static/5d89ee82afad6b391d45c37d/t/5e4e7777223f3d2c8b470561/1582200700456/Renewable+Energy_Working+Paper.pdf (accessed 26 December 2022).

ILO (2019). *Labour Force and Household Living Conditions Survey (LFHLCS) 2018–2019: Lebanon*. Available at https://www.ilo.org/beirut/publications/WCMS_732567/lang--en/index.htm (accessed 26 December 2022).

IPPC (2018). Global warming of 1.5 °C. Intergovernmental Panel on Climate Change. Available at http://www.ipcc.ch/report/sr15/ (accessed 26 December 2022).

IPCC (2021). Summary for policymakers. In *Climate Change 2021: The physical science basis*. Cambridge: Cambridge University Press, pp. 3–31. Available at https://www.ipcc.ch/report/ar6/wg1/downloads/report/IPCC_AR6_WGI_SPM.pdf (accessed on 26 December 2022).

IPCC (2022). *Climate Change 2022: Impacts, adaptation and vulnerability*. Cambridge: Cambridge University Press. Available at: https://www.ipcc.ch/report/ar6/wg2/ (accessed 26 December 2022).

IRENA (2019). Renewable Energy Outlook Lebanon: Multi-stakeholder meeting. 5–6 March. Available at https://www.irena.org/events/2019/Mar/Renewable-Energy-Outlook-Lebanon-Multi-stakeholder-meeting (accessed 26 December 2022).

IRENA (2020). *Renewable Energy Outlook: Lebanon*. Abu Dhabi: International Renewable Energy Agency. Available at https://www.irena.org/-/media/Files/IRENA/Agency/Publication/2020/Jun/IRENA_Outlook_Lebanon_2020.pdf (accessed 26 December 2022).

IRENA & UN ESCWA (2018). *Evaluating Renewable Energy Manufacturing Potential in the Arab Region: Jordan, Lebanon, United Arab Emirates*. Abu Dhabi: International Renewable Energy Agency. Available at https://www.unescwa.org/sites/www.unescwa.org/files/publications/files/evaluating-renewable-manufacturing-potential-arab-region-english.pdf (accessed 26 December 2022).

Jenkins, K. E. H. (2019). Energy justice, energy democracy, and sustainability: Normative approaches to the consumer ownership of renewables. In J. Lowitzsch (ed.), *Energy Transition: Financing consumer co-ownership in renewables*, pp. 79–97. Cham: Palgrave Macmillan. https://doi.org/10.1007/978-3-319-93518-8_4.

Kabakian, V., Kai, L., Naddaf, Y. & Sheikh, R. (2011). *Lebanon's Second National Communication to the UNFCCC*. Ministry of Environment, GEF & UNDP. Available at https://www.undp.org/lebanon/publications/lebanons-second-national-communication-unfccc (accessed 27 December 2022).

Kassem, Y., Gökçekuş, H., Çamur, H. & Esenel, E. (2022). A comparative study of a small-scale solar PV power plant in Nahr al-Bared, Lebanon. In H. Gökçekuş & Y. Kassem (eds), *Climate Change, Natural Resources and Sustainable Environmental Management*, pp. 139–46. NRSEM 2021. Cham: Springer. https://doi.org/10.1007/978-3-031-04375-8_16.

Kassem, Y., Gökçekuş, H. & Janbein, W. (2021). Predictive model and assessment of the potential for wind and solar power in Rayak region, Lebanon. *Modeling Earth Systems and Environment*, 7(3), 1475–1502. https://doi.org/10.1007/s40808-020-00866-y.

Kastrissianakis, K., Smaira, D. & Staeheli, L. A. (2019). 'Synthesis is not the same thing as uniformity': The cosmopolitics of youth citizenship in Lebanon. *Geopolitics*, 26(5), 1331–52. https://doi.org/10.1080/14650045.2019.1639043.

Khoury, J., Mbayed, R., Salloum, G., Monmasson, E & Guerrero, J. (2016). Review on the integration of photovoltaic renewable energy in developing countries: Special attention to the Lebanese case. *Renewable and Sustainable Energy Reviews*, 57, 562–75. https://doi.org/10.1016/j.rser.2015.12.062.

LCEC (2016). The National Renewable Energy Action Plan for the Republic of Lebanon 2016–2020. Ministry of Energy and Water/LCEC, Lebanon. https://www.fao.org/faolex/results/details/en/c/LEX-FAOC190114/ (accessed 27 December 2022).

LCEC (2017). Call for expression of interest (EOI) to participate in proposal submissions to build solar photovoltaic (PV) farms in Lebanon. Republic of Lebanon Ministry of Energy and Water. Available at https://lcec.org.lb/sites/default/files/2021-02/Call%20for% 20EOI%27s%20Solar%20Farms.pdf (accessed 27 December 2022).

LCEC (2018). History of LCEC. LCEC. Available at https://www.lcec.org.lb/our-identity/History-of-lcec (accessed 25 February 2023).

LCEC (2019a). *NEEREA*. LCEC. Available at http://lcec.org.lb/en/NEEREA/AboutUs (accessed 25 February 2023).

LCEC (2019b). The Solar Water Heater Subsidy Program. LCEC. Available at http://www.lcec.org.lb/en/LCEC/Projects/23/Solar-Water-Heaters (accessed 25 February 2023).

LCEC (2021). NREAP 2021–2025. Available at https://lcec.org.lb/our-work/LCEC/NREAP (accessed 17 August 2021).

Loveday, D. L., Bhamra, T., Tang, T., Haines, V. J. A., Holmes, M. J. & Green, R. J. (2008). The energy and monetary implications of the '24/7' 'always on' society. *Energy Policy*, 36(12), 4639–45. https://doi.org/10.1016/j.enpol.2008.09.067.

Machnouk, S., El Housseini, H., Kateb, R. & Stephan, C. (2019). Lebanon. In *The Energy Regulation and Markets Review, Eighth Edition*. ed. D. L. Schwartz, pp. 208–21. London: The Law Reviews. Available at https://www.hklaw.com/-/media/files/insights/publications/2019/07/colombia.pdf?la=en (accessed 27 December 2019).

Mannah, M. A., Nahas, M., Merhab, A. & Haddad, A. (2021). Evaluation of the effectiveness of standalone hybrid systems for small residential units: Case study Lebanon. In *2021 IEEE 3rd International Multidisciplinary Conference on Engineering Technology (IMCET)*, pp. 155–60. https://doi.org/10.1109/IMCET53404.2021.9665498.

Mehmood, F., Umar, M., Dominguez, C. & Kazmi, H. (2022). The role of residential distributed energy resources in Pakistan's energy transition. *Energy Policy*, 167, art. no. 113054. https://doi.org/10.1016/j.enpol.2022.113054.

Miller, C. A., O'Leary, J., Graffy, E., Stechel, E. B. & Dirks, G. (2015). Narrative futures and the governance of energy transitions. *Futures*, 70, 65–74. http://dx.doi.org/10.1016/j.futures.2014.12.001.

Ministry of Foreign Affairs of the Netherlands (2018). Climate change profile: Lebanon. Available at https://reliefweb.int/report/lebanon/climate-change-profile-lebanon (accessed 27 December 2022).

Moore, H. L. (2015). Global prosperity and sustainable development goals. *Journal of International Development*, 27(6), 801–15. https://doi.org/10.1002/jid.3114.

Moore, H. L. & Collins, H. (2019). Decentralised renewable energy and prosperity for Lebanon. *Energy Policy*, 137, 111102. https://10.1016/j.enpol.2019.111102.

Nasr, R. (2020). The Beirut River Solar Snake: The dawn of the solar market in Lebanon. Available at https://lcec.org.lb/our-work/MEW/BRSS (accessed 27 December 2022).

Nucho, J. R. (2017). *Everyday Sectarianism in Urban Lebanon: Infrastructures, public services, and power*. Princeton, NJ: Princeton University Press. https://doi.org/10.1515/9781400883004.

Nucho, J. R. (2022). Post-grid imaginaries: Electricity, generators, and the future of energy. *Public Culture*, 34(2), 265–90. https://doi.org/10.1215/08992363-9584764.

OECD (2020). *Innovative Citizen Participation and New Democratic Institutions: Catching the deliberative wave*. Paris: OECD Publishing. Available at: https://doi.org/10.1787/339306da-en (accessed 27 December 2022).

Olawuyi, D. S. (2021). From energy consumers to energy citizens. In R. Fleming, K. Huhta & L. Reins (eds), *Sustainable Energy Democracy and the Law*, pp. 101–23. Leiden: Brill Nijhoff. https://doi.org/10.1163/9789004465442_006.

Pietrostefani, E., Dabaj, J., Jallad, M., Maassarani, S., Makki, D., Mersalli, T., Mintchev, N., Sleiman, Y. Sleiman, M. & Moore, H. L. (2022). Prosperity report: El Mina, Tripoli. IGP. https://discovery.ucl.ac.uk/id/eprint/10156806/ (accessed 27 December 2022).

Ramadan, D. (2020). Shock value: A study of energy access, resilience, and how public-private electricity distribution can bring energy justice to Lebanon. MA thesis, American University of Paris. Available at: https://www.proquest.com/openview/555a1b6d3aea6fc0357101bac9dbcf84/1?pq-origsite=gscholar&cbl=2026366&diss=y (accessed 27 December 2022).

RELIEF Centre & UN-Habitat Lebanon (2020). *Hamra Neighbourhood Profile 2020*. Beirut: UN-Habitat Lebanon. Available at https://www.relief-centre.org/hamra-neighbourhood-profile (accessed 27 December).

Shehabi, A. & Al-Masri, M. (2022). Foregrounding citizen imaginaries: Exploring just energy futures through a citizens' assembly in Lebanon. *Futures*, 140, 102956. https://doi.org/10.1016/J.FUTURES.2022.102956.

Shehabi, A., Al-Masri, M., Obeid, J., Ayoub, M., Jallad, M. & Daher, D. (2021). *A Pilot Citizens' Assembly on Electricity and Energy Justice in Hamra, Lebanon*. London: IGP. Available at https://discovery.ucl.ac.uk/id/eprint/10129878/7/Shehabi_CA_Hamra_WP_JUNE21_v2.pdf (accessed 27 December 2022).

Shi, D., Wang, L. & Wang, Z. (2019). What affects individual energy conservation behavior: Personal habits, external conditions or values? An empirical study based on a survey of college students. *Energy Policy*, 128, 150–61. https://doi.org/10.1016/j.enpol.2018.12.061.

Snaije, B. (2022). Lebanon: Financial crisis or national collapse? *CIDOB Notes Internacionals*. Available at: https://www.cidob.org/en/publications/publication_series/notes_internacionals/275/lebanon_financial_crisis_or_national_collapse (accessed 25 February 2023).

Stel, N. & Naudé, W. (2016). 'Public-private entanglement': Entrepreneurship in Lebanon's hybrid political order. *Journal of Development Studies*, 52(2), 254–68. https://doi.org/10.1080/00220388.2015.1081173.

Szakola, A. (2022). 'National suicide': A breakdown of Lebanon's deepening dependence on diesel fuel for private generators. *L'Orient Today*, 14 January. Available at: https://today.lorientlejour.com/article/1287555/national-suicide-a-breakdown-of-lebanons-deepening-dependence-on-diesel-fuel-for-private-generators.html. (accessed 27 December 2022).

UN (2021). Around 1.5 million Lebanese in need, top UN humanitarian official there warns, *UN News*, 14 June. Available at https://news.un.org/en/story/2021/06/1094002 (accessed 27 December 2022).

UNDP (2017). *Lebanon: Derisking renewable energy investment*. New York: United Nations Development Programme.

UNDP (2019a). *Sustainable Development Goal 13: Climate action*. UNDP Lebanon. Available at https://lebanon.un.org/en/sdgs/13 (accessed 7 February 2023).

UNDP (2019b). *Sustainable Development Goal 9: Industry, innovation and infrastructure*. UNDP. Available at https://lebanon.un.org/en/sdgs/9 (accessed 7 February 2023).

UNDP/CEDRO (2018). Sustainable energy for Lebanese villages and communities: The Village 24 initiative. UNDP/CEDRO, Beirut, Lebanon. Available at: https://www.cedro-undp.org/Library/Assets//Gallery/Publications/SUSTAINABLE%20ENERGY%20FOR%20Lebanese%20villagers%20(1).pdf (accessed 27 December 2022).

UNDP/GEF (2014). *Lebanon's First National Survey Study of the Solar Water Heaters Market*. Available at: http://www.cedro-undp.org/content/uploads/publication/141204025125965~LCECCEDRO2014.Lebanon'sNationalSurveyStudyoftheSHWandPVMarkets.pdf (accessed 27 December 2020).

UN ESCWA (2018). Case study on policy reforms to promote renewable energy in Lebanon. E/ESCWA/SDPD/2017/CP.7. United Nations, Beirut. https://www.unescwa.org/sites/default/files/pubs/pdf/policy-reforms-promote-renewable-energy-lebanon-english.pdf (accessed 27 December 2022).

UNICEF (2021). Water supply systems on the verge of collapse in Lebanon: Over 71 per cent of people risk losing access to water. Press release, 23 July. Available at: https://www.unicef.org/press-releases/water-supply-systems-verge-collapse-lebanon-over-71-cent-people-risk-losing-access (accessed 27 December 2022).

USAID (2019). Lebanon climate risk analysis. Performance management and support program for Lebanon (PMSPL II). Available at: https://pdf.usaid.gov/pdf_docs/PA00WZTT.pdf (accessed 27 December 2022).

Vallvé, X., Petrick, K., Sallent, R., Chaar, R. & Hoballah, F. (2019). *Prioritization and assessment of value chains within the renewable energy sector in Lebanon*. MoEW, Kingdom of the Netherlands & UNDP. Available at https://reliefweb.int/report/lebanon/prioritization-and-assessment-value-chains-within-renewable-energy-sector-lebanon (accessed 25 February 2023).

Verdeil, E. (2016). Beirut, metropolis of darkness: The politics of urban electricity grids. In A. Luque-Ayala & J. Silver (eds), *Energy, Power and Protest on the Urban Grid: Geographies of the electric city*, pp. 155–75. Abingdon and New York: Routledge.

Von Borgstede, C., Andersson, M. & Johnsson, F. (2013). Public attitudes to climate change and carbon mitigation: Implications for energy-associated behaviours. *Energy Policy*, 57, 182–93. https://doi.org/10.1016/j.enpol.2013.01.051.

Wahlund, M. & Palm, J. (2022). The role of energy democracy and energy citizenship for participatory energy transitions: A comprehensive review. *Energy Research & Social Science*, 87, 102482. https://doi.org/10.1016/J.ERSS.2021.102482.

World Bank (2019). *Lebanon Electricity Transmission Project P170769*. World Bank. Available at http://documents.worldbank.org/curated/en/235831562864951356/text/Concept-Project-Information-Document-PID-Lebanon-Electricity-Transmission-Project-P170769.txt (accessed 27 December 2022).

World Bank (2020). Lebanon Economic Monitor: The deliberate depression. Available at:https://openknowledge.worldbank.org/bitstream/handle/10986/34842/LebanonEconomic Monitor-Fall2020.pdf?sequence=4&isAllowed=y (accessed 27 December 2022).

World Bank (2022). Lebanon Public Finance Review. Available at: https://openknowledge.world bank.org/bitstream/handle/10986/37824/P1733451f74154311fb4a149871a9041d2b54 5b62921.pdf?sequence=11&isAllowed=y (accessed 27 December 2022).

Youth Policy (n.d). Middle East and North Africa: Youth facts. Available at http://www.youthpolicy. org/mappings/regionalyouthscenes/mena/facts/ (accessed 27 December 2022).

Zaher, R. (2022). *Embodied Experiences, Troubled Livelihoods: Ethnographic observations from Ras Beirut*. PROCOL Working Paper. London: Institute for Global Prosperity. Available at: https://discovery.ucl.ac.uk/id/eprint/10156805/2/Zaher_Lives%20and%20Livelihoods% 20Working%20PaperVF_Sept2022_revised.pdf (accessed 27 December 2022).

Zbibo, Z. (2022) Lebanon's energy transition from no electricity to renewables. *Arab News*, 28 April. Available at: https://www.arabnews.com/node/2072436/middle-east (accessed 27 December 2022).

# 7
# Prosperity in crisis and the longue durée in Africa

Henrietta L. Moore

## 7.1 Introduction

This chapter uses data from research in Kenya and Zambia to discuss the relationship between rural life and various representations and experiences of it. The research literature on rural Africa is very rich, but understanding the changing nature of rural life in sub-Saharan Africa over time is not merely a matter of pursuing empirical investigation. As an object of study 'rural life' is a far from self-evident category, and its changing character is not a matter of straightforward chronology. Africa is a huge continent and the particularities and circumstances of each case are fundamental and binding, but what stands out is the fact that over long periods of time, rural Africa has often been portrayed as in crisis: a genuine crisis of resource and opportunity, and a rather more constructed one of agricultural production and social relations. The exact nature of this crisis has varied temporally and spatially, but its underlying motif has been one of failed prosperity. From the earliest attempts by colonial governments to extract labour and tax from rural areas to more recent anxieties about agricultural productivity, structural transformation and deagrarianisation, rural life has been found wanting. It has also, rather schizophrenically, and often simultaneously, been portrayed as the solution to the failures of African prosperity more generally, providing potential economic and social safety nets when other hoped-for transformations failed to materialise (World Bank, 2007). As a new debate on prosperity begins to take hold in the context of the aftermath of the 2008 crisis and the Covid-19 pandemic, climate change and the emerging post-growth agenda (see Chapter 1), it is instructive to revisit the particular articulations of crisis and failed prosperity that have shaped intervention, governance, aspiration and transformation in sub-Saharan Africa.

Recent revisions of the term prosperity have emphasised that it is not just a matter of wealth or income, but a larger terrain encompassing health, opportunity and quality of life. This enlarged notion of prosperity is increasingly part of policy aspirations in both the global North and the global South, and replaces – at least for some – a determined emphasis on gross domestic product (GDP) growth as the measure of economic success, as opposed to a broader emphasis on quality of life (see Chapter 1). However, while there is much talk recently of inclusive growth in relation to Africa, both research and policy still focus, for the most part, on high levels of GDP growth as the way out of crisis (Adam, Collier & Gondwe, 2014; Adam, Collier & Ndung'u, 2011; World Bank, 2016). In this chapter, I discuss how a continued focus on growth as the headline indicator for economic success perpetuates policy interventions that fail to recognise the real nature and character of structural transformation in Africa.

In particular, I discuss how visions of future prosperity based on standard models of agrarian transformation have failed to materialise because they have focused on agricultural productivity and market integration at the expense of quality of life and ecological wellbeing (Brockington & Noe, 2021). Understanding the evolution and tenacity of particular ways of envisaging economic growth and development for Africa requires a form of analytical history that examines how conceptual structures function over the longue durée (see Chapter 2). Such an approach is more than simply empirical analysis through time or a set of abstractions based on the self-understandings of historical agents. It involves the development of a hypothetical analytic structure which through its own forms of transformation eventually comes to play a role in shaping the lived world of participants, including researchers, policy makers and ordinary citizens (Moore & Vaughan, 1994). The effects of such transformations are often partial and incomplete, even contradictory, but they are of immense significance because of their entanglements with power and politics. Braudel's ([1949] 1995) original conceptualisation of the longue durée emphasised both the plurality of historical temporalities, and the significance of geography and the environment for historical analysis. His call was for disciplines to work collectively ([1958] 2009). Braudel proffered various formulations of the longue durée, including the geometric space of Western painting and the language of financiers ([1958] 2009, 179–80, 190–1). His point was that the longue durée is a methodological tool suitable for the analysis of particular problems rather than a theory in and of itself. He insisted on understanding the long-run structures of the economy, the continuities that exist between the present and the past which shape the character, flow and possibilities of people's lives without necessarily being apparent to them (see Chapter 2). Braudel was interested not just in capitalism, but in the economy understood as culture, as 'old habits of thought and action, of frameworks that strenuously resist dying, however illogical' ([1958] 2009: 180). How long such frameworks could endure varied, according to Braudel, but the principle was that by tacking back and forth from structure to data those limits could be determined ([1958] 2009: 195); see Chapter 2. For Braudel history was a science and its purpose was to help us understand the present.

My aim in this chapter is thus to demonstrate how a long-running – but temporally and spatially variable – focus on agricultural productivity has shaped the character of rural life in Africa, and why it has consistently failed to deliver enlarged forms of prosperity based on quality of life and ecological wellbeing. I am not concerned here with theorising Braudel or with different kinds of historical temporalities (longue durée versus conjoncture versus événement), but rather with exploring how long-run narratives and constitutive metaphors help us in understanding the emergence of rural Africa over the last 100 years, and its particular character. My own research history has been bound up with two different experiences of studying long-term change. Megan Vaughan and I studied Bemba agriculture in the Northern Province of Zambia over a hundred-year period from 1890 to 1990, based on a restudy of Audrey Richards's original work on land, labour and diet in the 1930s (Moore & Vaughan, 1994; Richards, 1939). In Kenya, I have been studying the same village in Elgeyo-Marakwet County since 1980, exploring changes in livelihoods, gender relations, rituals and environmental management (Davies & Moore, 2016; Moore, 1996, 1983).

The Kenyan and Zambian cases are exemplars not only of the historical and structural origins of rural crisis, but of the frameworks, narratives and constitutive metaphors used both to create and manage that crisis. The Bemba of the Northern Province provided the labour for the mines on the Copperbelt, linking agricultural production to migration, wage labour, extractive mining and world commodity prices. Elgeyo-Marakwet in northern Kenya was also a native reserve in the colonial period, and markets of all kinds, but most especially in land, came only tardily. The Bemba were drawn from the land by the industrial labour requirements of the colonial state, and the Marakwet were largely tied to it by restrictions on movement. They provide different ideas about what the rural has meant, and means, in some contexts in sub-Saharan Africa, and allow some reflection on the more general proposition that Africa's crisis as locally produced and experienced by rural residents, as a feature of development, as an imperative for governance, and as a framework for research, has much to do with the temporal and spatial images of the world we derive from our categories (see Chapter 2). It is also, and more importantly, the material consequence of the way successive generations have conceived of economic success, at the expense of social and ecological wellbeing.

## 7.2 The creation of a rural world in crisis

'What can be thought must certainly be a fiction' (Nietzsche, 1968: 291). In saying this, Nietzsche had in mind thought's limitations in relation to world. Thinking about the character and future of the rural world in Africa impressed upon me anew the fact that we impose patterns on historical time. What is evident is that for all social scientists, time has to be 'more than one damn thing after another' as Kermode would have it (2000: 47), and history as a human project can never be mere chronicle because it ignores whatever is not concordant (51). In social theory, as in other domains of life, we cannot humanise time without also humanising space. Many of our models of sociality, social change and processes of transformation seek to do just that; they create categories within which we can work: village, peasant, clan, woman-farmer, an MSM (a man who has sex with men) (Moore, 2011: 77–105). Such categories are often also the building blocks of governance and social policy, directing financial flows in the form both of inward transfers (aid budgets, cash transfers, agricultural subsidies) and of extractions (taxes, etc.; see Chapter 2)). Such categories are ways of cutting up the world to make it intelligible, but are also the product of imaginative structurings with their own material realities over time. In the case of rural sub-Saharan Africa, these material realities have been bound up since colonial times with the crisis of peasant agriculture, its failing productivity and its debilitated prosperity. Colonial and post-colonial governments, aid agencies and international development policy have all refigured the dream of the prosperous peasant. In this sense, Africa – like anywhere else – is the consequence of human design on the world. However, these categories of design are not things that lie outside the observer and just wait to be found, if Kermode is to be believed; they are also things that we need both emotionally and intellectually as residents, researchers and rulers. But how do these productive fictions coincide with reality? Science and social science alike depend on the 'necessary relation between the fictions by which we order our world and the increasing complexity of what we take to be the "real" history of that world' (Kermode, 2000: 67). Fictions and world coincide to a certain extent, but we also know that we cannot easily distinguish between a fact and our knowledge of the fact, for merely establishing facts inevitably links them to concepts (Moore & Vaughan, 1994: xii–xxv). We must acknowledge the historicity of facts, and while our personal satisfactions in science and in life demand a degree of compliance with reality as we imagine it, the questions and categories with which we begin are the stuff of human engagement and imagination, and not that of nature (see Chapter 2). As Whitehead remarked, 'Nature is patient of interpretation in terms of Laws that happen to interest us' (1967: 136).

Why does a sense of crisis pervade in relation to rural Africa? Partly perhaps, as Kermode suggests, because there is a resistance to 'humanly uninteresting successiveness' (2000: 46), and partly because of Africa's relation to the imaginative structuring of time and in particular that form of time that has perhaps been most important for representations of Africa, developmental time: the time of progress or rather the crisis of its lack (Moore & Moreno, 2022). Visions of modernity, as Jameson suggests, feed on notions of crisis, and tend to 'project an idea of the historical period as massive homogeneity (bounded on either side by inexplicable chronological metamorphoses and punctuation marks)' (1991: 55–6). As Latour puts it,

> The adjective 'modern' designates a new regime, an acceleration, a rupture, a revolution in time. When the word 'modern', 'modernization', or 'modernity' appears, we are defining, by contrast, an archaic and stable past. Furthermore, the word is always being thrown into the middle of a fight, in a quarrel where there are winners and losers, Ancients and Moderns. 'Modern' is thus doubly asymmetrical: it designates a break in the regular passage of time, and it designates a combat in which there are victors and vanquished.
>
> (1993: 10)

The point both make is that historical periodisation – where differences and non-linear features are subsumed – is implicit in categorisations, and even when criticised or repressed threatens to break into our forms of thought. Theories of crisis are the inevitable consequence of the entanglements of periodisations and categorisations, because transformations require rupture. In relation to rural Africa, the ideas, arguments and policies concerning the nature of its residents (modern peasants or traditional farmers), its economy (market-oriented or kinship-focused) and its potentialities (productive asset or backwater) have insistently referred to intertwined imaginings of time, place and categorisations.

The rural world of sub-Saharan Africa was not a pre-existing empirical entity or category, but something that had first to be specified in time and place. African societies were by definition non-European societies at a different stage of development. The requirements of colonial governance involved two contradictory processes: the first was to transform rural life and the second was to safeguard it in its structures and traditions. Bringing large sections of a vast continent, with its differing societies, forms of governance, networks of connection and productive possibilities, under the thin crust of colonial government was inevitably a variegated and uncertain process. The sparsely populated areas of Zambia and Kenya looked nothing like the rural areas of England, but they had to be imaginatively and productively transformed into spaces that could turn out labour and tax. Agricultural productivity was at the heart of this dilemma. It needed to be maintained to guarantee food supplies, but also to sustain what were seen as ideally self-sufficient traditional societies. However, the colonial authorities needed labour – partly for infrastructure projects and later for successful settler agriculture – and labour provided workers with money to pay taxes. The result was a contradiction at the heart of colonial rural policy: how to change a society and its productive system, and yet keep it the same. As early as 1901, the British South Africa Company official in charge of the Mpika station in Northern Rhodesia (Zambia) was caught in the dilemma of how to balance food production and labour requirements. He frequently found himself without labour because people were working in their gardens, or with no work to offer and only half the taxes collected. He could not afford to jeopardise the production of food in the area through forcible labour recruitment, and was also in competition with the local chiefs who viewed his demands on labour as rivalling their own. This turned out to be symptomatic of the situation for decades to come (Moore & Vaughan, 1994: 12).

The management of agriculture and labour was a key part of colonial governance, but it was also responsible for a reconfiguration of the landscape into different categories. Key to this process was control over people's movement. The insistence that 'native peoples' reside for the most part on land reserved for them reinforced particular understandings of the relationship between identities and productive systems. Anthropologists played an important role in documenting and consolidating such linkages, creating tribal societies with particular ways of life and modes of livelihood. However, from the very beginning of colonial rule anxieties were expressed about what were termed 'scattered settlements' and forms of 'shifting cultivation'. In the first decades of colonial rule, as Deborah Bryceson has noted, the wide variety of forms of African clans, lineages and age-grade systems which had functioned as flexible social organisations for facilitating territorial movement and minimising risk connected with shifting cultivation were being eroded. Pressure was being exerted on the dispersed loyalties and rights and obligations of individuals within lineage structures to consolidate and concentrate loyalties within household units where production, consumption and reproduction activities could intersect in ways that were comprehensible to those running systems of governance, whether of the economy or the soul (Bryceson, 2000: 45).

Central to this process was the imposition of hut and poll taxes which forced rural producers to earn cash for tax payment, generating the foundations for the continent's agricultural export economy and its industrial development. The Bemba went to the mines and the Marakwet to the highlands to work for white farmers. Taxation involved identifying a 'head of household' as the taxpayer, which encouraged the strengthening of more insular household relations, and coupled with a growing cash economy in some regions led to changing ideas of property ownership, and smaller households compared with larger collective units. In order for tax to be collected, chiefs and headmen had to function, and where they did not exist, as in Elgeyo-Marakwet, both they and the units over which they were supposed to have control, notably villages, had to be created. Villages in Marakwet were not a local category, and neither were the chiefs and the headmen who had to be created to run the villages and collect the tax. Even today, chiefs have difficulty actually controlling their populations, because within a local political system based on rule by male elders, they are, at best, *primus inter pares*. The result of the creation of traditional authorities was that villages were nested within tribes. Tribes remained the ultimate organising unit both of research and of governance, but villages acted as strategic points of entry, a way of delimiting the complexities of settlement and sociality as they spread out across the landscape. For anthropology, its study of kinship had to have a locale, a way of drawing boundaries around what was being studied, deciding who was in and who was out, with the result that much anthropology of the period between the 1940s and the 1970s in Africa struggled to make formal kinship models coincide with forms of lived settlement and sociality. But the fact of the matter was that village life in the sense that was being sought had never existed for the vast majority of the Bemba-speaking peoples. In the Northern Province of Zambia, ties were to people and to territories, rather than to villages per se (Moore & Vaughan, 1994: 132–3). Villages were not indigenous to other parts of Zambia either. Long-term research in Gwembe, in the Southern Province, documents neighbourhoods based on groupings of related families and collective ritual activities, cross-cut by matrilineal clans, which preceded colonial transformations and persist to the present (Cliggett, 2001). The Gwembe Tonga were displaced into villages in the 1950s, which then disintegrated when many people moved to open up new lands near the Kafue Reserve in the 1980s, and have since been reconsolidated to a certain extent after further devolution of power to local headmen in the 1990s made them conduits for food aid distribution and other state resources (Cliggett, 2000; Cliggett et al., 2007). Villages come and go, but what is clear is that they were not in the past, and are not now, the only, or even the major, way of organising the key ecologies of productivity, knowledge and resource on which people depend.

But even if the village was not necessarily the horizon of either sociality, or of meaning making, for the residents of the northern and southern provinces of Zambia, it was a spatial and temporal category essential to the problem of how to conceive of governance and development, because the notion of the rural which came to characterise the African landscape was one of populations characterised as village dwellers. Up until the 1940s in Zambia, the colonial government required people to reside within a registered village (Moore & Vaughan, 1994: 111), and in the first decade of independence (1964–74), village regrouping, as it was called, was a central tenet of rural development policy (Berry, 1993; Bratton, 1980: 125). In different historical periods, the non-existence of the village, or rather its ability to appear and disappear, has produced a sense of rural life in crisis. In the Northern Province of Zambia, colonial reports from the 1930s onwards take on an almost biblical tone, speaking of male labour migration to the Copperbelt in terms of exodus. The spectre was of ruined villages, deracinated male 'natives' and the breakdown of traditional society. Anthropologists from the 1930s to the 1960s were extremely anxious about what they termed 'detribalisation' and the impact of modern economies and urban living on traditional ways of life (Moore & Vaughan, 1994: 140). The result was a view that the underdevelopment of tribal areas was due to the disintegration of village life, and that the depredations of modernity were causing a crisis in the character and reproduction of the social realm, a view reproduced by successive governments well after independence and beyond. The possibility that rural life and livelihoods in the Northern Province depended on scattered settlement was no more acceptable to post-independence governments than it had been to the colonial authorities (Moore & Vaughan, 1994: 136–7). What was particularly strange about this concerted effort to create settled villages and permanent agriculture was that the authorities in all periods recognised, as did residents, that permanent settlement meant deforestation and soil degradation. Whatever the outcome of villagisation might be, it was most unlikely to be improved agricultural productivity.

## 7.3 Making agriculture pay

The creation of the rural world in the first 60 years of the twentieth century involved an imaginative engagement with people, land and livelihoods that gave rise to a series of material consequences. Landscapes had to be settled with villages and villages had to be inhabited by rural dwellers who were farmers. Smallholder agriculture was characterised as backward, and it needed to be replaced by more efficient agriculture. The colonial challenge, which post-colonial governments inherited, was how to make agriculture pay. The solution to this challenge was, in part, the improved farmer. He (and it was a man) would not only maintain the character of modern life, but also make agriculture productive. The authorities had been engaged from the 1950s onwards – and sometimes much earlier – in the production of someone called an improved farmer who would be an improvement on the subsistence farmer (Gertzel, 2008; Moore & Vaughan, 1994: 110–39; Vickery, 1986). The colonial notion of a progressive farmer in the Northern Province of Zambia implied a rejection of 'backward'-shifting agriculture and a commitment to full-time, settled agriculture. It carried with it assumptions about lifestyle that went beyond ways of working the land to encompass a series of transformations. A progressive farmer was a man who would wish to separate himself from kin networks, build a decent brick house, educate his children and be modern without being urbanised. His wife would be keen to learn the rudiments of domestic science.

However, progressive famers themselves often had other agendas, because becoming a farmer was an indication of wealth and a sign of status, and progressive farming was often a form of conspicuous consumption rather than a source of accumulation. It therefore required access to off-farm income and the management of multiple strategies for household reproduction. In the 1950s, very few people could rely on agricultural production alone (Moore & Vaughan, 1994: 115–16), and this is a situation that has persisted up to the present day. The uncertain nature not just of government policy and broken promises, but of risky input supply, poor transport and weak guarantees of a market meant that peasant farmers in the Northern Province continued and continue to engage with shifting cultivation in order to guarantee food supplies, manage cropping patterns and labour requirements, and diversify risks (Grogan et al., 2013). More importantly, investing in social networks to secure access to productive resources and to labour has remained crucial, and has continued to depend on membership in descent groups, as well as broader kin and non-kin networks (Berry, 1993: 136–59).

In the valley areas of Elgeyo-Marakwet, membership in descent groups allowed famers and households to benefit from the distributive effects of different ecological zones. After independence in 1963, restrictions on movement and settlement were lifted, and many men left to clear lands in the fertile forested areas of the Cherangani highlands (Cappon et al., 1985). Land also became available from the former white settler farms in Uasin Gishu and Trans Nzoia, and individuals most often acquired title to these lands through kinship links with family members employed by the government or parastatals. The post-colonial government, like the colonial government before it, wanted to reward followers and create loyal rural residents. Many men established second households in the Cherangani and made good use of the different cropping patterns, labour regimes and soils to diversify risk and gain access to commercial markets in the better-served highlands. Exchange of goods between households in the valley and the highlands was a common and regular feature of life, with maize and potatoes moving downwards to households and markets, and fruit and millet moving in the other direction. These exchange systems diversified consumption patterns, and research conducted in the valley area in the 1980s showed very clear processes of rural differentiation emerging between households who had secured access to land under title in the highlands and those who remained with only access to customary land in the valley. This process of differentiation accelerated from the 1970s onwards, as households in the highlands gained better access to education and urban wage opportunities. Differential access to land and other resources deepened social differentiation along lines of gender and generation, and even within lineages.

Cultivation in the valley was itself ecologically diverse, making use of a communally maintained system of irrigation canals to cultivate individual household plots near the foot of the escarpment, as well as communally cleared clan lands further into the valley floor, and small-scale plots of fruits and vegetables around the households on the escarpment side itself (Davies et al., 2014). From the 1930s onwards, cash came from selling fruits, animal skins, honey, tobacco and vegetables. Sweet potatoes, bananas and other fruit could be sold or bartered for foodstuffs from the highlands, as was common when I started work in Tot Division in the valley in 1980. Food production has historically been variable, and low yields leave little room for manoeuvre when things go wrong. In 2008, a study in the same area found that in order to counteract food shortages, 43 per cent of respondents engaged in casual labour, 10.87 per cent sold cash crops, 10 per cent purchased staple cereals from the market, 3.04 per cent borrowed food, 4.35 per cent sought relief food and 28.7 per cent sold animals (Kipkorir & Kareithi, 2013: 19). A series of government and non-governmental organisation (NGO)-backed initiatives to improve agricultural production have been proposed, sputtered into life and been extinguished again, partly as a result of lack of infrastructural support and state investment, partly because of the remoteness of the area, and partly because they were the designed plans of outsiders with no thought for the knowledge assets of local communities. However, while the agricultural system has been resilient, adapting to population growth and climate change, it has never produced sufficient income to drive long-term intensification and agrarian transformation (Davies & Moore, 2016; see Chapter 8). It has survived through diversification of social networks, ecological zones and sources of income (Pollard et al., 2015).

More than 68 per cent of all Kenyan households are involved in agriculture, and the mean size of agricultural holdings is roughly one hectare, larger than in many other sub-Saharan Africa countries (Food and Agriculture Organization, 2014). But land is an increasingly constraining factor of production for a sizeable and growing proportion of Kenya's population, and rising population is associated with shrinking farm sizes. This is contributing to land intensification, which does appear to increase the net value of crop production up to densities of about 550–600 persons/km$^2$ (Muyanga & Jayne, 2014: 103). Increased cash inputs and higher-value crops are observable forms of sustainable intensification under such conditions, but forms of intensification that are not sustainable include continuous cultivation and reductions in fallows without soil restoration (Powlson et al., 2011). This is evident from the fact that agricultural labour productivity does not rise with population density in a linear way, and above 550–600 persons/km$^2$ the net value of crop output per labour unit declines. This is likely the result of soil degradation (Valbuena et al., 2015). Smaller farm sizes may also impede surplus production, which in turn will impact on the financing of cash input purchases associated with land intensification. With declining land availability, increasing soil degradation and uncertain yields, the best prospect for these households could involve being pulled off land into non-farm sectors. However, findings from Kenya show that off-farm incomes are not increasing significantly, with large numbers of people working in petty trading in the informal sector and casual agricultural labour. These fragile non-farm/informal sectors cannot absorb the excess rural labour generated by declining land availability and productivity (Muyanga & Jayne, 2014: 110).

Research conducted in 22 districts in Kenya in the period 1997–2007 found that only a small fraction of households experienced an appreciable improvement or decline in their relative asset wealth over that timeframe. Households that did transition out of poverty were those that remained healthy, were not adversely affected by mortality, received more land from their parents when the household was formed, and had parents who were relatively well off and educated. Illness, death and minimal access to land undermined those households that reported declining prosperity. In such circumstances female-headed households were disadvantaged, largely as a consequence of women's insecure access to land and inherited assets, as well as their reduced receipt of human capital investment, notably education and health (Muyanga et al., 2013: 29–31).

Increasing population growth and land consolidation are driving agrarian change, but research from Kenya and Zambia suggests that this is not following a unilinear model of agrarian transformation and is not based on successful accumulation by small-scale farmers, throwing doubt on the idea that agricultural growth can effectively reduce rural poverty. However, if we look to recent drivers of change we see that between 2001 and 2011, Zambia did see a rapid increase in 'emergent' famers with landholdings between five and 20 hectares. An analysis of the historical trajectory through which these farmers achieved their scale of operation revealed that this was supported by significant state investment in input and output (price) subsidies for maize, and by settlement schemes and land legislation permitting the legal conversion of customary land to leasehold title (Lands Act, 1995; Sitko & Jayne, 2014: 196–7). Seventy-three per cent of the farmers sampled in the research achieved emergent farmer status through financing from off-farm income, principally from public-sector employment. The larger landholdings are concentrated among those with title to their land acquired after the 1995 Lands Act.

This is linked to state patronage, where farmers are given land primarily through settlement schemes as a reward for public service. From the early 2000s, Zambia experienced a recovery in global copper prices and between 2005 and 2015 sustained GDP growth rates of over 5 per cent. This further increased opportunities for the urban employed to invest in agriculture, buoyed up by enabling land legislation and supportive public spending on larger farms (Sitko & Jayne, 2014: 198–9).[1] Curiously, however, respondents operating on titled land cultivate on average less than 30 per cent of their land, in marked contrast to the overall smallholder population, where 87.3 per cent of all available land is cultivated (only 3 per cent of Zambian smallholders own six or more hectares of land). Taking the requirements of fallow into account, this underutilisation of land means that the employment effect per hectare on emergent farms is limited, and that land consolidation and peasantisation are not creating sustainable forms of agricultural productivity or a substantial agricultural labour market. In fact, those holding larger areas of land are utilising just a fraction of it for agricultural purposes. This suggests that state support for emergent farmers and land distribution are at the expense of poorer farmers, and are not driving large-scale agrarian transformation (Sitko & Jayne, 2014: 200–1).

## 7.4 Rural–urban connections

The long quest for prosperity understood as enhanced agricultural productivity has taken a variety of historical turns, but what is clear is that the urban, whether in terms of formal sector employment, retirement pensions, aspiration, or knowledge networks, has fundamentally shaped rural locales and environments. It is widely recognised that rural–urban migration is part and parcel of African rural life, and that migration is complementary to cultivation, rather than an alternative. The history of rural–urban migration in Kenya is a long one and the urban share of the population has grown from 7 per cent in 1960 to around 32 per cent today (Kenya National Bureau of Statistics, 2009; World Bank, 2007). However, while some research suggests that migration has changed its character over time from a predominantly circulatory form to one which is more pluralist, hybrid and translocal (Greiner & Sakdapolrak, 2013a), there is no clear unilinear trajectory. The importance of translocality and plurality across urban–rural divides was noted from the early 1970s in Kenya (Weisner, 1976), where the importance of socialities that stretch across the different locales has always been key. James Ferguson has argued for Zambia that there has been no unilinear historical development in terms of types of migration; rather, individual women and men have always pursued a variety of strategic alternatives to make use of the opportunities provided by the rural–urban division (1990: 411–12). Migration is rarely an individual or one-off decision; rural and urban family members in multilocational households – those spread across rural–urban locales – have a say in who migrates and for how long (Agesa & Kim, 2001; Greiner & Sakdapolrak, 2013b). Over a third of all Kenyan households divide their members between rural and urban homes, and more than 80 per cent of urban residents report maintaining a strong connection with their rural kin (Agesa, 2004). Migration, and the resulting remittances, are a household risk-mitigation strategy, especially under conditions of environmental stress and land shortage, and transfers of income, goods and services have long been recognised as key to household survival. The unidirectional nature of these flows has been interrogated by extensive research which emphasises that, with declining employment opportunities in urban areas and weaknesses in state safety net systems, reverse transfers are flowing from urban to rural contexts, with evidence of increasing urban–rural return migration (Djurfeldt & Wambugu, 2011; Falkingham et al., 2012; Oucho, 2007; Owuor, 2006, 2007), and even in some cases a stalling of urban growth (Beauchemin, 2011; Potts, 2010).

Many migrants and long-term urban residents – some of whom have never lived in the rural areas – claim that the farm is their real home, and that they wish to retire there and be buried there (Ferguson, 2013; Geschiere, 2014). Rural transformations are therefore not only bound up with essential urban linkages, but land and access to land are linked to forms of identity and belonging for rural and urban residents alike, as well as to livelihoods (Gugler, 2002; Owuor, 2007; Shipton, 2009). It is therefore increasingly difficult in contemporary Africa to divide the rural from the urban, experientially, emotionally, analytically or economically (Losch et al., 2013; Potts, 2005). Ferguson has recently argued persuasively that land in rural areas has to be seen not just – or even primarily – as a productive resource in the context of rural impoverishment and fragile livelihoods, but also as a space for leisure, comfort, connection and burial (Ferguson, 2013), in other words, as a resource for the imagination, as well as a practical investment for those who are urban rather than rural residents. There is no strict rural/urban divide in Kenya, but there are certainly differences structured by outlook, opportunity, geographical mobility and effective action spaces.

In Kenya, issues of financial inclusion, investment, information transfer and social networks are being transformed by the technology of the mobile phone. When mobile phones first came in, an important driver of phone ownership was access to non-farm income, but the cost of handsets and calls has fallen dramatically in the last five years. The Communications Authority of Kenya's 2015 report records 37.8 million mobile subscriptions in Kenya, with mobile penetration at 88.1 per cent of the population. Total internet subscriptions are 21.6 million, with an estimated number of internet users of 31.9 million, which is 74.2 per cent of the population (Communications Authority of Kenya, 2015). While they are personal – handsets have individual owners – the devices are also communal and shared, so that handsets help maintain social networks through exchange networks that involve the handset itself, as well as the information it conveys (Komen, 2014).[2] Managing multilocational households in Kenya is an intricate process, often happening over large distances. Phones clearly help spouses co-ordinate farm, household and community activities (Kusimba, Chaggar et al., 2013; Kusimba, Yang & Chawla, 2015; Oduor et al., 2014). In Elgeyo-Marakwet, personal calls merge greetings and staying in touch with requests for seeds, help to prepare land and money to pay children's school fees (Kirui et al., 2013). Implied in the Marakwet phrase 'takwessa tokol' (greet everyone) is a range of information about prices, politics, births, marriages and deaths that forms the real basis of exchanges dependent on labour, capital and knowledge, as well as the networks they create and reproduce (Oduor et al., 2014: 2709). Studies elsewhere in Kenya show that 70 per cent of women normally call siblings or other natal relatives, twice the rate for men (36 per cent), providing those married in patrilineal, virilocal societies with access to expanded networks of potential support and protection. Women in Marakwet also use mobiles to co-ordinate community activities, such as savings and church groups. More men make long-distance calls for work, reaching pastors, church leaders and government officials, further away. The mobile phone links family members to their kinship and social networks, and onwards to larger networks of resource, influence and power (Jack et al., 2013; Jack & Suri, 2014). This is key in the Kenyan context, where access to people is the surest route to gaining resources, education and even a job.

In contrast to discussions about the relevance of mobile phones to development in Africa which focus on their potential to facilitate market transactions and economic growth, development projects, the communication of public health messages, and other technical means for addressing poverty, it is important to recognise that they perpetuate and expand an older strategy for survival based on investment in people. The mobile phone allows those resident outside the rural area to send money – via

Mpesa, the mobile phone money transfer system (Mbiti & Weil, 2011; Morawczynski, 2009) – to cut down the costs and time of travel, to make an input into agricultural and household decisions, and to offer advice and comfort, as well as to interfere! Those resident in the rural areas reap the same benefits through greater communication and connectivity. Together they are the new digital farmers of Kenya.

Land remains an important resource for people in Elgeyo-Marakwet. New ways of working the land emerge as people invest in the crops that new consumption patterns bring: tomatoes, onions, watermelons, mangoes. Changing consumption patterns are linked to aspirations and ideas about the good life connected in people's imaginations with life 'in town'. Agrarian self-sufficiency is not a realistic option, since cash is needed to guarantee the satisfactions on which people rely for quality of life. Drawing on resources from kin settled in towns or on farms in the highlands, as well as entrepreneurial activities, loans and small-scale employment, those few who have resources are investing them in infrastructure, in roofed square houses, with water, solar-powered electricity, televisions and sofa sets. They are also persuading the young men to cut basic roads through the steep, rocky areas in which the settlements sit. They are investing in expensive church weddings, moving around on motor bikes, eating bread and watermelon. Class divisions are becoming very apparent and are driven by differential access to land and cash. Many smallholders are sinking into bare subsistence, but since rural locales are spaces where complex repertoires of economic activity are played out through both farm and non-farm activity, issues of quality of life are being shaped by changing aspirations and consumption patterns, even for those households for which they remain resolutely out of reach. The character of the rural is changing, but not because of improvements in agricultural productivity or accelerated agrarian transformation. There is less and less need to go to town – although everyone still does – because the village is becoming more like the town. The rural is beginning to have the same leisure facilities, comforts and entertainments as the town. And, as the residents will tell you, the food and water are better in the rural areas; there is no pollution; the quality of life is better. These comforts are not in any way excessive, but they are the comforts of home. The long-time absent, well-educated, formally employed professionals are all building large houses for their retirement, just as they hoped they would. But they are not the people who have transformed the rural area, although some of their income and resources will definitely have circulated in circuitous ways through many people's pockets. The valley has been transformed by its long-term residents, by their aspirations for a good life in a rural area. Rural livelihoods are evolving, but they are not always or even primarily based on agriculture in the sense of the cultivation of staples, but on complex ecologies of knowledge, resource, time and place.

## 7.5 Conclusion

In this chapter, I have suggested that understanding agrarian change and the evolution and persistence of particular ways of conceptualising it requires a form of analytical history based on the longue durée. Braudel's original insistence that the longue durée is a methodological tool rather than a theory, and that its purpose is to help us understand the present, is particularly germane for rural life in Africa. For one thing, it provides an analytical structure that allows us to lay out and comprehend the frameworks used both to create and to manage the ongoing crisis of rural livelihoods and their failed prosperity. For another, it emphasises the material consequences of interventions and of the way successive generations of analysts and policy makers have repeatedly tried to mould the nature of rural transformation through the imposition of models that have indelibly marked its present with its past.

Looking afresh at the changing character of rural lives and livelihoods, it is clear that the *sine qua non* of survival in many rural African contexts is diversification. Rural residents have responded and continue to respond to changes in market access, prices, state subsidies, global commodity prices, new technologies, new crops, digital inclusion, and even online extension services for farmers. Resources have been, and continue to be, patchily distributed across rural landscapes in Kenya and Zambia, and significant inequalities between regions within individual countries are important, but what emerges is a concerted effort to use social networks to knit together resources in innovative ways. Dichotomous boundaries between the rural and the urban make little analytical sense, especially since urban growth seems stalled in many parts of sub-Saharan agriculture, and employment opportunities have failed to keep pace with demographic change. Getting an education and going to town are no longer the real or imagined road to prosperity. The result is that the visions of African agrarian transformation espoused to varying degrees by rulers, residents and researchers have failed to live up to any sustained or sustainable model of unilinear development, whether based on agricultural intensification, educational opportunity, urbanisation or industrialisation.

This is a far cry from the prosperous peasant farmers and rising agricultural productivity and incomes envisaged in various five-year plans and development visions over the long decades of the twentieth century. There is no doubt that rising populations and declining size of landholdings, combined with reversals of agricultural policies, failure to reform land acquisition and registration, the erratic nature of the world economy, and the deepening ecological crisis of rising temperatures and acidifying soils are all working against the vision of an African agriculture that would not only support rural populations but engage with export trade and raise government incomes. There is much to be said for the argument that the ongoing crisis of rural Africa is not the product of farmer resistance – whether this be figured as tradition, lack of productivity, lack of market integration, etc. – but of a series of futures only equivocally offered, a failure to envisage what prosperity might mean and entail for Africa on its own terms and through the visions of its citizens. Growth rates in many sub-Saharan countries have been solid in the last 10 years, and there have been marked improvements also in maternal and child health, in transport infrastructures, in educational attainment and in communication technologies. But overall improvements in quality of life for most rural residents – the prosperity gain – from such growth have been minimal. We live in an age that is fully aware that its fictions are themselves models of human design on the world. Small-scale African farmers take this as pretty much axiomatic and continue to seek prosperity through the complex forms of ecology, resource, capital and place that are based on social relations in an effort to mitigate the consequences of others' designs and to try and advance their own whenever opportunity arises.

## Notes

1. Since 2016, the Zambian economy has slowed markedly again with exposure to reduced copper prices (World Bank, 2017).
2. In the rural areas, ownership is still differentiated by gender, and for women without a handset borrowing from friends or family is the most common way to gain access to a phone (Murphy & Priebe, 2011; Oduor et al., 2014: 2711).

## Bibliography

Adam, C. S., Collier, P. & Gondwe, M. (eds) (2014). *Zambia: Building prosperity from resource wealth*. Oxford: Oxford University Press.
Adam, C. S., Collier, P. & Ndung'u, N. (eds) (2011). *Kenya: Policies for prosperity*. Oxford: Oxford University Press.

Agesa, R. U. (2004). One family, two households: Rural to urban migration in Kenya. *Review of Economics of the Household*, 2(2), 161–78. https://doi.org/10.1023/B:REHO.0000031612.77882.29.

Agesa, R. U. & Kim, S. (2001). Rural to urban migration as a household decision: Evidence from Kenya. *Review of Development Economics*, 5(1), 60–75. https://doi.org/10.1111/1467-9361.00107.

Beauchemin, C. (2011). Rural–urban migration in West Africa: Towards a reversal? Migration trends and economic situation in Burkina Faso and Côte d'Ivoire. *Population, Space and Place*, 17(1), 47–72. https://doi.org/10.1002/psp.573.

Berry, S. (1993). *No Condition Is Permanent: The social dynamics of agrarian change in sub-Saharan Africa*. Madison: Wisconsin University Press.

Bratton, M. (1980). *The Local Politics of Rural Development: Peasant and party-state in Zambia*. Hanover, NH: University Press of New England.

Braudel, F. [1949] (1995). *The Mediterranean and the Mediterranean World in the Age of Philip II* (trans. S. Reynolds). Berkeley: University of California Press.

Braudel, F. [1958] (2009). History and the social sciences: The longue durée (trans. I. Wallerstein). *Review* 32(2): 171–203.

Brockington, D. & Noe, C. (eds) (2021). *Prosperity in Rural Africa? Insights into wealth, assets, and poverty from longitudinal studies in Tanzania*. Oxford: Oxford University Press.

Bryceson, D. F. (2000). African peasants' centrality and marginality: Rural labour transformations. In F. Bryceson, C. Kay & J. E. Mooij (eds), *Disappearing Peasantries? Rural labour in Africa, Asia and Latin America*, pp. 37–63. London: Intermediate Technology Publications.

Communications Authority of Kenya (CAK) (2015). First quarter sector statistics report for the financial year 2015/2016 (July–September 2015). Nairobi: Communications Authority of Kenya.

Cappon, J. C., van den Goorbergh, M., Mwangi, M. S. & Saina, C. M. (1985). *District Atlas Elgeyo Marakwet*. Iten: Ministry of Planning and National Development, Republic of Kenya.

Cliggett, L. (2000). Social components of migration: Experiences from Southern Province, Zambia. *Human Organization*, 59(1), 125–35. http://dx.doi.org/10.17730/humo.59.1.f29132613q2k543p.

Cliggett, L. (2001). Survival strategies of the elderly in Gwembe Valley, Zambia: Gender, residence and kin networks. *Journal of Cross-Cultural Gerontology*, 16(4), 309–32. https://doi.org/10.1023/A:1014546709621.

Cliggett, L., Colson, E., Hay, R., Scudder, T. & Unruh, J. (2007). Chronic uncertainty and momentary opportunity: A half century of adaptation among Zambia's Gwembe Tonga. *Human Ecology*, 35(1), 19–31. https://doi.org/10.1007/s10745-006-9080-7.

Davies, M. I. J., Kiprutto, T. K. & Moore, H. L. (2014). Revisiting the irrigated agricultural landscape of the Marakwet, Kenya: Tracing local technology and knowledge over the recent past. *Azania: Archaeological Research in Africa*, 49(4), 486–523. https://doi.org/10.1080/0067270X.2014.979527.

Davies, M. I. J. & Moore, H. L. (2016). Landscape, time and cultural resilience: A brief history of agriculture in Pokot and Marakwet, Kenya. *Journal of Eastern African Studies*, 10(1), 67–87. https://doi.org/10.1080/17531055.2015.1134417.

Djurfeldt, A. A. & Wambugu, S. K. (2011). In-kind transfers of maize, commercialization and household consumption in Kenya. *Journal of Eastern African Studies*, 5(3), 447–64. https://doi.org/10.1080/17531055.2011.611671.

Falkingham, J., Chepngeno-Langat, G. & Evandrou, M. (2012). Outward migration from large cities: Are older migrants in Nairobi 'returning'? *Population, Space and Place*, 18(3), 327–43. https://doi.org/10.1002/psp.678.

Ferguson, J. (1990). Mobile workers, modernist narratives: A critique of the historiography of transition on the Zambian Copperbelt [part one]. *Journal of Southern African Studies*, 16(3), 385–412. https://doi.org/10.1080/03057079008708243.

Ferguson, J. (2013). How to do things with land: A distributive perspective on rural livelihoods in Southern Africa. *Journal of Agrarian Change*, 13(1), 166–74. https://doi.org/10.1111/j.1471-0366.2012.00363.x.

Food and Agriculture Organization (FAO) (2014). *The State of Food and Agriculture: Innovation in family farming*. Rome: Food and Agriculture Organization.

Gertzel, C. (2008). East and Central Africa. In M. Crowder (ed.), *The Cambridge History of Africa. Volume 8: From c. 1940 to c. 1975*, pp. 383–457. Cambridge: Cambridge University Press.

Geschiere, P. (2014). The funeral in the village: Urbanites' shifting imaginations of belonging, mobility, and community. In M. Diouf & R. Fredericks (eds), *The Arts of Citizenship in African Cities: Infrastructures and spaces of belonging*, pp. 49–66. New York: Palgrave Macmillan.

Greiner, C. & Sakdapolrak, P. (2013a). Rural–urban migration, agrarian change, and the environment in Kenya: A critical review of the literature. *Population and Environment*, 34(4), 524–53. https://doi.org/10.1007/s11111-012-0178-0.

Greiner, C. & Sakdapolrak, P. (2013b). Translocality: Concepts, applications and emerging research perspectives. *Geography Compass*, 7(5), 373–84. https://doi.org/10.1111/gec3.12048.

Grogan, K., Birch-Thomsen, T. & Lyimo, J. (2013). Transition of shifting cultivation and its impact on people's livelihoods in the miombo woodlands of northern Zambia and southwestern Tanzania. *Human Ecology*, 41(1), 77–92. https://doi.org/10.1007/s10745-012-9537-9.

Gugler, J. (2002). The son of the hawk does not remain abroad: The urban–rural connection in Africa. *African Studies Review*, 45(1), 21–41. https://doi.org/10.2307/1515006.

Jack, W., Ray, A. & Suri, T. (2013). Transaction networks: Evidence from mobile money in Kenya. *American Economic Review*, 103(3), 356–61. https://doi.org/10.1257/aer.103.3.356.

Jack, W. & Suri, T. (2014). Risk sharing and transactions costs: Evidence from Kenya's mobile money revolution. *American Economic Review*, 104(1), 183–223. http://dx.doi.org/10.1257/aer.104.1.183.

Jameson, F. (1991). *Postmodernism, or, The Cultural Logic of Late Capitalism*. London: Verso.

Kenya National Bureau of Statistics (KNBS) (2009). *Kenya Census 2009*. Nairobi: Kenya National Bureau of Statistics.

Kermode, F. (2000). *The Sense of an Ending: Studies in the theory of fiction: With a new epilogue*. Oxford: Oxford University Press.

Kipkorir, D. & Kareithi, J. (2013). Indigenous irrigation and food security in Tot Division, Kerio Valley, Kenya. *Journal of Anthropology & Archaeology*, 1(1), 12–27.

Kirui, O. K., Okello, J. J., Nyikal, R. A. & Njiraini, G. W. (2013). Impact of mobile phone-based money transfer services in agriculture: Evidence from Kenya. *Quarterly Journal of International Agriculture*, 52(2), 141–62.

Komen, L. J. (2014). Mobile assemblages and maendeleo in rural Kenya: The case of Marakwet. PhD thesis, University of East London.

Kusimba, S., Chaggar, H., Gross, E. & Kunyu, G. (2013). Social networks of mobile money in Kenya. IMTFI Working Paper no. 2013-1. Institute for Money, Technology and Financial Inclusion, University of California.

Kusimba, S., Yang, Y. & Chawla, N. V. (2015). Family networks of mobile money in Kenya. *Information Technologies & International Development*, 11(3), 1–21.

Lands Act (1995). Ministry of Legal Affairs, Government of the Republic of Zambia. Available at: http://www.parliament.gov.zm/sites/default/files/documents/acts/Lands%20Act.pdf (accessed 1 January 2023).

Latour, B. (1993). *We Have Never Been Modern* (trans. C. Porter). Cambridge, MA: Harvard University Press.

Losch, B., Magrin, G. & Imbernon, J. (eds) (2013). *A New Emerging Rural World: An overview of rural change in Africa*. Montpellier: CIRAD.

Mbiti, I. M. & Weil, D. N. (2011). Mobile banking: The impact of M-Pesa in Kenya. NBER Working Paper no. 17129. National Bureau of Economic Research, Cambridge, MA. https://www.nber.org/papers/w17129 (accessed 1 January 2023).

Moore, H. L. (1983) Anthropology and development: Some illustrations from the Marakwet of Kenya. In B. E. Kipkorir, R. C. Soper & J. W. Ssennyonga (eds), *Kerio Valley, Past, Present and Future: Proceedings of a seminar held in Nairobi at the Institute of African Studies, University of Nairobi, May 21–22, 1981*, pp. 132–8. Nairobi: Institute of African Studies, University of Nairobi.

Moore, H. L. (1996). *Space, Text and Gender: An anthropological study of the Marakwet of Kenya*, 2nd edn. New York: Guilford Press.

Moore, H. L. (2011). *Still Life: Hopes, desires and satisfactions*. Cambridge: Polity.

Moore, H. L. (2015). Global prosperity and sustainable development goals. *Journal of International Development*, 27(6), 801–15. https://doi.org/10.1002/jid.3114.

Moore, H. L. & Moreno, J. M. (2022). Tilting relationalities: Exploring the world through possible futures of agriculture. *Sociological Review*, 70(2), 313–29. https://doi.org/10.1177/00380261221084778.

Moore, H. L. & Vaughan, M. (1994). *Cutting Down Trees: Gender, nutrition, and agricultural change in the Northern Province of Zambia, 1890–1990*. Portsmouth, NH: Heinemann.

Morawczynski, O. (2009). Exploring the usage and impact of 'transformational' mobile financial services: The case of M-PESA in Kenya. *Journal of Eastern African Studies*, 3(3), 509–25. https://doi.org/10.1080/17531050903273768.

Murphy, L. L. & Priebe, A. E. (2011). 'My co-wife can borrow my mobile phone!': Gendered geographies of cell phone usage and significance for rural Kenyans. *Gender, Technology and Development*, 15(1), 1–23. https://doi.org/10.1177/097185241101500101.

Muyanga, M. & Jayne, T. S. (2014). Effects of rising population density on smallholder agriculture in Kenya. *Food Policy*, 48, 98–113. https://doi.org/10.1016/j.foodpol.2014.03.001.

Muyanga, M., Jayne, T. S. & Burke, W. J. (2013). Pathways into and out of poverty: A study of rural household wealth dynamics in Kenya. *Journal of Development Studies*, 49(10), 1358–74. https://doi.org/10.1080/00220388.2013.812197.

Nietzsche, F. W. (1968). *The Will to Power* (trans. W. Kaufmann & R. J. Hollingdale). New York: Vintage Books.

Oduor, E., Neustaedter, C., Judge, T. K., Hennessy, K., Pang, C. & Hillman, S. (2014). How technology supports family communication in rural, suburban, and urban Kenya. In *Proceedings of the 32nd Annual ACM Conference on Human Factors in Computing Systems*, pp. 2705–14. New York: Association for Computing Machinery. Available at: https://dl.acm.org/doi/abs/10.1145/2556288.2557277 (accessed 1 January 2023).

Oucho, J. O. (2007). Migration and regional development in Kenya. *Development*, 50(4), 88–93. https://doi.org/10.1057/palgrave.development.1100425.

Owuor, S. (2006). *Bridging the Urban–Rural Divide: Multi-spatial livelihoods in Nakuru town, Kenya*. Leiden: African Studies Centre. https://scholarlypublications.universiteitleiden.nl/handle/1887/4637 (accessed 1 January 2023).

Owuor, S. O. (2007). Migrants, urban poverty and the changing nature of urban–rural linkages in Kenya. *Development Southern Africa*, 24(1), 109–22. https://doi.org/10.1080/03768350601165926.

Pollard, G., Davies, M. I. J. & Moore, H. L. (2015). Women, marketplaces and exchange partners amongst the Marakwet of northwest Kenya. *Journal of Eastern African Studies*, 9(3), 412–39. https://doi.org/10.1080/17531055.2015.1089699.

Potts, D. (2005). Counter-urbanisation on the Zambian Copperbelt? Interpretations and implications. *Urban Studies*, 42(4), 583–609. https://doi.org/10.1080/00420980500060137.

Potts, D. (2010). *Circular Migration in Zimbabwe and Contemporary Sub-Saharan Africa*. Woodbridge: James Currey.

Powlson, D. S., Gregory, P. J., Whalley, W. R., Quinton, J. N., Hopkins, D. W., Whitmore, A. P., Hirsch, P. R. & Goulding K. W. T. (2011). Soil management in relation to sustainable agriculture and ecosystem services. *Food Policy*, 36 (Supplement 1), S72–S87. https://doi.org/10.1016/j.foodpol.2010.11.025.

Richards, A. (1939). *Land, Labour and Diet in Northern Rhodesia: An economic study of the Bemba tribe*. London: Oxford University Press.

Shipton, P. M. (2009). *Mortgaging the Ancestors: Ideologies of attachment in Africa*. New Haven, CT: Yale University Press.

Sitko, N. J. & Jayne, T. S. (2014). Structural transformation or elite land capture? The growth of 'emergent' farmers in Zambia. *Food Policy*, 48, 194–202. https://doi.org/10.1016/j.foodpol.2014.05.006.

Valbuena, D., Groot, J. C. J., Mukalama, J., Gérard, B. & Tittonell, P. (2015). Improving rural livelihoods as a 'moving target': Trajectories of change in smallholder farming systems of Western Kenya. *Regional Environmental Change*, 15(7), 1395–1407.

Vickery, K. P. (1986). *Black and White in Southern Zambia: The Tonga Plateau economy and British imperialism, 1890–1939*. Westport, CT: Greenwood Press.

Weisner, T. S. (1976). The structure of sociability: Urban migration and urban–rural ties in Kenya. *Urban Anthropology*, 5(2), 199–223.

Whitehead, A. N. (1967). *Adventures of Ideas*. New York: Free Press.

World Bank (2007). *World Development Report 2008: Agriculture for development.* Washington, DC: World Bank.

World Bank (2016). Kenya – Country Economic Memorandum: From economic growth to jobs and shared prosperity. Available at: https://documents.worldbank.org/en/publication/documents-reports/documentdetail/763771468197384854/kenya-country-economic-memorandum-from-economic-growth-to-jobs-and-shared-prosperity (accessed 25 February 2023).

World Bank (2017). The World Bank in Zambia. Available at: http://www.worldbank.org/en/country/zambia/overview (accessed 1 January 2023).

# 8
# Emergent prosperity, time and design: farming in Marakwet, Kenya

Matthew Davies, Samuel Lunn-Rockliffe,
Timothy Kipkeu Kiprutto and Wilson Kipkore

## 8.1 Introduction

Since at least the 1930s, the Marakwet people of north-west Kenya (Moore, 1983, 1986) have been both lauded and criticised for their complex system of intensive agriculture. While many visitors have praised the ingenuity of the hundreds of kilometres of gravity-fed irrigation channels (or furrows) and a plethora of landrace crops and soil management techniques (Davies, Kiprutto & Moore, 2014; Davies & Moore, 2016), many observers have simultaneously assumed that such modes of production are inefficient and at imminent risk of failure and ecological collapse (Hennings, 1941; Huxley, 1959; Watson et al., 1998; Caretta & Börjeson, 2015; Kipkorir & Kareithi, 2013; cf. Davies & Moore, 2016). Outside observers have often been unable to see beyond periodic and localised patterns of soil erosion and crop failure, to consider how such systems actually work in time and space. This myopic thinking recursively builds on, and feeds into, a prejudicial inability to imagine African smallholder farmers as anything but a static relic of tradition in need of immediate modernisation (see also Chapter 7).

A more nuanced temporal and spatial understanding, however, provides a set of alternative narratives that suggest the Marakwet system of cultivation and the communities it has served have remained remarkably resilient in the face of multiple challenges (Davies, Kiprutto & Moore, 2014; Davies & Moore, 2016). While the Marakwet have faced recurrent food shortages and conflicts, local agricultural systems have proved highly adaptable over the last century, seeing the growth of irrigation-based farming, the accommodation of a threefold population increase and the weathering of major climatic fluctuations.

So why have regular and repeated warnings of collapse from outside observers and 'experts' proved so pervasive? We argue that the continued portrayal of the Marakwet as highly sophisticated farmers who are nevertheless perpetually on the precipice of agricultural failure represents a particular condition of modernity built upon singular notions of teleological progress curated through Western economic and scientific norms. Such frameworks of linear development leave little room for alternative technologies, knowledges and ideas, even when they are clearly effective. As explored below with particular reference to a recent case, these assessments buttress the rationale to implement externally designed development initiatives aimed at improving local livelihoods, despite the fact that such schemes repeatedly fail (Derbyshire & Lowasa, 2022).

Conversely, we contend that the Marakwet improve their own lifeways through creative experimentation, improvisation and innovation in ways that allow them to thrive. Here people work towards prosperous livelihoods conceptualised not simply as the accumulation of wealth, although this is no doubt important, but rather with a more holistic understanding of *maisha bora* (Swahili) or *tasampo tai* (Marakwet), translated as 'the good life' (see also Woodcraft et al., 2020). Ongoing research in Marakwet identifies the need for quality education, human health, clean and healthy environments, inter-clan solidarity, secure housing and work and a voice in decision-making processes. But, more than this, we argue that good lives in Marakwet have to exist through time and across generations. As we attempt to show below, we see this evidenced by the maintenance of lifeways, including forms of farming and food production, the persistence of households, lineages and clans, and overall increases in population, the retention and evolution of local social institutions, and a wider maintenance of biodiversity. These features of Marakwet life have persisted under threat, whether that be from climatic change, deforestation or the interventions of the state or outside experts. We contend that this persistence can be viewed as a practical lived prosperity through time that is often overlooked or ignored by external agents.

In this chapter we therefore build on a long intellectual history that critiques the 'received wisdoms' of these external agents and the 'anti-political' historical reductionism of later twentieth-century development planning (Moore, 2015; Anderson, 1984; Ferguson, 1994; Leach &

Mearns, 1996; see also Chapter 7). However, we aim not simply to show how wrong these external assumptions have been, nor to explain why such interventions have failed. Rather we more fundamentally attempt to demonstrate how they begin from a deeper flawed assumption that prosperous lives can be generated through singular acts of design embedded in teleological visions of the past and the future. Taking a lead from thinkers such as Santos (2014) and Arturo Escobar (2017, 2018), we argue instead that the Marakwet have, through time, maintained their own ways and means of addressing and solving ecological, economic and engineering challenges so as to generate forms of lived prosperity. Such processes have often been enacted in antithesis to the design intentions of external actors which, in many ways, have been distractions from everyday life.

Key to our argument, then, is the contention that the ability to generate prosperous lives principally resides with the people who live that prosperity. We illustrate how the capacity to generate prosperity does not exist in some atemporal space (as a timeless characteristic or potential of all moments) to be realised through the enactment of a singular 'developmental' design or blueprint. Rather, the generation of prosperity resides in a multitude of momentary experiences, actions and decisions that play out through time. As discussed in Chapter 1 of this volume, we might thus see the realisation of prosperity as a temporally contingent emergent phenomenon of complex socio-natural systems. While this 'emergence' of prosperity can be guided by forethought and planning, it can only be properly realised/generated through iterative processes of shaping by daily living. It cannot be realised in some abstracted future but is created in the here and now.

This chapter therefore draws on long-term archaeological, historical and ethnographic data to present the case of rural farmers in Marakwet as an example of such emergent prosperity. We first introduce the reader to the study area before juxtaposing failed developmental designs projected onto Marakwet farmers with alternative narratives of relatively successful community-led agricultural development. In so doing, we aim to show how prosperous forms of living are self-made in the contemporary moment through the ongoing shaping of emergence. While we firmly recognise that such forms of prosperity are not perfect, we conclude by arguing for forms of support for rural agricultural communities that harness and catalyse such generative capacities so as to accelerate and strengthen the emergence of prosperous lifeways.

## 8.2 Introduction to agriculture in Marakwet

The Marakwet are members of the Kalenjin group of southern Nilotic speakers and predominantly reside in Elgeyo-Marakwet County, northwest Kenya (Kipkorir & Welbourn, 2008; Moore, 1986). With a population of 119,969 (Kenya National Bureau of Statistics, 2019), their agropastoral farming activities extend from the semi-arid plains of the Kerio Valley (*c.* 1,000 metres above sea level [masl]), through to highland forests (*c.* 2,500 masl) and up to the ericaceous moors (*c.* 3,500 masl). These diverse ecological zones facilitate a dynamic regional food system; people exploit altitudinal variation to grow an array of foodstuffs throughout the year. Generally speaking, the cooler, wetter areas at higher altitudes are reserved for growing potatoes and a range of leafy greens. As elevation decreases, maize becomes the dominant cultivar, alongside beans, onions, spinach and avocado. In the Kerio Valley maize is intercropped with sorghum, and finger millet alongside cassava, tomatoes, pulses, bananas, mango trees and a variety of other fruits and vegetables.

We focus our attention on the lower slopes of the Elgeyo Escarpment and the village centre of Tot-Sibou (Figure 8.1), where agriculture has remained the primary livelihood for a majority of people since the migration of Marakwet populations into the region some 250 years ago (Moore, 1983, 1986; Dietz et al., 1987; Davies & Moore, 2016; Lunn-Rockliffe, 2019; Kay, 2021). Food is grown at the household level and with short fallow regimes in semi-permanent fields, and around homesteads and commercial centres at the foot of the escarpment. Larger tracts of uninhabited land on the flatter plains of the Kerio Valley allow for complementary shifting cultivation, with long fallow periods and management at the communal level. This patchwork has created a highly fluid agricultural landscape, where individuals and groups employ a variety of techniques, such as intercropping, cover cropping and fallowing, as they respond to changing ecological conditions (drought, erosion, fertility) and societal pressures (demographic change, conflict, residential mobility). Access to a range of resources is achieved across altitudinal and ecological zones, both through direct cultivation of plots at higher elevations, and through complex social and kin networks and regional markets (Pollard et al., 2015). As discussed in more detail below, the system is sustained by a sprawling network of irrigation furrows that channel water from the wetter highland forests to the drier ecology of the Kerio Valley floor. The lower reaches of furrows are intended to shift over time as farmers plant different crops, rotate fields or move to better soils (Davies, Kiprutto & Moore, 2014).

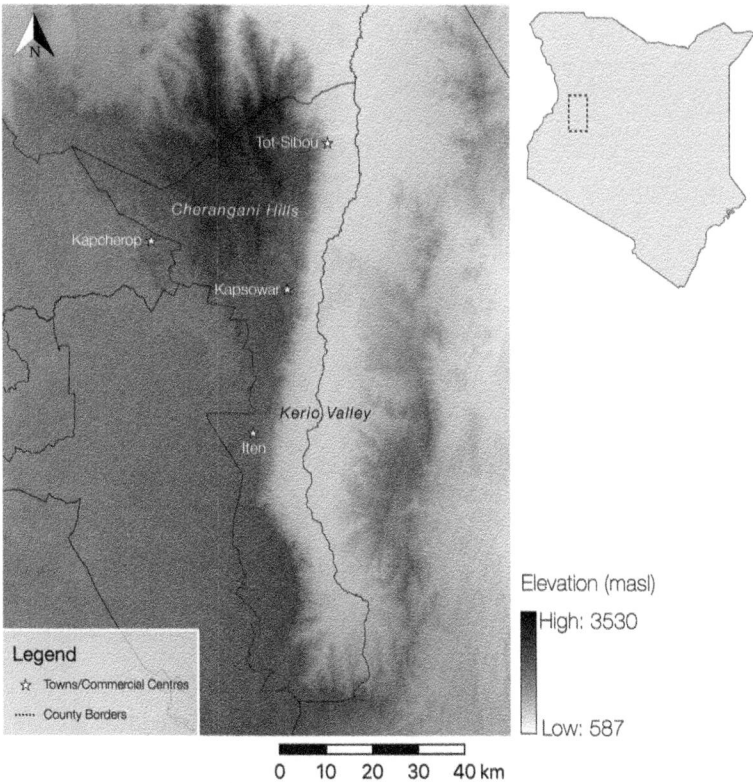

**Figure 8.1**  Location and geography of Elgeyo-Marakwet.

## 8.3 Development interventions and attempts to design agricultural prosperity in Marakwet

The Kerio Valley has been subjected to a plethora of development initiatives aiming to improve food security and livelihoods (Kipkorir, 1983; Moore, 1983; Dietz et al., 1987; Davies & Moore, 2016). One of the more recent of these was the establishment of a new 500-acre irrigation scheme funded by the Canadian Red Cross near the village of Sibou and the neighbouring commercial centre of Tot (Figure 8.2). Established in 2012 and operational for the first time in 2014, the scheme channelled water through a major pipeline across the floor of the Kerio Valley to irrigate 250 acres[1] of arable land for the Marakwet, and 250 acres for the neighbouring Pokot communities living in Baringo County to the east of the River Kerio. The scheme was designed to encourage cash

**Figure 8.2** Noah Kiplagat, PROCOL Kenya citizen scientist, helps to dig a trench for the piping of the irrigation scheme.

Source: Davies, 2014

cropping through the establishment of reliable irrigation pipes and the distribution of hybrid seed, inorganic fertilisers and pesticides.

While implemented with honest intentions, the scheme was planned around a set of assumptions that framed local practices as inefficient and in need of modernisation. The project thus failed to recognise the creative capacity of farmers and the multiple responses that would ensue. Indeed, many farmers realised that the largest potential from the scheme lay not in the cash cropping of maize, but in the selective planting of diverse horticultural products with high market value. Maize seed was stowed, sold or planted elsewhere, depending on individual needs. Similarly, chemical fertilisers intended for intensifying maize cultivation were saved for future use or sold to release immediate capital.

More problematically, the newly implemented system of fixed-pipe irrigation stood in stark contrast to the fluid and flexible existing system of shifting irrigation and cultivation. Many farmers complained that the plastic fixtures of the irrigation pipes were repeatedly broken by wandering livestock, that water pressures were low, and that the concentrated influx of new foodstuffs attracted wildlife that destroyed produce. Furthermore, the allocation of land for the project disrupted delicate pre-existing land tenure and management systems, fuelling existing tensions between Marakwet communities. Ultimately, the Red Cross withdrew operational activities and, with broken equipment and increasing levels of insecurity, the project was largely abandoned by community members after only two seasons of use.

The Red Cross project is part of a much longer history of development schemes that have attempted to reshape agricultural practice in Marakwet. The first half of the twentieth century saw a range of colonial interventions to establish demonstration farms to modernise farming techniques through the introduction of cash crops such as tobacco, cotton, sisal, pineapples, chillies, castor, mangoes, pawpaw, sugar cane and varieties of banana (Davies & Moore, 2016; Kipkorir, 1983). These activities were scaled up in the mid-twentieth century with the establishment of the African Land Development Program (ALDP), when development officers were put in place to encourage additional cash-cropping regimes and systems of ridge and furrow to improve soil quality and water retention. The ALDP also 'up-graded' indigenous irrigation systems with new concrete structures and plastic piping, much of which was ineffective, broke or became clogged with foliage and was consequently replaced by locally designed structures over the following decade. Similar attempts to introduce tractor ploughing stood at odds with deeper understandings of land tenure and divisions of labour at household and communal levels (Kipkorir, 1983).

Throughout the 1980s and 1990s the parastatal Kerio Valley Development Agency (KVDA) and a number of other institutions (notably World Vision and the Catholic Church) continued to engage in agricultural development activities. These included regular donations, continued attempts at renovating irrigation channels and yet more cash-cropping schemes, including cotton, rice, grain-seed and sugar cane. Of particular note was a feasibility study for an irrigation scheme at the confluence of the rivers Embobut and Kerio. These plans continued to view local agriculture as retrogressive (Kipkorir, 1983), and while the scheme was not formally established at the time, it provided the rationale and blueprint for the implementation (and inevitable failure) of the Red Cross project some 30 years later.

Each of these periodic planned development initiatives, from the colonial period to the Red Cross in 2014, has largely been predicated on the assumption that local forms of agriculture in Marakwet were inefficient and facing impending collapse, yet these initiatives have broadly proved fragile. Local agriculture has at best been seen as a barrier to more modern forms of agricultural livelihoods and at worst as symptomatic of a state of crisis. Yet, as we explore below, agricultural history in Marakwet can be read very differently.

## 8.4 An alternative narrative: agriculture in Marakwet as a form of long-term emergent prosperity

Contemporary farming in Marakwet is not an ahistorical and static system passively waiting to be modernised by external interventions, but a constantly changing temporal construct that has emerged out of centuries of intergenerational experimentation and adaptation. Such change is in part underpinned by patrilocal clan-based systems of land tenure that have resulted in a constantly shifting kaleidoscope of settlement (Davies & Moore, 2016; Lunn-Rockliffe, 2019; Kay, 2021; Moore, 1986). Within these patrilocal systems, clans have finite territories that become increasingly subdivided over generations. Consequently, as populations increase, so does localised pressure on land and resources. Farmers respond to this challenge by exploiting the dynamics of an agricultural landscape that operates at multiple scales, including horticultural plots at the household level, semi-permanent fields located at different elevations, and communally farmed fields in the largely uninhabited plains of the Kerio Valley. Across this landscape, farmers creatively experiment with agronomic intensification through soil conservation measures (for example, terracing, fallowing, manuring, mulching, afforestation) and diverse cropping practices (for example, intercropping landrace crops with cash crops).

The system as a whole relies upon an intricate network of irrigation furrows, totalling some 315 km in length, that distributes water from the highlands into the Kerio Valley for both agricultural and domestic purposes (Davies, Kiprutto & Moore, 2014; Figure 8.3). These furrows are highly flexible, being opened, closed and temporarily diverted at various locations on the escarpment and valley floor to replenish soils and irrigate crops. This fluidity of the irrigation system is intimately tied to shifting agricultural practice over multiple generations. Indeed, mapping by the IGP local citizen science teams reveals that, since 1980, 30 new main irrigation channels totalling over 60 km have been established (Soper, 1983; Davies, Kiprutto & Moore, 2014). Such fluctuations may occur as individuals and family units gradually relocate household compounds within their clan territory to different elevations on the escarpment on temporary, semi-permanent and permanent bases as they move farmland to the fringes of available water sources, manage erosion and soil fertility, and maintain access to a range of resources across ecological zones. The ramification of this process is that, when viewed diachronically, agricultural settlement may move spatially over several generations along with concomitant furrows and fields (Davies, 2013).

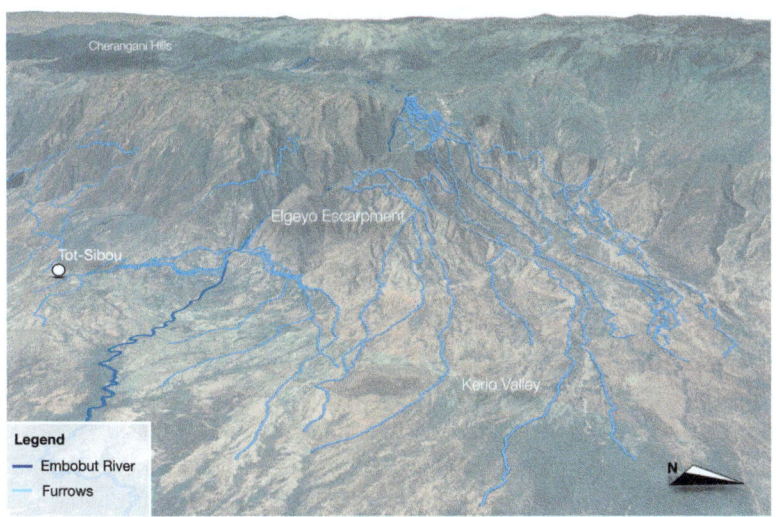

**Figure 8.3** Digital elevation model of the Elgeyo Escarpment displaying the distribution of irrigation furrows. For more detailed diagrams see Davies, Kiprutto & Moore, 2014.

These emergent changes are evident over broad temporal cycles as crops, vegetation, field boundaries, terraces and irrigation channels become altered, reused or abandoned to meet the needs of gradually shifting livelihoods (Davies, 2014; Davies, Kiprutto & Moore, 2014).

The ongoing reorganisation of irrigation and land use stems from, and feeds into, a deeper need and ability of farmers to accommodate ever-shifting socio-ecological conditions. Regional climatic records reveal major fluctuations over the course of the last three centuries (Anderson, 2016; Davies, 2012), including major dry episodes during the periods 1760–90, 1820–40, 1890–1940 and 1970–85 interspersed with more humid conditions in the early eighteenth century, the mid- to late nineteenth century, and much of the second half of the twentieth century. Similarly, demographic surveys attest to considerable increases in population (Dietz et al., 1987), with national census data demonstrating that the population of Elgeyo-Marakwet County has more than tripled in the past 40 years, increasing from 148,868 in 1979 to 454,480 in 2019 (Davies & Moore, 2016; Kenya Bureau of National Statistics, 2019).

Data outlined here, and reported in more detail elsewhere, therefore attests to vibrant systems of cultivation which have been largely able to accommodate population changes and major climatic events over the twentieth century and beyond without large-scale environmental collapse

(Davies, Kiprutto & Moore, 2014; Davies & Moore, 2016). Looked at from a historical perspective, these systems work because they allow for certain degrees of flexible movement around the landscape. At any one time, part of the system may appear to be in decline (the abandonment of settlements, fields and irrigation channels, erosion, soil depletion) but other parts will be experiencing new (or renewed) settlement, the construction or shifting of irrigation features, and the planting of new fields. Such changes at generational scales and across wide landscapes may be partially imperceptible to those engaged within the system, but they are often especially overlooked by outside analysts, policy makers and developers who spend only short periods conducting the research on which they base their interventions; this may in part explain why such interventions are often largely ineffective.

More broadly, however, this 'untidy' mix of spatial and temporal activities (often mistaken for decline or collapse) constitutes what we would consider a good example of the shaping of emergent phenomena in which well-understood ecological parameters are managed through a series of established yet diverse mechanisms which allow for fluid forms of response and adaptation.

## 8.5 Shaped emergence

The historical narrative of resilient flexible agriculture presented above might be seen as evidence of a broader shaping of emergent prosperity enacted through several important social mechanisms and practices. To unpack these dynamics further, we identify four key parameters with corresponding institutions.

### 8.5.1 Networked knowledge and pooled resources

Multiple social mechanisms have been widely retained in Marakwet which ensure the sharing of knowledge, ideas, practices and materials (such as seeds, fertilisers and tools) across wide landscapes and diverse ecologies. Strong patrilines link core family members, creating adjacent farms with familial ties and concomitant agricultural activities. At the same time, valued matrilineal (*kamamaa*) relations extend knowledge-sharing networks more widely and across broader ecological and altitudinal zones, from the Kerio Valley to the highland forests, and may even be used to allow families access to land in other parts of the region.

Strong knowledge-sharing relationships also exist beyond that of kin networks, the most evident of which are defined by individuals who share the same age-set. Age relationships operate for both men and women and are often drawn upon in the establishment of more formal male and female 'friendships' known as *tilia* (Pollard et al., 2015). *Tilia* relations in particular involve the exchange of seed, grain and livestock; they not only operate within the Marakwet but can extend into neighbouring pastoralist communities, linking people across ethnic identities and providing access to a wider pool of recourses. Work with female entrepreneurs in markets and commercial centres across the region has shown how *tilia* relations often act as a support network for partners in difficulty, as well as underpinning more formal business relations and the wider exchange of goods across the region (Pollard et al., 2015).

Broadly, then, these networks cut across diverse social and ecological landscapes, allowing members to gather knowledge and ideas from multiple sources to share and exchange practices. This amplifies access to diverse resources, spreads risk and buffers families in times of difficulty (Bollig, 1998). More generally, these networks enable the widespread sharing of ideas and materials, which farmers are able to experiment with to enhance best practice and more readily respond to ecological and climate-related challenges. At a more fundamental level, these dynamics provide an integral foundation for farmers to thrive within a spatially and temporally unpredictable world.

### 8.5.2 Distributed decision making

The pooling of networked knowledge across ecological zones ties in with more formal mechanisms for communal decision making beyond the individual household. Perhaps most significant of these is the institution of the *kokwo*, a meeting of circumcised men (women attend *kokwo* but are not permitted to stand and speak) which functions in part to collate networked knowledge and then to discuss and decide on multiple issues, including those of landscape and water management (Adams et al., 1997; Davies, 2009; Ssennyonga, 1983). Within the *kokwo* respected elders are endowed with authority, and explicit and implicit rules of etiquette govern who can talk, in what order and on what authority. The membership of a *kowko* is flexible and contingent on the matter at hand, so that a *kokwo* discussing land tenure and ruling on a land dispute may have a different constituent membership to one addressing an issue of irrigation water rights. Indeed, claims to land and resources are in themselves flexible, being based both on ideas of history and inheritance, and on contemporary use. Therefore members of a *kokwo* might claim the right to attend and to speak on the matter at hand. *Kokwo* might be called upon to decide who should have access to land and who should not, to reprimand those who fail to look after the land or who engage in problematic practices (for example, cutting down riverine trees without discussion), to decide on allocations of water, and to decide what should be grown where, and when. The workings of the *kokwo* include the mobilisation of communal labour to undertake tasks, including repairing irrigation furrows, addressing erosion and clearing ground for communal shifting cultivation.

*Kokwo* are not just discussion forums but have effective powers to impose fines (the penalty may be, for example, the payment of a goat, or restricted access to irrigation water) and support those in need (for example by allocating irrigation water out of turn). While male charisma is often dominant at *kokwo*, women do attend and their needs and concerns can be heard (Moore, 1986; Adams et al., 1997). Thus, while the diversity of knowledge represented at *kokwo* may be biased towards male knowledge, it is not exclusively so and it does serve as an effective mechanism for pooling knowledge across generations as well as for centralising information from the wider networks discussed above. We have explained some of the mechanisms of *kokwo* in more detail elsewhere (Davies, 2009; see also Kipkorir & Welbourn, 2008; Moore, 1986), and have argued there that it is a highly formulised political process well adapted to rapid and efficient communal decision making. To extend that definition here, we would argue that the pooling of knowledge and responsiveness to change that *kokwo* allows is a key formal mechanism through which farmers in Marakwet are able to collectively shape their world and respond to the unexpected challenges it throws up.

### 8.5.3 The maintenance of diversity

Pooled knowledge and distributed decision making both enhance the ways in which Marakwet farmers maintain diversity. At one level, the networks that cut across ecological zones provide families with direct access to land in other ecologies and climates as well as indirect access to the resources of those locations. We see in these networks both a valuing of diversity and a direct way of reciprocally sharing interest in its maintenance. Farmers also prize access to diverse forms of land and cultivation in their immediate environs. In Tot-Sibou, for example, there is a continuity of types of farmland, from highland finger millet fields, to smaller domestic fields around homesteads, larger semi-permanent household fields around the foot of the escarpment and forms of communal shifting cultivation and riverine cultivation on the valley floor (Davies & Moore, 2016; Davies, Kiprutto & Moore, 2014). Most families hold access to land of each of these types and may variably choose to use, experiment upon and enhance each of these classes of land. Land of different types offers distinct microclimatic, hydrological (irrigation- versus rain-fed) and soil qualities, each suited to different combinations of species and landraces of crops with varying levels of resilience to water, soils and pests. Different types of land are given differing forms and degrees of management, with more fixed fields around homesteads and at the base of the escarpment organised around household decision making and needs, while shifting cultivation on the valley floor is organised communally in terms of shared labour, fencing, pest management, crop choice and irrigation.

Land or fields may be accessed through a diversity of forms of tenure, with at least 11 main types and several sub-variations, including forms of paternally and maternally inherited land as well as land loaned, rented, exchanged, bought, held in custodianship or gifted, women's land and community land. A fuller examination of each type is not possible here, but we note that these variable forms of claiming and accessing land provide farmers with a great flexibility that allows them to shape their responses further to emergent socio-ecological phenomena.

Across this landscape there is thus a great diversity of possible combinations of production by elevation, soil, hydrology, crop and land tenure (see Chapter 7). The management of water for farming exemplifies the ways in which these diverse subsystems of production are fluidly integrated. For example, as farmers shift the focus of production spatially to address soil type, depletion or erosion, so the lower secondary and tertiary branches of major irrigation furrows can be diverted with relative ease, allowing farmers to exploit new areas or switch between rain-fed and irrigated cultivation and between different crops with variable water needs (Davies, 2014). In several places fields might be amenable to watering from multiple secondary branches, which provides farmers with multiple options over the timing of water and in their negotiations at *kokwo*. Thus, at the same time that farmers exploit diverse forms of access to land, they are also able to exploit a diverse range of sources of water and to combine and recombine these as required.

Diversity in systems of access to land and water is complemented by diversity of crop types. A fuller examination of the ethnobotany of food crops is not possible here beyond the fact that there is a complex history of successive crop introductions with diversity broadly added through time.

Preliminary data from Tot-Sibou published in Davies and Moore (2016) outlines some 40 food plants, of which nine are wild and 22 are regularly recurring cultivars with African, Asian and American origins. Of these 22, of particular note are the cereal crops sorghum, finger millet and maize. Though maize dominates, varieties of sorghum and finger millet remain widely grown and, importantly, retain some seven landraces of sorghum and 15 of finger millet alongside older and more modern varieties and hybrids. The landraces of both sorghum and millet are especially significant, in that they suggest the active curation of older varieties and their retention due to diverse ecological characteristics that can be experimentally matched with diverse combinations of soil and water. A wide variety of legumes are regularly intercropped with the cereals to enhance the potential of this diversity, while soil conservation and fertility enhancement techniques abound, including terracing, mulching and manuring. Again we argue that Marakwet farmers combine knowledge pooling and distributed decision making with the maintenance of diverse and flexible physical subsystems that relate to water, land/soils, crops and other techniques. This allows experimental combinations to constantly emerge in response to complex opportunities and challenges.

### 8.5.4 Lived innovation and experimentation

Finally we argue that innovation and experimentation are central aspects of what it means to live as a farmer in Marakwet. It is the coalescence of the factors above into a process of experimental living which shapes unpredictable emergent phenomena into manageable responses and opportunities. For example, multiple repeat interviews, participant farm mapping and citizen-collected smartphone data (Davies, Moore, Kiprutto et al., 2022) from Tot-Sibou and around the larger town of Iten in Elgeyo-Marakwet County have shown how farmers maintain highly diverse fields with multiple combinations of crops and cropping practices. These tend to mix not only cereals and legumes but also fruit trees, root and leafy vegetables, fodder crops and trees grown for wood fuel or timber. Moreover, the combinations of these are constantly changing from year to year as farmers experiment with rotating and intercropping different cultivars.

Intricate cropping regimes involving both landrace and hybrid plants are complemented by equally complex uses of organic and synthetic inputs that defy simple characterisations as either 'traditional' or 'modern'. The combinations are often innovative in that farmers regularly try new things, both derived from their own experience and imagination and also (as noted above) taking inspiration from neighbours, kin and age-mates, as well as things heard on the radio, seen on TV, or shared on social media. Our interviews suggest that farmers are adept at learning from such experiments and drawing on such learning, both to enhance their practice and to respond to unpredictable events such as drought and pests, the latter in particular being exemplified in recent responses to plagues of locusts in 2021 (Davies, Moore, Kiprutto et al., 2022).

This living experimentation forms the nexus of how farmers navigate and shape ever-emergent socio-ecological phenomena through time. In particular, knowledge and materials flow from diverse wider networks (kinship links, age-sets and *tilia*) into distributed forms of decision making (e.g. *kokwo*), influencing the development of diverse biophysical subsystems (land tenure, irrigation, soil maintenance, crops) and allowing for regular daily experimentation. The outcomes of this experimentation recursively feed back into these dynamics, influencing decisions at *kokwo*, shaping the collective management of the biophysical and redistributing knowledge and practice through wider networks of kin, age and friendship. In short, we argue that these are integrated social, technical and ecological landscapes that are themselves constituted by a continual recursive shaping of emergent phenomena.

## 8.6 Temporalities of 'progress' and change in complex systems

In the introduction to this chapter we suggested that many external development designs were out of touch with the lived realities of agrarian life in Marakwet (see also Chapter 7). In fact, rather than improving livelihood security, agricultural interventions have often disrupted the gradual and iterative shaping of complex and emergent social and ecological systems. External technical experts struggle to comprehend how Marakwet farmers subtly navigate this complexity because it plays out across multiple spatial and temporal dimensions – between people, plants and animals, across homesteads, villages, clans and landscapes and across seasons, years and generations. From individual on-farm innovation, to intergenerational landscape management and knowledge sharing, to community-based negotiation such as the *kokwo*, the most effective methods for shaping the Marakwet world are produced by the very people who encounter the emergent complexities of daily living. In short, the Marakwet people and the world in which they live are not separate but mutually constituted and thus the key nexus for generating prosperity are the people who live that prosperity.

Understandings of temporality and progress are critical here in the unpicking of the failures of external design to generate prosperity. Much Western technical and development practice tends to conceptually dislodge people from the spatiotemporal context within which they are situated and suspend them as ahistorical communities conditioned by a timeless past and aspiring to a developed future. To improve such people's livelihoods, development planning attempts to deploy a singular act of change to relocate people from the static past into the static modern future. It is assumed in such acts that there are clear start and end destinations, a singular path or trajectory between them, and a broadly singular process (even if punctuated by distinct phases and operations) of change from one to the other. This has multiple effects – in particular it reduces the contemporary moment from being a period of 'living', to being a necessary transition to be endured prior to a better form of modern 'living'. In such thinking 'to live' is about temporal stasis, equilibrium and stability. In contrast, progress is the process of non-equilibrial change from one static state of 'living' to another. This gives rise to the notion that people undergoing change (those who are 'developing') are not 'living', let alone thriving, and that their current state is inadequate or inauspicious. Consequently, by focusing only on future states to be realised through punctuated processes of change, we become blind to how prosperity and aspects of good lives are being forged in the here and now.

## 8.7 Design and contemporary experience

The problem outlined above has been neatly distilled by Santos (2014), who argues that such understandings of development or progress constitute a 'winnowing' of contemporary experience. This is because it is assumed that people living outside of the 'already modern' global North are in a transitional phase, being consigned to an atemporal past, and that their futures are already mapped out by the dimensions of universal, directional and globalised modernity. This winnowing not only hampers our ability to draw on non-Western knowledges and practices in processes of future building, but even more problematically generates a failed model for 'change' (see Chapter 7). Such a model deploys design and planning in the abstract as a controlled process for moving communities from a static state of perpetual underdevelopment to a future state of modernity and progress. Singular acts of atemporal design, however, are highly underdetermined by the knowledge and information of recipient peoples and struggle to accurately shape the lives they wish to influence, not least because of the complex nature of human agency and the unpredictability of interconnected socio-natural systems.

At best such abstracted acts of design are worked upon, selected, rejected and made real by actors who problem-solve in the moment and who draw on varieties of lived social and natural resources to do so. Whether applied to the construction of a building, the founding of a business or the management of a farm, it is these acts of intuitive, imaginative and improvised problem solving that operationalise design. In some instances, where conditions are controlled and designs comprehensive, the need for such improvisation may be minimal. But in the design of entire socio-natural systems we would argue that a majority of development designs, particularly those from global North to global South, have been lamentably inadequate and are often founded on weak starting principles, especially so in comparison to the knowledge of the actors who live and make do in such worlds.

Where planned acts of development design work, we contend that this is due in part to the abilities of the recipient communities to shape and integrate such plans into daily living through ongoing processes of autonomous design (Escobar, 2018). This kind of design philosophy allows for the 'creation of conditions for the community's ongoing self-creation and successful structural coupling with their "increasingly globalized" environments' (Escobar, 2017: 45). In such instances, communities are able to forge their own worlds, which are not on a simple journey from past to present or from tradition to modernity, but are lives lived in the here and now.

## 8.8 Conclusions: emergent prosperity

In conclusion, prosperity is not something that can be designed as a singular act; rather it must be brought into being through the process of living in the world through time. It must be realised not in an abstract (and unpredictable) future but in contemporary moments. Borrowing from complex systems theory, we can view this process of bringing into being as a process of 'emergence', where we might say that prosperity is an 'emergent' contemporary experience rather than a singularly designed future phenomenon (see Chapters 1 and 2). We argue then that in contrast to the failed singular designs of modernity, Marakwet farmers act intuitively through a range of distributed actions across multiple temporal and spatial scales to shape the emergence of certain forms of socio-natural prosperity. They do so in multiple holistic daily acts of decision making, constantly weighing up a host of factors based on deep-seated historical, experiential and experimental knowledge, often balancing the longer-term sustainability of soils, the propagation of plants and fluctuations of climate with the demands of the market and the needs of households. Sometimes they choose to deplete soils to meet social demands, at others they choose to maintain the health of their land to enhance sustainability and resilience. Sometimes they choose to use modern chemical and hybrid inputs, at other times they choose to use organics and to maintain landrace varieties. Sometimes they invest in communal acts of labour to reshape their landscape while at other times they allow infrastructure and land to fall into disuse.

This is a creative curation of a varied assemblage from which a flexible prosperity can and does emerge in contemporary moments. This is not to say that people in Marakwet do not need forms of external support. Increasing the opportunities open to Marakwet farmers and families, allowing them to choose how to thrive autonomously, should be a priority. Marakwet is not a romantic garden of Eden; challenges of many kinds persist, but, as we hope we have shown here and elsewhere (Lunn-Rockliffe et al., 2020), it is those communities who live prosperity who must be the ones who shape its emergence. This means strengthening rather than eroding the many local values, customs, practices and institutions that have continued to sustain communities across the challenges of the last century. It requires a shift away from singular designs to distributed lived experimentation, in short, empowering people to do better what they already do best.

## Note

1. Originally this was intended to be 500 acres and the community expended much energy to clear this amount of land, only to have the scheme scaled back by the Red Cross afterwards.

## Bibliography

Adams, W. M., Watson, E. E. & Mutiso, S. K. (1997). Water, rules and gender: Water rights in an indigenous irrigation system, Marakwet Kenya. *Development and Change*, 28(4), 707–30. https://doi.org/10.1111/1467-7660.00061.

Anderson, D. M. (1984). Depression, dust bowl, demography, and drought: The colonial state and soil conservation in East Africa during the 1930s. *African Affairs*, 83(332), 321–43.

Anderson, D. M. (2016). The beginning of time? Evidence for catastrophic drought in Baringo in the early nineteenth century. *Journal of Eastern African Studies*, 10(1), 45–66. https://doi.org/10.1080/17531055.2015.1134532.

Bollig, M. (1998). Moral economy and self-interest: Kinship, friendship, and exchange among the Pokot (N.W. Kenya). In T. Schweizer & D. R. White (eds), *Kinship, Networks and Exchange*, pp. 137–57. Cambridge: Cambridge University Press.

Caretta, M. A. & Börjeson, L. (2015). Local gender contract and adaptive capacity in smallholder irrigation farming: A case study from the Kenyan drylands. *Gender, Place & Culture: A Journal of Feminist Geography*, 22(5), 644–61. Available at: https://www.tandfonline.com/doi/abs/10.1080/0966369X.2014.885888?journalCode=cgpc20 (accessed 16 September 2022). https://doi.org/10.1080/0966369X.2014.885888.

Davies, M. I. J. (2009). An applied archaeological and anthropological study of intensive agriculture in the northern Cherangani Hills, Kenya. DPhil thesis, University of Oxford.

Davies, M. I. J. (2012). Some thoughts on a 'useable' African archaeology: Settlement, population and intensive farming among the Pokot of northwest Kenya. *African Archaeological Review*, 29, 319–53. https://doi.org/10.1007/s10437-012-9118-8.

Davies, M. I. J. (2013). Forced moves or just good moves? Rethinking environmental decision-making among East African intensive cultivators. In M. I. J. Davies and F. N. M'Mbogori (eds), *Humans and the Environment: New archaeological perspectives for the twenty-first century*, pp. 57–76. Oxford: Oxford University Press.

Davies, M. I. J. (2014). The temporality of landesque capital: Cultivation and the routines of Pokot life. In N. T. Håkansson & M. Widgren (eds), *Landesque Capital: The historical ecology of enduring landscape modifications*, pp. 172–96. Walnut Creek, CA: Left Coast Press.

Davies, M., Haklay, M., Kiprutto, T., Laws, M., Lewis, J., Lunn-Rockliffe, S. P., McGlade, J., Moreu, M., Yano, A. & Kipkorir, W. (2022). Supporting the capacities and knowledge of small-holder farmers in Kenya for sustainable agricultural futures: A Citizen Science pilot project. UCL. https://doi.org/10.14324/111.444/000155.v1.

Davies, M. I. J., Kiprutto, T. K. & Moore, H. L. (2014). Revisiting the irrigated agricultural landscape of the Marakwet, Kenya: Tracing local technology and knowledge over the recent past. *Azania: Archaeological Research in Africa*, 49(4), 486–523. https://doi.org/10.1080/0067270X.2014.979527.

Davies, M. I. J. & Moore, H. L. (2016). Landscape, time and cultural resilience: A brief history of agriculture in Pokot and Marakwet, Kenya. *Journal of Eastern African Studies*, 10(1), 67–87. https://doi.org/10.1080/17531055.2015.1134417.

Derbyshire, S. & Lowasa, L. (2022). The ruins of Turkana: An archaeology of failed development in northern Kenya. In N. Berre., P. Geissler & J. Lagae (eds), *African Modernism and its Afterlives*, pp. 267–82. Bristol: Intellect.

Dietz, A. J., van Haastrecht, A. & Moore, H. L. (1987). *Locational Development Profile: Endo, Mokoro and Embobut Locations, Elgeyo Marakwet District, Kenya*. Iten: Arid and Semi-Arid Lands Programme.

Escobar, A. (2017). Response: Design for/by [and from] the 'global South'. *Design Philosophy Papers*, 15(1), 39–49. http://dx.doi.org/10.1080/14487136.2017.1301016.

Escobar, A. (2018). *Designs for the Pluriverse: Radical interdependence, autonomy, and the making of worlds*. Durham, NC: Duke University Press.

Ferguson, J. (1994). *The Anti-Politics Machine: 'Development', depoliticization, and bureaucratic power in Lesotho*. Minneapolis: University of Minnesota Press.

Hennings, R. O. (1941). The furrow makers of Kenya. *Geographical Magazine*, 12, 268–79.

Huxley, E. (1959). African water engineers. *Geographical Magazine*, 32, 170–5.

Kay, D. (2021). Unsettled settlements: Continuity and change in the Marakwet habitation of the northern Elgeyo Escarpment, northwest Kenya, from c. 1850 to the present-day. PhD thesis, University of Cambridge. Available at: https://doi.org/10.17863/CAM.80367 (accessed 16 September 2022).

Kenya National Bureau of Statistics (KNBS) (2019). *2019 Kenya Population and Housing Census. Volume I: Population by County and Sub-county*. Nairobi: Kenya National Bureau of Statistics. https://www.knbs.or.ke/?wpdmpro=2019-kenya-population-and-housing-census-volume-i-population-by-county-and-sub-county (accessed 1 January 2023).

Kipkorir, B. E. (1983). Historical perspectives of development in the Kerio Valley. In B. E. Kipkorir, R. C. Soper & J. W.Ssennyonga (eds), *Kerio Valley, Past, Present and Future: Proceedings of a seminar held in Nairobi at the Institute of African Studies, University of Nairobi, May 21–22, 1981*, pp. 1–11. Nairobi: Institute of African Studies, University of Nairobi.

Kipkorir, D. & Kareithi, J. (2013). Indigenous irrigation and food security in Tot Division, Kerio Valley, Kenya. *Journal of Anthropology and Archaeology*, 1(1), 12–27.

Kipkorir, B. E. & Welbourn, F. B. (2008). *The Marakwet of Kenya: A preliminary study*, 2nd edn. Nairobi: East African Literature Bureau.

Leach, M. & Mearns, R. (eds) (1996). *The Lie of the Land: Challenging received wisdom on the African environment*. Oxford: James Currey and Heinemann.

Lunn-Rockliffe, S. (2019). Beyond the ruins of Embobut: Transforming landscapes and livelihoods in the Cherangani Hills, Kenya. *Journal of Contemporary Archaeology*, 6(2), 274–96. https://doi.org/10.1558/jca.38591.

Lunn-Rockliffe, S., Davies, M., Willman, A., Moore, H. L., McGlade, J. M. & Bent, D. (2020). *Farmer Led Regenerative Agriculture for Africa*. London: Institute for Global Prosperity.

Moore, H. L. (1983) Anthropology and development: Some illustrations from the Marakwet of Kenya. In B. E. Kipkorir, R. C. Soper & J. W. Ssennyonga (eds), *Kerio Valley, Past, Present and Future: Proceedings of a seminar held in Nairobi at the Institute of African Studies, University of Nairobi, May 21–22, 1981*, pp. 132–8. Nairobi: Institute of African Studies, University of Nairobi.

Moore, H. L. (1986). *Space, Text and Gender: An anthropological study of the Marakwet of Kenya*. Cambridge: Cambridge University Press.

Moore, H. L. (1987). Problems in the analysis of social change: An example from the Marakwet. In I. Hodder (ed.), *Archaeology as Long-Term History*, pp. 85–104. Cambridge: Cambridge University Press.

Moore, H. L. (2015). Global prosperity and sustainable development goals. *Journal of International Development*, 27(6), 801–15. https://doi.org/10.1002/jid.3114.

Pollard, G., Davies, M. I. J. & Moore, H. L. (2015). Women, marketplaces and exchange partners amongst the Marakwet of northwest Kenya. *Journal of Eastern African Studies* 9(3), 412–39. https://doi.org/10.1080/17531055.2015.1089699.

Santos, B. de Sousa (2014). *Epistemologies of the South: Justice against epistemicide*. Abingdon: Routledge.

Soper, R. C. (1983). A survey of the irrigation system of the Marakwet. In B. E. Kipkorir, R. C. Soper & J. W. Ssennyonga (eds), *Kerio Valley: Past, present and future: Proceedings of a seminar held in Nairobi at the Institute of African Studies, University of Nairobi, May 21–22, 1981*, pp. 75–95. Nairobi: Institute of African Studies, University of Nairobi.

Ssennyonga, J. W. (1983). The Marakwet irrigation system as a model of a systems-approach to water management. In Kipkorir, B. E., Soper R. C. & Ssennyonga, J. W. (eds), *Kerio Valley: Past, present and future*, pp. 96–111. Nairobi: Institute of African Studies, University of Nairobi.

Watson, E. E., Adams, W. M. & Mutiso, S. K. (1998). Indigenous irrigation, agriculture and development, Marakwet, Kenya. *Geographical Journal*, 164(1), 67–84. https://doi.org/10.2307/3060546.

Woodcraft, S., Osuteye, E., Ndezi, T. & Makoba, F. D. (2020). Pathways to the 'good life': Co-producing prosperity research in informal settlements in Tanzania. *Urban Planning*, 5(3), 288–302. https://doi.org/10.17645/up.v5i3.3177.

# Epilogue
Henrietta L. Moore

Redefining prosperity for the twenty-first century is among our most urgent tasks. We need to fundamentally rework the relationship between the economic and the social. Without accomplishing this task, we will not be able to tackle climate change and biodiversity loss, nor the failure of the most developed countries in the world to protect their populations from declining standards of living, nor develop social protection programmes for emerging economies, nor tackle diminishing trust in governments, nor arrest contracting forms of social capital that are corroding our ability to live with differences between ourselves and others. One has only to reflect on the question of migration and the poisonous politics it engenders to comprehend how all these challenges are interconnected. Rethinking the relationship between the economic and the social involves developing alternative approaches for understanding values and outcomes. This is 'a large subject', as Kermode would have it, 'because the instrument of change is the human imagination. It changes not only the consoling plot, but the structure of time and the world' (Kermode, 2000: 31).

As this volume has demonstrated, change is already underway; there is an emerging recognition that maximising GDP should not necessarily be the paramount goal of national policy, and that there are winds of change that cannot be assuaged by current economic policies and models. In reality, growth is increasingly elusive, and possibly, as Tim Jackson says, we have been slow to recognise that we are already in a post-growth world (Jackson, 2018). Suddenly, large numbers of commentators seem to be referencing the fact that workers' wages as a share of national income in the most developed countries of the world have been declining since the 1970s, or even the 1960s! A 60-year failure for economic orthodoxies that has apparently gone unnoticed until it is too late, perhaps. Beliefs and ideologies are often oppositional, and for some this point is of little significance, while for others it is the crux of the matter, the clear evidence that trickle-down economics is not the solution for the present or the future.

As we have argued in this volume, these new ideas and debates are useful in providing an emerging critique of how we think about the intersections between economy, society and politics. Arguably, there is a more rigorous debate than at any time in living memory about the orthodoxies of untrammelled markets, and the damage of extractive economies, with their inevitable consequences for people and planet. Yet, dominant economic models still hold sway and progress on climate change and biodiversity loss is glacial. The world may be warming, but politics are frigid, stuck in the mud of nationalist policies and chilled by the air of self-interest. Consequently, this volume has sought to move beyond critiques of the status quo and generalised accounts of what a new economy might look like to engage with local, co-designed ideas about prosperity and the redefinition of its constitutive elements for the twenty-first century. It has pursued new theories, frameworks and models of prosperity, and advanced a critique of the value of the economic in social life, challenging the structural features of the dominant economic models on which we depend and the value premises on which they are built. However, it has also moved beyond merely discussing new ideas to explore how such ideas open the door to innovative practices that will allow us to address inequalities in new ways. What makes the approach laid out in this volume distinctive is that instead of focusing just on how to define and measure prosperity (providing alternatives to GDP), it has set out what we need to do to make prosperity a realisable proposition for specific people living in specific locales, delineating possible pathways to prosperity. This pushes the debate on prosperity forward substantially, emphasising that visions of the good life are diverse and require empirical work co-designed with local communities and stakeholders, in order to develop well-founded frameworks and pathways for sustainable prosperity that can be operationalised by communities, policy makers, business, civil society and government.

Overall, the volume emphasises the diversity and non-linearity of concepts, frameworks and pathways, insisting on the fact that there are many paths to achieving improvements in quality of life for people and planet, but that they need to be locally grounded. In recognition of this fact, the framework adopted embraces a whole-systems approach, where the interplay of intersecting factors is always more critical than any single factor. Key here is the contention that social innovation is critical to sustainability and improved prosperity, drawing on novel forms of collaboration, knowledge sharing and multi-stakeholder value creation. The evident need for new institutions and forms of governance is something that is currently being explored in ongoing work at the Institute for Global Prosperity, but what is already clear is that if societal goals shift from maximising the growth of the market economy, then existing institutions can be repurposed to better deliver the goals of social innovation. The inclusion and empowerment of local actors is fundamental for successful contextual innovation and for problem solving. Working under conditions of profound and pervasive uncertainty, co-ordination, co-design and collaboration deepens, strengthens and reshapes democratic participation, refocusing it on solutions in context. This is a process which requires consensus through experimentation, and one in which social solidarity – the creation of social value – is key to innovation.

Many of our current economic problems around the world are blamed on poor productivity, and commentators bemoan the fact that productivity growth is negligible. However, the approach adopted in this volume focuses more concretely on social rather than economic productivity, on how social value drives economic value, and on how, through new forms of governance and collaboration, quality of life for people and planet can be improved. The reality, as many critics have identified, is that our economies are good at producing some things and not others. A twenty-first-century economy needs to produce more of what we need, in other words, to assure the supply of essential goods on which we all depend: soil, water, biodiversity, healthcare. There is something both depressing and very alarming about the fact that the real productivity failures in our current economies are in delivering the common good, for both people and planet. The fundamental shift required is one that moves away from asking whether change can take place to exploring how it can be delivered in diverse contexts, involving diverse stakeholders, to improve diverse forms of prosperity. This is the challenge this volume addresses.

## Bibliography

Jackson, T. (2018). The post-growth challenge: Secular stagnation, inequality and the limits to growth. CUSP Working Paper no. 12. Centre for the Understanding of Sustainable Prosperity, University of Surrey. Available at: https://cusp.ac.uk/wp-content/uploads/WP-12-The-Post-Growth-Challenge-1.2MB.pdf (accessed 1 January 2023).

Kermode, F. (2000). *The Sense of an Ending: Studies in the theory of fiction: With a new epilogue.* Oxford: Oxford University Press.

# Index

actors 7, 30, 39, 40, 42, 63, 69, 156, 219
   diverse 62
   external 17, 205
   and growth 116–17
   and inclusion 116
   interdependent 147
   institutional 14
   local 225
   political 113
   social 51
Africa 19, 181, 183, 184, 187–8, 193, 195, 197–8
   clans in 187
   farmers in 203
   inclusive growth in 182
   modernity in 184–5, 194
   Prosperity Co-Laboratory and 7, 16
   societies in 186
   structural transformation in 182
   sub-Saharan 191, 198
      rural life in 181–6
   rural transformation in 194, 197
African Land Development Programme 209
agency 7, 16, 27, 31, 38, 40, 132–3, 219
   language and 61
   local 30
aggregate 7, 9, 26–7, 39, 41–2, 62, 65, 81, 83, 87, 95, 102, 114, 129, 166 *see also* macroeconomics
agrarian change 182, 192–3, 196–7 *see also* sub-Saharan Africa
agriculture 174
   in Africa 198
   in Bemba 183
   colonial governance and 186
   community-led development and 205
   impacts of colonialism on 208–9
   in Kenya 191
   investment in Zambia 193
   in Marakwet 16, 206, 210, 212
   productivity and 183, 189, 193
   retrogressive 209
   smallholders and 189
   in Kenya 191
Airbnb 92
Al-Masri, Muzna 171
Amin, Ash 132
Aristotle 89
artificial intelligence 173
aspiration 2, 16, 17, 19, 25, 32, 55–6, 61–2, 69–70, 78, 83, 87, 89, 93, 95, 119, 131, 135, 137, 182, 193, 196–7

assemblage 7, 17, 19, 68–70, 220
   emergent 19, 174
   in Marakwet 220
   in naming prosperity 62–4
   prosperity assembled and reassembled 17, 69
   prosperity dynamic and emergent 19
   in relation to complex systems and prosperity 38–40, 174
assets 7, 39–40, 65
   community 161, 191
   environmental 31
   knowledge 191
   life outcomes 38
   liquid 53
   in relation to livelihood security 108–14, 118, 122–3
   local 42
   skills as 41
   women and 192
AUB Policy Institute 153
Australia 117
autonomy 29, 97, 107

basic services 111, 155, 161 *see also* public services
belonging 2, 5, 32, 91, 97, 107–8, 130, 147, 161, 170, 194
biodiversity 17, 32, 51, 204, 223–5
biophysical systems 14, 18
Bolivia 4
Bourdieu, Pierre 55, 63, 69, 120
Braudel, Fernand 182–3, 197
British South Africa Company 186
Bryceson, Deborah 187
buen vivir (living well) 4
'build back better' 6, 25, 108, 113, 115

Canada 5
Canadian Red Cross 207–9
capabilities (and capacities) 7, 19, 29, 40–4, 62, 119, 122, 151–2
   and life opportunities 38
carbon net-zero 43
caring 2, 87, 96, 109, 110, 112, 113
Cassiers, Isabelle 57
CatalyticAction 143, 145
Charities *see also* NGOs
childcare 87, 101, 110–13
Chile 4
Citizens' Assembly 170–2

225

citizenship
  energy 170, 173
  national and urban 146
civic participation 89, 91, 96
civil society 1, 7–8, 14, 28, 39, 42, 116, 153, 172, 224
class 37, 61, 99, 110, 111, 133, 135, 141, 196
climate change 10, 14, 16, 26, 49, 50, 55, 152–3, 181, 191, 223–4
  as linked to economic growth 10
  and migration 14
Club of Rome 1
co-design
  in Bar Elias 15, 130, 134, 145, 147
  household survey and 32
  and inclusive intervention 133–4, 140, 145
  and local communities 6, 35, 62, 95, 171
  in policy 119
  practice of 63, 133
  prosperity model and 32–3, 35, 62, 67, 161, 224–5
  differing stakeholders in 1, 63
  in the UK 118
collectivism 39, 62, 93, 101, 119, 141, 160–1, 173, 182, 187–8, 214, 217
colonialism 15
  linked to the Marakwet 16, 183, 209
  in sub-Saharan Africa 181, 184, 186–90
Community Energy Efficiency and Renewable Energy Demonstration Project for the Recovery of Lebanon (CEDRO) 159
community wealth-building 116, 120
complex systems (theory and change) 18, 27, 38–40, 217, 219 *see also* emergence
concepts (related to theories, methods and metrics) 65–6
Costanza, Bob 3
Covid-19 2, 10, 27, 77, 94
  in Marakwet 16
  in Lebanon 140, 151, 155, 157–8, 181
  and recovery planning 6, 87, 102, 108, 115
  and system failure 18, 26
  in the UK 99, 101, 113–14, 123
culture 2, 7, 14, 28–9, 32, 42, 44, 61, 68–9, 79, 97, 161, 183

Davos 8, 58
deindustrialisation 86
democratic deficit 108, 118, 121, 123, 171
deprivation 29, 80, 86–7
detribalisation 188–9
development agendas (Marakwet) 16, 207–10, 218
Dews, Peter 60
discourse analysis 8, 49, 51–2
diversity 18, 28, 42, 114, 119, 173
  in Bar Elias 133–5
  foundation on prosperity 131–2
  in redefining prosperity 7, 9, 28, 65, 78–9, 93
  social inclusion 118
  superdiverse 86
Doyal, Len 29

Eco, Umberto 52–3, 58
'economics first' 26, 55
ecosystems 11, 15, 31, 51
Electricité du Liban (EDL) 154–5, 157–8, 160

Elgeyo-Marakwet 183 *see also* Marakwet people
  agronomic intensification in 210
  biodiversity in 16, 204
  Cherangani highlands 190
  colonial intervention in 209
  crops in 203, 206, 208, 215–16
  generational scale change 212
  irrigation in 16, 204, 208, 210, 215
  Iten 216
  Kerio Valley 206–7, 210
  land ownership in 190, 196, 210, 215
  Pokot 207
  population of 210
  Sibou 207
  socio-ecological conditions in 211
  soil degradation in 18
  soil management in 16, 203, 210, 215
  Tot-Sibou 206, 214–15
  water in 18, 215
emergence of prosperity 7, 17, 19, 38–40, 44, 57, 62, 64, 70, 174, 205, 211–12, 215–17, 219–20
employment 12, 43
  in Lebanon 132, 140, 171, 173
  in London 86, 94, 100, 109, 111, 113
  LOOT framework and 38
  prosperity indicators of 94, 99, 120–1
  in sub-Saharan Africa 192–4, 196–7
England 43, 86, 87, 186
entrepreneurs 91–2, 173, 196, 213
European Bank for Reconstruction and Development 159
European Union 11
evaluation and monitoring 122
exclusion 79, 91, 107

farmers 16, 39, 184, 186, 190, 192–3, 197–8, 204–6, 208, 210–11, 213–17, 219–20
  and digital world 196
  colonial notion of 189
  smallholders, African 203
  white 187
Federal Ministry for Economic Affairs and Climate Action (BMWK) (Germany) 4
Ferguson, James 193–4
financial stress 96, 98, 100–1
Finland 5
food 62, 110, 119, 196
  as basic need 29, 110, 113, 123
  distribution 101, 188
  growing (production) 17, 91, 152, 186, 190–1, 204, 206, 215, 216
  system, global 18, 151
  insecurity 10–1, 99, 133, 155, 203, 207
  nexus 16, 167
fossil fuels
  linked to economic growth 10–11 *see also* climate change
  in Lebanon 153, 158, 171
Foundational Economy Collective 27
future generations 5, 93

'games' 60
gender 61, 110, 111, 135, 145, 183, 190
German government 4

Gidley, J. and theory of social
    inclusion 117–18
Glasgow (Govanhill) 118
global financial crash (2008) 1, 94, 181
global North 12, 182, 218–19
global South 8, 12, 15–16, 119, 182, 219
globalisation 4, 39
    impact on east London 90
    impact on the global South 15–16
Gough, Ian 29
governance 34, 37, 42, 58, 66, 69, 132, 225
    and collaboration 27
    devolved 7
    indicators 94
    Lebanon 157, 171
    sub-Saharan Africa 182, 184, 186–8
great reset 5–6, 25
green (new) deal 5, 25
green spaces 10, 31, 62
Greenpeace 172
gross domestic product
    beyond GDP 2–7, 26–7, 65, 223–4
    climate change and 55, 152
    economic growth as the policy goal 7–9, 18, 26, 50–1, 57, 94, 115
    income-based indicators 13, 65, 77, 79, 102
    indicator for wellbeing 38, 94, 182
    Lebanon 11, 154
    post-GDP 28, 78
    Zambia 193
growth, economic
    a-growth 12
    moving beyond 25
    degrowth vs green growth 11–14, 19, 56
    discourse on 8, 51, 53, 55–6
    failure of growth in GDP 1–2, 38–9, 43, 94, 121
    in Africa 181–5, 195, 198
    green growth 11–12, 51
    inclusive growth 5–7, 25, 56, 108, 114–20, 122–3
    in (macro)economic policy 3, 26, 78, 94, 99, 108, 111, 113, 120
    no-growth 12
    'growth plus' model 115
    post-growth 5, 12, 19, 28, 181, 223
    relative and absolute decoupling 11–12
    as synonym for prosperity 9, 15, 51, 57, 77

Haddad, Camille 171–2
happiness 89
    critique of GDP growth 26, 38, 78
Hartlepool 114
Hesse, Mary B. 59
heating systems 43
Hijri New Year 141
housing 13, 62, 66, 99
    in Lebanon 10, 130, 133, 156, 161–2
    in sub-Saharan Africa 17, 204
    in the UK 43, 85–94, 96, 99–100, 108–16, 118–20, 123
Human Capital Index 151

Iceland 5
identities 40, 52, 61, 123, 186
    diversity 110, 111
    in the Marakwet 213
    prosperity model 32, 97
inclusion 1, 9, 70, 87–9, 96, 98, 107, 110, 116–23, 225
    in Bar Elias 131, 134, 147
    digital 197
    financial 194
    social 84
inclusive economy 115–16
inequality 26, 114, 116
    related to the Covid-19 pandemic 87, 94, 115
    related to economic growth/GDP 2, 4, 26, 43, 58, 79
    horizontal forms of 110
    intra-urban 107
infrastructure 27
    in Bar Elias 134, 146–7
    material infrastructures 112
    material infrastructure in Lebanon 130
    in terms of secure livelihoods 112–14
    social infrastructures 112–13
    theory 112–14
insecurity 90
    and energy 99, 133
    in Lebanon 133
    in sub-Saharan Africa 208
    in the UK 79, 90, 101, 110, 112, 114, 117, 123
International Panel on Climate Change (IPCC) 153
International Renewable Energy Agency (IRENA) 158, 173

Jackson, Tim 3, 223
Jameson, Fredric 185
Johnson, Boris 92
Jordan 132
justice 28
    and energy 170
    intergenerational 9, 102
    social 12–13, 29, 118

Kabrikha 159
Kenya
    locusts 202, 217
    mobile phones 195–6
    population intensification 191–2
    rural-urban migration 193–4
Kerio Valley Development Agency 209
Kermode, Frank 184–5, 223
kin networks 206, 212–13
kinship 187, 217
knowledge 12, 16
    citizen-led 78, 119, 122–3
    co-production and 7, 40–2, 102, 118, 120–1
    context-specific (and local) 30–1, 62–3, 84, 108, 161, 191
    embodied 84, 188
    expert-led 102
    forms of 'lived and learned' 115
    non-Western 5, 15, 197, 204, 218–20
    policy-relevant 10, 99, 108
    sharing (or networked) 17–18, 25, 38, 44, 173, 193, 195, 212–14, 216–17, 225

Lacan, Jacques, theory of language 60
Laclau, Ernest 52
Lagos 8
Latour, Bruno 185
Lebanon
  Bar Elias 15, 130, 134–7, 140, 145, 147, 50
  Baaloul Project 160
  Banque de l'Habitat 158
  Beirut 130, 140–1, 151, 155
    explosion 140, 151
  Beirut River Solar Snake 157, 159
  Beqaa Valley 15, 134, 155
  Civil War 130, 163
  economic crisis in 129, 130, 132, 140–1, 145, 151
  El Mina 161–9
  gas 11, 153
  Hamra 34, 67, 141, 161–7, 170
  impacts of climate change 152
  infrastructure 129–30
  migration
  National Energy Efficiency Action Plan (NEEAP) 156–8
  National Energy Efficiency and Renewable Energy Action Plan (NEEREA) 157–8
  National Renewable Energy Action Plan (NREAP) 156–7
  net-metering 158–9
  oil imports 153
  private (diesel) generators (and owners) 153, 155–7, 159–60, 162–4, 167, 173
  Prosperity Co-Laboratory 7
  Ras Beirut 161, 167–8, 169
  solar photo voltaic (PV) 157–60, 173
  solar water heaters (SWHs) 157–8
  Tfail 159
Lebanese Center for Energy Conservation (LCEC) 154, 158
Lebanese Central Bank (BDL) 157
Legatum Prosperity Index 27, 35–6, 66, 78
  in east London 81–3
levelling up 6, 78, 112
  as a metaphor 54, 58
localism 101, 174
locale 7, 13, 19, 27–8, 34, 161, 172, 187, 193–4 *see also* self-determination
  form of entanglement 9, 70
  in redefining prosperity 6, 30, 32, 65, 68, 224
London
  Barking and Dagenham 8, 58
  east 9, 33, 77, 79, 80, 83–8, 90, 94, 96–7, 100, 102
    secure livelihoods, in 107–8, 110, 112, 114, 118, 122–3
  East Village 85, 91–3, 100
  Hackney 81–3, 85–7, 90–1, 94, 124
  Hackney Wick 85–6, 90–1, 94, 98, 100–1
  Newham 81–3, 85–7, 92
  Stratford 85, 89–91, 94
  Tower Hamlets 81, 85–6, 92, 118
  Waltham Forest 81, 85
LOOT Framework 38, 44

macroeconomics 9, 14, 19, 26, 40–1, 119–20, 152
  context 27
  policy levers 7

maisha bora (Kiswahili) 16, 204
Māori knowledge 4
Marakwet people 203–4, 206
  intergenerational prosperity 16, 204
  kokwo 213–14, 217
  matrilineal relations (*kamamaa*) 212
  patrilocal clan-based system 210
  tilia 213, 217
Mayer, Colin 3
McCloskey, Deirdre 53
Medusa 64
MENA (Middle East and North Africa) 151, 170
Menjez 260
meso level 37
metaphor
  constitutive 56
  cultural 56
  in economics 50–56
  market 50
  in policy formation 49
  Ricoeur on 49–50
migration 14, 129, 131, 223
  rural-urban 193–5
Moltaka Shabab Bar Elias 145

narratives 11, 34, 56, 58, 62–3, 69
  in Africa 183, 203, 205
  in Lebanon 136, 147, 171
  prosperity 1–2, 8, 87, 90–1
natural capital 39
neoliberalism 3–4, 12, 117, 131
New Zealand 5
NGOs 32, 35, 62, 122, 191
Nicaragua 4
Nietzsche, Friedrich 184
nomological networks 65–6
non-encampment policy 132
Nussbaum, Martha 29

Olympic Games 79–80
  host boroughs 81
  legacy 79, 81, 85–6
Olympic Park 81, 83, 85–6, 91, 98, 100
OTB Consult 172–3
Organisation for Economic Cooperation and Development (OECD) 11
  Better Life Initiative 27, 66

Palestinian national day (Independence Day) 141
participation 30, 70, 107, 118, 153 *see also* inclusion
  approaches to policy making in the UK 118–20
  civic 91, 96, 112
  community 96, 109, 122, 147
  cultural 97
  democratic (also political) 8, 59, 66, 91, 97, 225
  in energy policy 170–1
  in terms of needs 29
  of refugees 146
participatory spatial intervention (PSI) 133–9
  evaluation 140–6
  in relation to social and material infrastructure 146

partnerships
    cross-sector 122
    innovative 14
    local communities and 9, 70, 94, 147
    in redefining prosperity 63, 69
Peru 4
place *see also* locale
    in redefining prosperity 19, 28, 121
    meso level and 37
    in UK policy 107
political freedom 9, 102
poverty reduction 111, 116
power (in terms of relations) 16, 31, 39–40, 90, 112, 182
    and language 49, 58, 61, 63, 68–9
    in Lebanon 130, 135, 153
    prosperity model and 32
    in sub-Saharan Africa 188, 195
private rented sector 92
Prophet's Birthday 141
Prosperity Co-Laboratory 7, 10
Prosperity Model 32–6, 65–7
    co-designed 63, 79, 83, 94–5, 161–2
    in whole-system change 44
*prosperus* 57
public services 27, 31–2, 116
    in Lebanon 14–15, 132, 135, 151–2, 161–2
    in the UK 9, 26, 87–8, 99, 101–2, 108–10, 112, 116, 119, 123
purchase power agreement (PPAs) 157

Ramadan 141
real household disposable income (RHDI) 100
redevelopment 130–1
regeneration 89
    environmental 6, 173
    economic (and development) 80–1, 85–6, 90–1, 110, 112
refugees 14–15, 18
    and economic benefits 131
    and history in Lebanon 129–30
    'hosting fatigue' 133
    infrastructures 147 *see also* participatory spatial intervention
    Palestinian 134
    Syrian life in Lebanon 132
relationality 36–7, 39, 68, 112
    in redefining prosperity 14, 30–1, 93
RELIEF Centre 152, 161
Richards, Audrey 183
Ricoeur, Paul 49–50
Royal Society of Arts (RSA) Inclusive Growth Commission 118

Santos B. de Sousa 203, 218
Sawalha, Aseel 131
Scotland 5
sectarianism 10, 130, 133, 151, 154, 171, 173
self-determination 16, 31 *see also* self-realisation
self-realisation 2, 31, 57 *see also* self-determination
semiotics 8, 49
Sen, Amartya 41
Shehabi, Ala'a 171
Shell 10
Singapore 8

social capital 39, 44, 66, 81, 101–2, 112, 223
social cohesion 13
social diversity 17, 134
social instability 134
social justice 12, 13, 29, 118
social needs 89
social networks 9, 17, 113, 146
    in London 101, 112
    in sub-Saharan Africa 190–1, 194–5, 197
social progress 12, 15, 28
social solidarity 17, 43, 160, 204, 225
social transformation 49, 62–3
Social Progress Imperative 27
socio-ecological systems 18
socio-natural systems 17, 205, 219
Solidere 131
solidarity 38 *see also* social solidarity
Sonatrach 155
subjectivity 79, 132
Sustainable Development Index 27
Sustainable Development Goals 11, 27, 167
Sustainable Livelihoods Approach 112
Syrians 14, 134–5, 141, 143, 146, 159, 166, 169

Tanzania 16, 33, 37–8
    Dar es Salaam prosperity index 35
tasampo tai (Kimarakwet) 16, 204
Total Energies 10
transition 6, 12–14
    related to energy in Lebanon 153, 156, 170–2, 174
    into modern living 218
    out of poverty (Kenya) 192
translocality 192
Trowbridge Estate 86
trust 11–12, 101, 112
    in governments related to indicators 94–5
    in Lebanon 151, 171
    in redefining prosperity 39, 223
Tsing, Anna 70
Turkey 132

Ukraine 10, 18, 99, 151, 155
unemployment *see also* employment
United Kingdom 42–3, 81, 83, 86, 90
    cost-of-living crises in 99, 77
    Covid-19 114–15
    Employment in 113
    levelling-up White Paper 6, 95
    policy 58, 113, 116, 118, 123
    'productivity puzzle' 78
    Prosperity Co-Laboratory 7, 37
United Nations (UN) 119, 134
United Nations Development Programme (UNDP) 152
United Nations Environment Programme (UNEP) 10, 11
United Nations Economic and Social Commission for Western Asia (UN ESCWA) 173
universal basic income 13
universal needs 29
urban development 81, 86, 101

Vaughan, Megan 183
voice 7, 9, 15, 17, 19, 31–2, 65, 70, 95, 97, 117, 123, 131, 147, 204
vulnerabilities 15, 136

Wales 5, 87, 118
water services 39–40, 152
wellbeing
  as alternative to GDP in policy 5, 12, 15, 28, 78
  compared with prosperity 66–7, 69, 93
  community 2, 29
  ecological 182–3, 184
  Economy Governments (WEGo) 5
  individual 7, 29, 31, 93
  in Lebanon 143, 151–2, 161
  as metaphor 59
  planetary 4
  in the UK 101–2
Western (also non-) 15–16, 89, 182, 204, 218

Wittgenstein, Ludwig 59–60
Whitehead, A. N. 185
whole-systems
  approach 7, 13–14, 171–2, 174, 224
  change 51
  problems 42
women
  in Lebanon 142
  in sub-Saharan Africa 192, 195, 213–15

Yellen, Janet 3
young people 62
  in Lebanon 172
  in the UK 88, 91, 96, 99–100

Zambia 17, 181, 186, 193–4, 197
  and agrarian transformation 192
  Bemba agriculture in 183, 188–9
  Gwembe 188
zero-hours contracts 101, 109

The manufacturer's authorised representative in the EU for product safety is Easy Access System Europe, Mustamäe tee 50, 10621 Tallinn, Estonia, (gpsr.requests@easproject.com).

Printed and bound by CPI Group (UK) Ltd, Croydon, CR0 4YY

21/04/2026

02094480-0001